MAKING SENSE OF THE JONESTOWN SUICIDES

A Sociological History of Peoples Temple

JUDITH MARY WEIGHTMAN

Studies in Religion and Society

Volume Seven

The Edwin Mellen Press
New York and Toronto

Library of Congress Cataloging in Publication Data

Weightman, Judith Mary.
    Making sense of the Jonestown suicides.

    Bibliography: p.
    Includes index.
    1. Peoples Temple. 2. Jones, Jim, 1931-1978.
I. Title. II. Series: Studies in religion and society
(New York, N.Y.) ; v. 7.
BP605.P46W39 1983   306'.6   83-21999
ISBN 0-88946-871-0

Studies in Religion and Society   ISBN 0-88946-863-X

The Edwin Mellen Press
P.O. Box 450
Lewiston, New York   14092

Printed in the United States of America

For Karen Brown

with love, admiration, and gratitude

TABLE OF CONTENTS

PEOPLE ASSOCIATED WITH THE PEOPLES TEMPLE

Jack Beam: Associate Pastor of the Temple since the early 1960s, a member of the elite until the final White Night.

Ross Case: Associate Pastor of the Temple from the late 1950s through the mid 1960s; left the Temple when it moved away from traditional Christianity.

Stanley Clayton: Left Jonestown during the final White Night rather than join the other members of the Temple in committing suicide.

Concerned Relatives: A group of ex-members and families of members who urged investigation of the Temple and were instrumental in urging Congressman Ryan to go to Jonestown.

Archie Ijames: Associate Pastor of the Temple since its founding in the late 1950s, he was eased out of a power position by Jones in 1974. He was a member of the Temple at the time of the suicides, but was in San Francisco and did not die.

Maria Katsaris: Joined the Temple in the early 1970s, rising to a powerful position in the hierarchy as Jones's mistress.

Steven Katsaris: Maria's father, an important member of the Concerned Relatives group.

Anthony Karsaris: Maria's brother, he was on the final trip to Jonestown with Congressman Ryan. He was wounded in the airstrip ambush.

Larry Layton: The first member of the Layton family to join the Temple, he instigated the ambush in which the Congressman, three reporters, and a defector were killed.

Deborah Layton Blakey: Larry's sister, she defected prior to the suicides and attempted, through a legal affidavit, to alert authorities of the danger of mass suicide.

Carolyn Moore Layton: Larry's first wife, she became, with Maria Katsaris, one of Jones's two most important mistresses.

Al and Jeannie Mills: Changed their names (from Elmer and Deanna Mertle) on the advice of their lawyer following their defection from the Temple in the 1970s because of the many incriminating documents they had signed. Important members of the Concerned Relatives group.

Gerald Parks: Defected with his family on the day of the final White Night. His wife Patricia was killed in the airstrip ambush.

Odell Rhodes: Left Jonestown during the final White Night to avoid suicide.

Tim Stoen: Temple attorney and Jones's confidante. Defected and became member of Concerned Relatives group.

Grace Stoen: Tim's wife during their membership (they have since divorced), she preceded him out of the Temple. Important in the Concerned Relatives group.

John Victor Stoen: Grace and Tim's son, whom Jones claimed to be his. Center of a custody battle.

INTRODUCTION

On 18 November 1978, the Peoples Temple brought itself to the attention of the world by committing mass suicide.* Most of the analyses of this virtually unprecedented event have not, in fact, really be analyses. They have been, instead, explanations based on unexamined assumptions about brainwashing and the danger of the cults to the American Way of Life. Further, most of these explanations are based on an assumption that members of the Peoples Temple were "not like us"--that they were in some very fundamental way different, other. The assumption of the argument to be presented here, on the other hand, is that the members of the Peoples Temple were like me, like you, like us all. It attempts to take seriously the potential within us all for just such an act.

Given this assumption, it is not surprising that the methodological starting point should be Max Weber's concept of Verstehen, or understanding. According to Weber, this is achieved when a

> particular act has been placed in an understandable sequence of motivation, the understanding of which can be treated as an explanation of the actual course of behavior. Thus, for a science which is concerned with the subjective meaning of action, explanation requires a grasp of the complex of meaning in which an actual course of understandable action belongs.[1]

This complex of meaning, in the case of the Peoples Temple, was their understanding of revolutionary suicide.

---

*Following Temple usage, I have referred to the Temple throughout as the Peoples (not People's) Temple. In addition, following both Strunk and White's Elements of Style (New York: Macmillan, 1959, p. 1) and Turabian's Manual for Writers (Fourth Edition: Chicago: University of Chicago Press, 1937, 1955, 1967, 1973, p. 31), I have formed the possessive of the name Jones as Jones's, not Jones'. Alternative forms of these two constructions are common, and are not indicated by "sic."

1

Gerald Parks, whose family left the Temple with Congressman Ryan the day of the suicides and whose wife was killed in the ambush at the airstrip, describes this understanding in an interview. He begins by talking about socialism:

[T]he philosophy of it sounds good, people controlling the distribution of the wealth and everybody having everything equal--that would be nice, but it just doesn't work. Evidently the human race isn't ready for it, not at that price.

But anyhow, the ones that want to overthrow the capitalist government or dictatorship that controls--one man controls everything--they start their revolution. And they're dedicated to it, they'll give their lives for this revolution, give their lives to make this change, to kill the dictator, to change the government and get a socialist government, communist government in there running things. So they become very dedicated to their cause and their purpose. So this is basically what Jones taught, and this is what they're teaching in other countries that leans--that has a party that leans to the left. So when they talk about revolutionary suicide: when it gets to the point, you know, you've gone as far as you can go with your revolution, then you are able, rather than let them take your life, or take it away from you, or put you in jail where you'll no longer be any good to anybody yourself--you can commit what you call revolutionary suicide, singly or en masse, if you want. So this is a sick way of looking at anything, and I knew it. So in one of these white nights Jones would call over there, the first time I had heard about anybody committing revolutionary suicide, over there, was then, this white night . . . .

[A]s far as the revolutionary suicide, everybody there would raise their hand, and the first time, I didn't raise my hand. So if you didn't raise your hand, you know, they were watching you, guards standing around watching, he was watching, you know--so if you didn't raise your hand, you were singled out for why. Or then he would ask you if you wasn't willing to raise your hand, course I stuck my hand up. And he had you come up front of the crowd and give your reason why. So I told him, I said, "I didn't come over here to commit suicide." I said, "I have no reason to commit suicide, I don't believe in committing suicide."

And so then I begin to recollect the times that he had said . . . "If you commit suicide, you retrogress 500 generations" it was or however you want to look at it. If you believe in reincarnation, you're gonna go back 500 generations, you know, to the Stone Age and have to live it all over again and come back to this era, which is beyond me, but anyhow, that's what he said. So I thought of that, so I just put it to him, he was sitting up there on his damn throne and surrounded by his followers, and I said, "I thought you said if you committed suicide you was gonna retrogress 500 generations." I said, "Now you're asking me if I'll commit suicide." I said, "How do you equate the two?"

He said, you know, something screwy. And he said, "Well," he said, "If you just commit suicide, you know, for no apparent reason." He said, "This is a good cause, for a good reason." He said, "If you commit suicide, revolutionary suicide," he said, "then you're dying with dignity." He said, "You're not snuffing your life our for nothing." He said, "You're doing it for a cause and a good reason." Then he said, "That's what we call revolutionary suicide."[2]

This concept of revolutionary suicide—what was, in effect, a theology of suicide—is the "complex of meaning" within which the collective act of mass suicide took place. The members of the Temple saw themselves to be doing something with a purpose, not performing the act which the rest of the world perceived as meaningless.

The perception that the mass suicide was a meaningful act is merely the starting point of the present analysis. The question which arises from such a perception is, of course, how could the members of the Temple get to the point where they found such an act meaningful? The argument developed herein attempts to suggest some of the elements involved in such resocialization. How does one go about gathering the data through which to discover this process?

The acquisition of data is the primary methodological problem of a sociological analysis of the Peoples Temple. Because the act which brought the Temple to the world's attention, mass suicide, also effectively put it beyond the possibility of traditional sociological method (e.g., participant observation, questionnaires and interviews), the problem of data is fundamental. The primary source of information is individuals, and these individuals, for the most part, are not believers. They are ex-members, apostates, who have repudiated their association with the Temple, and they are non-member relatives of individuals who were in the Temple. Few members who survived are willing to maintain their commitment to the beliefs and practices of the Temple--and the testimony of the individuals who are is generally discounted, a priori, as arising out of diminished capacity (i.e., the believers are assumed to be brainwashed).

By far the most important source of information about the Temple is the apostates, former members who have turned against the Temple. As Anson Shupe and David Bromley point out in their discussion of apostates and atrocity stories, such repudiation is necessary for the ex-believers to reaffirm normative boundaries and be readmitted to the larger society, a society which, by definition, disapproves of the deviant group.[3] The repudiation takes the form of denigrating the group involved, its beliefs and practices, and, most especially, the motives of its leaders. The specific form used, the atrocity story, is generally revisionism: describing one's activities within the group in terms of the norms and reality of the larger society, and not the sub-society.

Much of the material available on the Temple is suspect, because the vast majority of it has been obtained from ex-members, almost all of whom were in opposition to the Temple even before the suicides. Thus, an evaluation of information about the Temple is the first, and most problematical, step in analysis. The 19 books which have been published as of September 1983 are of various degrees of value. They are of three main types: histories of the Temple, first person accounts, and polemical analyses. (Naturally, these are not clear-cut divisions, for both histories and analyses are very dependent on first person accounts for information.) The analysis presented here is based primarily on information from the histories and the first person accounts. The histories are, again, of varying quality. Not surprisingly, those which came out in the immediate aftermath of the suicides are of limited factual

usefulness. Far and away the best is Tim Reiterman's
Raven,[4] which should prove to be the definitive history
of the Temple. Reiterman, one of the reporters in the
Congressman's entourage, did extensive interviewing and
research to provide a richly detailed portrait of the
Temple. Although it was not published until November 1982,
after the first draft of this study had been completed, it
has served as a source against which to double check the
information already used.

Most of the information for this study was garnered
from first person accounts, both published and personally
gathered. I interviewed Gerald Parks (who is quoted
above); Steven Katsaris, member of the Concerned Relatives
group and father of Maria, one of Jones's most important
mistresses; Anthony Katsaris, Maria's brother, who was in
Jonestown the day of the suicides and who was shot in the
ambush; and Ross Case, assistant pastor of the Temple until
he broke with the church in the mid 1960s. In addition, in
the spring and summer of 1979 I corresponded with both Rev.
Case and Jeannie Mills, one of the most prominent defectors
and a members of the Concerned Relatives group.

All material on the Temple needs to be evaluated for
accuracy. For instance, two books by peripheral ex-members
which claim to provide the true inside story (both published by Christian presses within a few months of the suicides)[5] are not heavily relied upon. When individuals
such as Jeannie Mills[6] had more detailed inside knowledge, their position as apostates needs to be more carefully considered. These individuals are cited more frequently, but only in particular instances, taking into
account the possibility of revisionism. Ultimately, I have
been forced to rely on intuition as to who is telling a
fairly straightforward story and who is reaffirming normative boundaries. Although most of the first person stories
are cited at some point, only one is consistently cited:
Ethan Feinsod's Awake in a Nightmare,[7] which presents the
stories of Stanley Clayton and Odell Rhodes, who escaped
during the final White Night. These two rank and file
members, although no longer believers, have not repudiated
their membership in the Temple. Their accounts are cited
frequently because they are able to describe their
experiences without denying their value and meaning to
them.

The gathering of data is only the first step in sociological analysis: the second step, of course, is the

analysis itself. The fundamental approach being used here
is the sociology of knowledge, based primarily on Peter
Berger and Thomas Luckmann's <u>Social Construction of Reality</u>. As they state in their Introduction,

> the sociology of knowledge must concern itself
> with whatever passes for "knowledge" in a socie-
> ty, regardless of the ultimate validity or in-
> validity (by whatever criteria) of such "know-
> ledge." And insofar as all human "knowledge" is
> developed, transmitted and maintained in social
> situations, the sociology of knowledge must seek
> to understand the processes by which this is
> done in such a way that a taken-for-granted
> "reality" congeals for the man in the street.[8]

The reality being investigated is one in which mass suicide
for socialism--dying with dignity--makes sense. The sociology of knowledge approach is used most explicitly in Chapter Four, in the discussion of resocialization, but it
underlies most of the rest of the argument. The one exception is the discussion of the commitment process in Chapter
Two. A functionalist approach is necessary at that point
for reasons which are discussed there.

There are two further premises on which this argument
is based: that the Temple was political in nature <u>in addition to</u>, and not instead of, religious; and that the Temple
should be understood as a cult, and not as a new religion.
Let us briefly examine the reasoning behind these two premises.

First, the prevailing assumption seems to be that the
religious techniques that Jones used--healings, revivals,
and so on--were calculated techniques for mobilizing the
religiously oriented. Jones himself explains the Temple in
this way (see below, p. 10). The question necessarily
hinges on the definition of religion being used.

The starting point for the definition of religion
being used here is Joseph Fichter, who calls religion "a
probing relationship in search of truth, transcendence, and
the sacred."[9] "The sacred" can be removed from this
definition without undue damage, insofar as "sacred" is an
<u>ex post facto</u> label applied to events and experiences of
the transcendent or to persons or objects that are seen to

be in some form of communication with the transcendent.
Sacredness is thus secondary and derivative.[10]   Although
it is highly unusual to have a religion which does not rely
heavily on the understanding of the sacred, it is not
necessary, as long as the other three terms are there.
Religion is a _search_ for _truth_ and _transcendence_.

What is politics? In its broadest sense, politics is
essentially about power relationships, the interactions of
various groups in an effort to control resources. Jones
clearly dabbled in politics, as we will see from his usage
of the Temple as a voting bloc and tool, by means of which
he was able to gain political positions such as Chairman of
the San Francisco Housing Commission.

Politics, however, is not only about the actual interactions of individuals and groups in this quest for
power.   It is also about the understandings that these
individuals and groups have about the nature of the inter-
action--ideology. It is because of Jones's--and hence the
Temple's--ideology[11] that the question of whether the
movement was primarily political or primarily religious
becomes problematical for so many people.   If Jones had
been a capitalist or a Randite, the distinctions could be
made more clearly, but Jones was a Marxist/socialist.
Marxism, like religion, is about truth and transcendence--
just as religion, like politics, is about power. Marx had
a vision of a conflictless society, a society in which
politics and religion would no longer be necessary for the
oppression of groups and thus would wither away.   Marx
foresaw an egalitarian society, a communal society; Marx
dreamed of a society very much like the Christian Kingdom
of God.

The Peoples Temple worked in a number of concrete
ways to move toward this vision of society, primarily
through their support of liberal politicians and radical
figures (e.g., Angela Davis, Dennis Banks).   Insofar as
many mainline churches work for political causes, this was
not problematical; insofar as the means were sometimes
questionable, it became more so. Regardless of the Temple's violation of their Section 501 (tax-exempt) status,
however, what we see is the political being used to further
the religious vision, and vice versa.

This brings us back to religion. We have defined
religion as the search for truth and transcendence.   The
Peoples Temple was clearly involved in a search.   This is

shown, for instance, by their actual physical wandering-
from Indianapolis to Redwood Valley to San Francisco to
Guyana--as they looked for a place where their vision could
be worked out.

Truth is a hard word to define. Truth is relative
and protean in its manifestations. Truth can never be
arrived at finally, for as the situation changes, the Truth
will as well. (The Temple's tolerance for the mutability
of truth, while an interesting question, will not be dealt
with here.) The Temple's experiments with racial integration and economic communalism, however, would seem to be
the earmarks for a quest for truth.

Transcendence is another hard word to define. In
general it involves experience which goes beyond the obvious, the material, to a "higher" (different) level of
experience and understanding.[12] This transcendent atti-
tude is manifested in the theology of suicide, as Gerald
Parks described it above. There is, however, a certain
ambiguity in Jones's thought on this point. Although Parks
says that Jones "said there is no God, there's no heaven
and no hell and no damnation and no life hereafter,"[13] he
did profess belief in reincarnation, a clearly transcendent
conception of the human essence. Regardless of the exact
nature of his true beliefs on this point, however, it is
clear that many of his followers believed that there was a
life hereafter: "'We'll all fall tonight,' one communard
said, stepping forward for his cup of poison, 'but he'll
raise us tomorrow.'"[14] Even if this is a minority view,
the suicides should still be seen in a transcendent light:
their deaths were not just deaths, but a major statement
about the evil nature of the world.

This positive conception of suicide was itself the
result of a political view. Jones's starting point was
Huey Newton's distinction between reactionary and revolutionary suicide:

> Reactionary suicide was carried out by those who
> were demeaned and demoralized beyond redemp-
> tion. This form of suicide did not inevitably
> imply a literal taking away of life. Reaction-
> ary suicide could mean the death of a spirit,
> the flight into liquor and drug addiction. The
> majority of American Blacks had had their spir-
> its slaughtered. Their lives, like their actual
> deaths, were emblematic of their powerlessness

and subjugation. Revolutionary suicide is the exact opposite of this passive moribundity. It begins to occur when the slave rises up and says "no" to his oppressor.   The death of such a man is a positive act. It is positive because it springs not out of defeat and self-contempt but out of self-assertiopn and calculated disobedience.   Both his life and his death thereby acquire meaning . . . . Life gives meaning to death. Death gives meaning to life.[15]

Another way of approaching this interrelationship of the religious and the political is through John R. Hall's analysis of the Temple as an apocalyptic group.   He concludes that:

The Peoples Temple could not begin to achieve revolutionary immortality in historical time because it could not even pretend to achieve any victory over its enemies. If it had come to a pitched battle, the Jonestown defenders--like the Symbionese Liberation Army against the Los Angeles Police Department S.W.A.T. Team--would have been wiped out.
    But the Peoples Temple could create a kind of immortality that is not really a possibility for political revolutionaries.   They could abandon apocalyptic hell by the act of mass suicide. This would shut out the opponents of the Temple . . . . Mass suicide bridged the divergent threads of meaningful existence at Jonestown-- those of political revolution and religious salvation.   It was an awesome vehicle for a powerful statement of collective solidarity by the true believers among the people of Jonestown--that they would rather die together than have their lives together subjected to gradual decimation and dishonor at the hands of authorities regarded as illegitimate.[16]

In short, I am arguing that the Peoples Temple was both a political and a religious group, and that, in fact, it makes no sense to talk about one aspect without the other.

Granting that the Peoples Temple was a religious

group, what kind was it? The church/sect typology developed by Ernst Troeltsch in 1912[17] has proven problematical over the years, even with the addition of the third type of "cult." In the early 1970s, the word "cult" was abandoned by most scholars in favor of the term "new religion," both because of the methodological imprecision and because of the overwhelmingly pejorative connotations it had taken on in a world trying to make sense of the Moonies, the Hare Krishnas, the Children of God, et (many) al.

What these scholars do not seem to have recognized, however, is that there was a qualitative change in the nature of the phenomenon at the time of this terminological shift. The new religions appeal to white, middle class young adults, while the cults appeal to the marginal in society. This change in phenomenon can be discerned through the changing nature of legal cases concerning the First Amendment rights of the groups. During the 1930s, First Amendment cases were being tested by the Jehovah's Witnesses who were dealing with a public reluctant to allow them to proselytize. This public reluctance arose not out of fear that they, or their children, would be converted, but rather out of a desire to maintain the peace of their suburban neighborhoods. In the 1970s, on the other hand, the cases were on the First Amendment questions of brainwashing and deprogramming. The possibility of proselytizing middle class children was real, as it had not been real in the 1930s.

There is, then, a meaningful distinction to be maintained between new religions and cults (which might perhaps be better called "marginal religions" to avoid the pejorative connotations of the word "cults"). The Peoples Temple clearly appealed to the marginal in society. The membership was 80% black, and the whites were primarily lower and lower middle class. The significance of this distinction will be developed in counterpoint to the rest of the argument.

As stated above, the premise underlying the following analysis is that the mass suicide of the members of the Peoples Temple was an act meaningful to them. The problem is to discern in the practices of the Temple the ways in which such a belief could be inculcated. Chapter One describes the history of the Temple in order to provide a baseline of facts. Chapter Two is an analysis of the appeals of Temple membership and the process through which individuals became committed to the Temple. It will be argued that these processes are similar to those involved in commitment to any group, although in a more extreme form. Chapter Four examines the leadership structures of the Temple, most specifically the charismatic nature of that leadership, and suggests the implications of this for the fate of the Temple. Chapter Four discusses the process of socialization into the subsociety of the Temple, contrasting a sociology of knowledge understanding of this process with the generally accepted "brainwashing" explanation. Finally, Chapter Five examines the responses to the suicides, describing them in terms of Shupe and Bromley's typology of atrocity stories.[18] ✳

As with any project of this size, there are so many people to thank that I can only apologize in advance for any who may inadvertently have been forgotten.

On the Peoples Temple end, thanks must go first and foremost to Steven Katsaris. He has lent me books, given me materials, let me go through his files, arranged interviews, shared his thoughts with me, and supported and encouraged me. In many ways this project would not have been possible without him. Thanks also to his son Anthony, who has always done his best to answer my questions, no matter how unexpected. I would also like to thank the other individuals I interviewed--Ross Case, Carlton Goodlett, and Gerald Parks. Posthumous thanks to Jeannie Mills, with whom I corresponded during the spring and summer of 1979.

On the technical end, heartfelt thanks to Karen Brown, who has been godmother to this project since its first incarnation as a term paper. Like a good mother, she has pushed me when I needed to be pushed, and coddled me when I needed to be coddled. I would like to thank David Graybeal, Sidney Greenblatt and Neal Riemer for their comments on early versions of this manuscript. Thanks also to Charles Selengut, Arthur Pressley, and Michael Ryan, among many others, for helpful conversations about the Temple.

Many people have clipped articles for me about the Temple, notably: Brenda Adamczyk, Eileen Barker, Stan

Bindell, Karen Brown, Beverly Busch, Rene Carlson, Jack Gaylord, Angus Gillespie, David Harrell, Pat Macpherson, Alan Padgett, Art Pressley, Bob Price, Ruth Richardson, Neal Riemer, Helen Weightman and M. A. Weightman.

Thanks to Robin Zucker who typed the first good draft of this manuscript and to Donna Speer who prepared the final manuscript for publication.

Finally, I would like to thank my family and friends—especially Ruth Richardson—for their support and encouragement during the long gestation of this study.

FOOTNOTES

[1]*Economy and Society*, Volume I, edited by Guenther Roth and Claus Wittich (Berkeley, Ca.: University of California Press, 1978), p. 9.

[2]Gerald Parks, interview, Ukiah, California, 26 June 1981, emphasis in original.

[3]Anson D. Shupe, Jr., and David G. Bromley, "Apostates and Atrocity Stories," in *The Social Impact of New Religious Movements*, edited by Bryan Wilson (New York: Rose of Sharon Press, 1981), pp. 179-215. This is a condensed version of the argument they present in *The New Vigilantes* (Beverly Hills, Ca.: Sage Publications, 1980).

[4]Tim Reiterman with John Jacobs, *Raven* (New York: E. P. Dutton, 1982).

[5]Phil Kerns with Doug Wead, *People's Temple: People's Tomb* (Plainfield, N.J.: Logos, 1979); Bonnie Thielmann with Dean Merrill, *The Broken God* (Elgin, Ill.: David C. Cook, 1979).

[6]In addition to my correspondence with her, I relied on her book *Six Years With God* (New York: A&W, 1979), which describes her experience with the Temple.

[7]Ethan Feinsod, *Awake in a Nightmare* (New York: W. W. Norton, 1981).

[8]Garden City, New York: Doubleday Anchor, 1966, p. 3.

[9]Joseph Fichter, "Youth in Search of the Sacred," in *The Social Impact of New Religious Movements*, p. 22.

[10]Emile Durkheim's *Elementary Forms of the Religious Life*, translated by Joseph Ward Swain (New York: Free Press, 1915) has obviously influenced this definition, despite the radically different use made of the experience/label split. Also influential was Robert M. Pirsig, *Zen and the Art of Motorcycle Maintenance* (New York: Bantam, 1974).

[11]In this case, it should be referred to as a utopia in Karl Mannheim's sense. _Ideology and Utopia_, translated by Louis Wirth and Edward Shils (New York: Harcourt, Brace and World; 1936).

[12]Cf. F. C. Happold's characteristics of mystical states: ineffability, noetic, transciency, passivity, consciousness of the oneness of everything (optional), timelessness, and egolessness. _Mysticism_ (Baltimore: Penguin Books, 1963, 1964, 1970), pp. 45-50.

[13]Gerald Parks, interview, 6/26/81.

[14]Carey Winfrey, "Why 900 Died in Guyana," in _New York Times Magazine_, 25 February 1979, p. 40.

[15]Shiva Naipaul, _Journey to Nowhere_ (New York: Simon and Schuster, 1980, 1981), pp. 286-287. Newton does not think that Jones understood what he meant by this, but does not clarify where he sees the difference to lie. Ibid., p. 288.

[16]John R. Hall, "The Apocalypse at Jonestown," in _In Gods We Trust_, edited by Thomas Robbins and Dick Anthony (New Brunswick, N.J.: Transaction Books, 1981), p. 188.

[17]_The Social Teaching of the Christian Churches_, translated by Olive Wyon (New York: Macmillan, 1932), Volume I, pp. 328-349.

[18]_The New Vigilantes_, Chapter Three, "The Anti Cult Movement Ideology."

CHAPTER ONE

THE HISTORY OF THE PEOPLES TEMPLE

James Warren Jones was born in Lynn, Indiana, a tiny town whose primary industry was casket building, on 13 May 1931. He was brought up with little attention from either of his parents. His father had returned from World War I with lung trouble (having been gassed in the trenches in France), and was in ill health during Jones's childhood. Even while alive, James Thurmond Jones had little attention to spare for his son. Early reports claimed that he was preoccupied with his activities with the Ku Klux Klan, but this is questionable. He was not an open member of the active local chapter, and did not appear at the cross burnings that were held regularly; nor, apparently, did he make anti-black, anti-Jewish, or anti-Catholic statement.[1] Jim's mother, Lynetta, was frequently gone from the home, working in a series of factory jobs to support the family. She was a strong-willed woman who was not swayed by popular opinion. Jones revered his mother deeply. A 1953 article about Jones (which appears to be the first) has him attributing his social conscience and activism to her example. Titled "'Mom's' Help For Ragged Tramp Leads Son To Dedicate His Life To Others," the article describes an encounter between the young Jones and a "tattered knight of the road," who told him:

> "I don't have a friend in the world. I'm ready to give up."
> The boy, barely through his first year of school, looked at the tired, beaten old man and said firmly: "What do you mean, mister? God's your friend and I'm your friend. And Mom will help you get a job!"
> And "Mom," Mrs. Lynetta Jones, did just that.[2]

Jones's early religious guidance, however, came from a neighbor, Myrtle Kennedy, who took care of him during his youth. She would take him on her lap and tell him Bible stories, which enthralled him. A member of the Nazarene Church, she frequently took him to services, which were energetic participatory affairs:

> One of the most common sights in most Nazarene
> Churches is the large number of young people at-
> tending the services. They, along with others,
> are attracted by the freedom of the services, by
> the spontaneity of the singing, and by the evi-
> dent friendliness and concern of the people--a
> concern which continually finds expression in
> aggressive evangelism and ever-widening areas of
> service.[3]

Jones's early attachment to Mrs. Kennedy was marked when he
brought twelve busloads of his parishioners with him when
he visited her in 1976 and paid tribute to her as his
"second mother."[4]

The Nazarene Church was not the only one he attended,
however. "'He was allowed to go to any church and he went
to all of them,' a neighbor said.   'You never knew when he
got ready to go to Sunday school where exactly he was
going.'"[5] Specifically, he is known to have attended
Pentecostal services. This brand of enthusiastic religion,
featuring speaking in tongues and all night worship services, would later be reflected in the Temple.

Naturally, those recalling him as a child in the
light of the suicides find that there was much that was
exceptional about him even then. He held "uncanny" power
over other children and over animals.[6] He performed
funerals for a variety of small animals, and preached
enthusiastically to his young playmates. Another trait--
one, like his compassion, learned from his mother--was his
foul mouth. It was apparently quite common for him to
greet the neighbors with a cheery "Good morning, you son of
a bitch." The older boys would respond by chasing him down
the street.[7]

Lynetta and James Thurmond Jones divorced in 1945,
and Lynetta and her son moved to Richmond, Indiana, a
larger town in the same area as Lynn.   This is where he
attended high school.   On 12 June 1949, he married Marceline Baldwin, a nurse about four years older than himself.   He had met her at Reid Memorial Hospital, where he
worked as an orderly.   According to the "Ragged Tramp"
article quoted above, he:

> . . .once considered entering the field of medi-
> cine. Undecided but knowing his life's work
> must include helping other people either spiri-

tually or physically, Jones entered Indiana
university (sic). Finally in April 1952, . . .
he decided. It would be the ministry.[8]

Jones was soon to drop out of Indiana University.
His roommate there, Kenneth E. Lemmons, describes him as
"maladjusted and ignored" and suggests that "Marceline was
a 'mother figure' to Jones.   'He called her at work every
day.'"[9]

In 1950 the Joneses moved to Indianapolis, where Jim
became student pastor at the Somerset Methodist Church in
June of 1952. It was during this time that he first began
to synthesize and move beyond denominational lines.   The
"Ragged Tramp" article was primarily about a youth center
for which he was raising money.   Although sponsored by the
Methodist Church, it was to be "open to children of all
faiths." The article goes on to outline his theological
stance:

> As a foundation for his all-faith youth center,
> the Rev. Mr. Jones has established a church
> program at Somerset almost unheard of under the
> strict rules of doctrine outlined by most reli-
> gious sects.
> In his program, Jones preaches no doctrine,
> but simply points out moral lessons taken from
> the Bible. His inter-community church has be-
> come acceptable to all denominations and the
> knowledge that no group is discriminated against
> has aided greatly in winning new members.[10]

Jones and the churches he was affiliated with went
through a number of changes during the early 1950s. Somerset Methodist changed to Somerset Christian Assembly, which
fell apart, and the Community Unity Church was formed.   Due
to burgeoning numbers of worshippers, Jones moved for a
time to be Associate Pastor at the Laurel Street Taberna-
cle. He began to travel the evangelistic circuit throughout the Midwest, attracting new followers everywhere he
went.   Then, in 1955, Jones had finally raised enough money
to open his own Church: The Peoples Temple Full Gospel
Church.

In 1953, Jones claimed that the basic conflict in his
life was between medicine and religion. The third main
force in his life was politics. He was convinced that his
political aims could best be achieved through a religious
movement:

At the age of 18, Jones told his wife that his hero was Mao Tse-Tung, who had recently over-thrown the government of Nationalist China. Within three years, according to his wife, he had become convinced that such dramatic social changes could be effected only by unifying people through religion.[11]

Jones was to explain later that integration, too, was merely a means to this end:

> Integration was a big issue with me . . . . What a hell of a battle that was. I thought, "I'll never make a revolution. I can't even get these f----rs to integrate, much less get them to any Communist philosophy." I thought, "There's no way I'm going to politicize these f----rs if I can't get them to sit together." And it was a hell of a job. I'd get these Pentecostalists in and all the Methodists would leave. C.T. Alex-ander [the Pastor at Somerset Methodist] called me and asked, "What's going on over there?"
> I decided, "We'll piss on you, man, you didn't put me in this church, and I'm not going to let you put me out." So I conspired with the whole goddamn church to withdraw from the Metho-dist denomination . . . . I got a whole bunch of people together to vote the goddamn church out of the conference and named it another church. . . . Church was nothing, handful of old bigots until I brought in some blacks. And that is how the goddamn religious career got rolling. I was preaching integration, against war, throwing in some Communist philosophy.[12]

The first Peoples Temple was an integrated church in a section of Indianapolis that was changing from a primar-ily white to a primarily black population. The congrega-tion was expanding, as was Jones's family. He and Marcie had adopted their first child, a Korean girl; they were to adopt five more (including blacks and orientals) and have one son of their own, Stephan Gandhi, in 1959. This was a very important period for Jones: he was creating many of the structures, many of the appeals that the church was to feature until the end: the interracial congregation, the enthusiastic worship, the tests of commitment,[13] the healings, the travel, the evangelism. It was at this time, too, that he did his first serious study of a specific role model: Father Divine.

Jones visited the Peace Mission in Philadelphia in the summer of 1956. He wrote a little tract on his experiences with the Mission three years later, passing it out wherever he preached. In this tract he says:

> I had always been extremely opposed to adulation or worship of religious leaders. In order to stop flesh exaltation which seemed to be developing in my own healing ministry I publicly insisted that no one even refer to me as Reverend. Naturally, one can imagine the revulsion I felt upon entering their church and hearing the devoted followers of Mr. Divine refer to him as Father . . . .
>
> It has to be the spirit of truth that stimulated me to return to their atmosphere because my every natural inclination was opposed to it. I was nauseated by what seemed to be personal worship to their leader. Nonetheless when I would pause to think and be fair in my judgement, I could not help but see a peace and love that prevailed generally throughout the throng of enthusiastic worshipers. Every face was aglow with smiles and radiant friendliness. . . .
>
> I know it will seem strange to you, dear reader, that a person could be benefited spiritually by people who propagate the teaching of the deification of a person, which we have always considered to be gross misconception. But I must honestly state the facts: as the Holt Writ declares: "give honor where honor is due."[14]

Jones saw in the Mission a "flower garden of integration" which manifested "cooperative communalism," and declared, "I have never seen a demonstration of democracy comparable to this in any other religious circles."[15]

He was to learn well from the Peace Mission's example. Integrated communalism <u>could</u> work, and social service was a powerful attraction. By the early 1960s, the Peoples Temple would be providing a soup kitchen (a "free restaurant"), a free grocery, and a free clothing center. Many of his followers, both at this time and throughout the Temple's existence, were drawn by this concrete activist Christianity.

In order to have an effective group, however, it is necessary to have a committed cadre of people. Jones soon

began to develop structures for solidifying and strengthening the group. Soon after Jones's visit to Divine, for
instance, he instituted an "interrogation committee":

> Doubters, malingerers, and those who failed to
> keep up their tithes were subject to home visits
> from the church's board of directors. Jimmy
> himself usually presided over these visits,
> assisted by Jack Beam and other board members.
> The interrogations and the verbal abuse often
> got brutal--especially when Jack Beam had the
> floor. The committees of interrogation knew
> best how to reach every individual in Peoples
> Temple, for Jimmy had requested, during ser-
> vices, that all his followers write down their
> fears and turn in the lists to Beam or Ijames or
> himself. As the number of followers grew, the
> committees stopped going to individual homes.
> Those who violated the rules would be notified
> by telephone that they would be brought before
> the board to appear. The subpoenas of the board
> were infinitely more fearsome than those of a
> court of law.
>   If there were any lingering wounds from the
> interrogation committee's ego effacements, they
> weren't allowed to fester for long. At the con-
> clusion of each service, while Loretta Cordell
> played the organ and the teary-eyed parishioners
> hugged one another in an effusive display of
> brotherly love, Jimmy stood at the pulpit,
> available for confessions. Transgressors were
> encouraged to come forward and kneel before
> Jimmy and confess not their sins but their ill
> feelings toward others. Jimmy would direct the
> supplicants to make peace with their adversaires
> by verbalizing their animosities. Once stated,
> the ill feelings would vanish in a tearful out-
> pouring, to be replaced by gusty emotions of
> unity, brotherhood, and Christian fellow-
> ship.[16]

In addition, the first of the disaffected members
left around this time. Thomas Dickson, explaining later
why he left, said, "He'd take the Bible--as he called it
the black book--and throw it on the floor and say, 'Too
many people are looking at this instead of me.'"[17] Many
others, however, were not disturbed by the lessening of
emphasis on traditional fundamentalist preaching, finding
that Jones was acting out his--and their--beliefs in a way

that was not only satisfactory, but attractive.

It was during this period that Jones began to share his socialist beliefs with his followers.   He held special Sunday afternoon meetings in which he outlined them, although they were still presented within the general context of Christian idealism. As Klineman (a non-member) reconstructs these sessions, Jones taught:

> Race? Class? Money? Hunger? All creations of the capitalist exploiters, they made artificial distinctions among the Children of God. In the world of Jimmy's utopian vision, there would be no race or class distinctions, there would be no need for money, there would be no hunger or sickness or pain. Jimmy did his best to make his ideals reality.[18]

One of the ways in which Jones ministered to his flock was through faith healing. He later described this period:

> . . . I heard all these healers, and I thought, "Well, if these sons of bitches can do it, then I can do it too," and I tried my first faith healing. I don't remember how. Didn't work too well, but I kept watching those healers.   I thought, "These a------s, doing nothing with this thing."   I couldn't see nobody healed. But crowds coming. . . . So I thought there must be some way that you can do this for good, that you can get the crowd, get some money, and do some good with it . . . .
> Packed out the biggest auditoriums in Indiana and Ohio.   I should've left it that way. But I'd have been dead.   People passing growths and then by sleight of hand I'd started doing it, and that would trigger others to get healed . . . Carried the entire operation on myself. And I don't know how the hell I got by with it. It wasn't days before people were saying, "You're Jesus Christ."   Hell, it didn't make me believe anymore in the living deity than I did before, I can tell you that . . . .   I didn't know how to explain how people got healed of every goddamn thing under the sun, that's for sure, or apparently got healed.   How long it lasted, I don't know . . . .[19]

Naturally, however, he claimed that the power to heal came from "the Christ within" him, which was able to reach "the Christ within others." He:

> blasted "faith healers and fundamentalists" . . . for failing to utilize the "wonderful healing powers of God" correctly.
> The Rev. Mr. Jones, standing before a sign which proclaimed he wore "modest and worn clothing," declared:
> "They (faith healers) call for the coming of Christ and go out to meet him in a brand new Lincoln Continental" as well as build magnificent, useless edifices and squander $40,000 on bulls [sic]."[20]

In Jones's perception, the mix of politics and religion was not completely successful:

> I could not get the cadre of people to get together politically. Could get the crowd, but I couldn't get them politicized. Never misused the money. Money always went for good causes. The money went for some f-----g strange causes too. Very early, I had treasurers channel money to places where they didn't know what the hell they were doing. I personally always kept out of that money business . . . . Sent money through a church foundation and then on to help some of the people on trial for political reasons. I got money to them . . . . [21]

He was achieving his political aims through the Temple, but only indirectly, due to the membership's reluctance to make that ideological shift. Jones thus began to act directly, but as a (well-respected) individual.

Jones's interracial family and interracial congregation brought him to the attention of the local politicos, who found him an ideal figure with which to start Indianapolis's movement toward integration--no easy task, Indianapolis being the national headquarters of the Ku Klux Klan. In February 1961, Jones was appointed to a $7,000 a year job as director of the Indianapolis Human Rights Commission. This brought him more fully into the public eye, especially because of the harrassment he and his family received at the hands of never-to-be-identified racists.

Bill Wildhack reported in the **Indianapolis News** (11 August 1961):

> He has become the victim of a letter-writing campaign. His name is forged to letters making insulting statements about minority groups. The letters are mailed to Negroes and others known to be interested in the problem of racial relations.[22]

Other members of the Commission and other activists in Indianapolis at the time were not harrassed in any similar manner.

The early 1960s featured two primary socio-political moods in the United States. We have seen how Jones reflected the first, the move toward integration. He was also very much affected by the second, the fear of nuclear warfare. In January, 1962, **Esquire** magazine published an article entitled "Nine Places to Hide."[23] Among them were Belo Horizonte, Brazil, and Eureka, California. Now Jones had had a vision, in September, 1961, of the destruction of Indianapolis. Given the mood of the times, it was only reasonable to assume that this destruction would be nuclear. Ross Case, an Associate Pastor of the Temple, urged that the Temple act on this vision and move to safety:

> It had long occurred to me that the great majority of people **drift** rather than **decide** to change, as disaster gradually threatens and then overtakes them. I felt that the vision was given to us at Peoples Temple because we were not cut from the common pattern, that we were capable of acting on such a warning. Then, again, the vision fit in with something I had read previously [:] . . . a prophecy of Nostradamus . . . .
> I felt that the Peoples Temple was an unusual congregation in that it was a Bible-believing congregation, and also that it was without racial prejudice. Many congregations which were conservative theologically were also conservative on the race issue . . . . So I pushed the idea that we should move the church so that we would be alive to evangelize what was left of the world after the holocaust hit.[24]

Jones was originally negative, but ultimately became persuaded that the move would be a good idea. In 1962, he
took his family to Belo Horizonte, one of Brazil's "syn-
thetic" industrial cities of the interior.

Jones spent two years in Brazil, doing some social
work, such as feeding some of the swarms of hungry children
in the streets of the town. He met a missionary family,
the Malmins, whose daughter Bonnie practically became
another daughter to Jim and Marcie. She was to move in and
out of close involvement with them for another fifteen
years. Her version of the story, The Broken God[25] indicates that by the time Jones arrives in Brazil, he was
fully convinced of the imminence of nuclear war:

> Anytime we were out in the city and saw any
> large pointed shape--even a large church steep-
> le--he would begin to rave about missiles.
> "They don't know what they're doing," he would
> say. "They don't know what's going to come." I
> was a naive sixteen-year-old, of course, so I
> dismissed it as one of his idiosyncrasies. Even
> when he showed me a picture of him and Marceline
> standing on either side of Fidel Castro, who
> they had met during a Cuban stopover en route to
> Brazil, I wasn't particularly alarmed.[26]

Bonnie reports that Jones investigated a number of
religions during this time. He visited Spiritist and other
native groups, and saw David Martine de Miranda, "Envoy of
the Messiah," a famous healer. Jones often discussed religion with Bonnie's father, who "eventually became frustra-
ted with a man who seemed to drink the water offered to him
and then spit it back out again."[27]   Jones struggled with
theological topics like the Virgin Birth and the Trinity,
ultimately being unable to make sense of them.[28]   He
remained fascinated with the power of religion:

> Strangely enough, however, Jim was deeply at-
> tracted to my father's Bible. He constantly
> wanted to hold it. "I feel such power when your
> Bible is in my hands," he said. "I feel a surge
> of strength everytime I hold it."[29]

One new element which appeared around this time was
Jones's talk about reincarnation. This rather upset Bonnie, a Bible-reared Christian, but she had been somewhat
prepared by a book she had read in an attempt to be open-

minded.   Jones began by telling her that he had been Ikhnaton, the Egyptian heretic monotheist. Bonnie had been his
and Marcie's child in previous lifetimes:

> But Jim was not finished.   He had also been
> Buddha,   and   Lenin, and even Jesus Christ, among
> others.   Life was a tapestry, he explained, and
> each of us, as various threads, had come back to
> the surface again and again.[30]

Jones returned to Indianapolis in 1964, travelling
there by way of British Guiana.[31]   By this time, Ross
Case had already left for California (being unable to find
a job in Eureka, one of the "places to hide," he settled in
Ukiah, where he could).   Jones followed with a hundred or a
hundred and thirty of his flock, settling in Redwood Valley. Ukiah and Redwood Valley are two small, very conservative[32] towns in the agricultural area about a hundred
miles north of San Francisco. Case broke with Jones around
this time because:

> When he returned he [Jones] had changed in these
> areas: (1) He no longer accepted the Bible as
> true or authoritative in any sense, but rather
> denounced it bitterly, and (2) he sought to re-
> place Jesus Christ in the devotion of Peoples
> Temple by himself. He sought to do this by such
> strategems as claiming that he, himself, was the
> reincarnation of Jesus Christ, that he, himself,
> was God, the Father, and by bolstering these
> claims by carefully contrived deceptions.[33]

So, once again, with the move and the new emphasis, there
was a paring down of the congregation; this paring down,
however, served to unify the group and solidify their devotion to Jones. The congregation soon began to grow again
in size.

Life in Mendocino County featured most of the characteristics of the Temple in Indianapolis, with many of them
further refined.   The faith healings continued, both fake
and apparently genuine.[34]   It was at this time that
Jones's claims in the area began to expand somewhat. From
merely healing the sick and preventing death (he claimed
that there had been no deaths among the membership),[35] he
went on to claim ability to raise the dead. The sermons go
a little longer, from three or four hours to five or six,
but, as Jeannie Mills reports:

> We began to appreciate the long meetings, be-
> cause we were told that spiritual growth comes
> from self-sacrifice. Jim's sermons no longer
> seemed long or boring. Now we listened to every
> word he said so that we could learn to make the
> world a better place for everyone.[36]

The emphasis on community within the congregation got a
little more concrete: people began to sell their homes,
give the proceeds to Jones, and move into Temple housing.
The practices of the Temple in the interrelated areas of
sexuality and punishment began to move away from the norms
of the larger society as distinctive ideologies around
these issues emerged.

Tim Reiterman, in his definitive history of the
Temple, describes the development of the ideology of
punishment:

> Like so much with the church, the physical dis-
> cipline began in a small way and only gradually
> reached extremes. It had started with a few
> light spankings for children. Then a paddle-
> like one-by-four inch "Board of Education" was
> introduced. The paddlings became more severe
> and were often administered by a rotund black
> woman named Ruby Carroll, who was chosen for her
> physical strength, not a mean disposition. Like
> a master of ceremonies, Jones supervised, but
> the audience participated, particularly when the
> disciplined person was deserving or disliked.
> The swats varied in number and intensity. Some
> were spanked almost half-heartedly, or in fairly
> good humor. Other spankings qualified as
> beatings. In one of the most extreme, teen-age
> Linda Mertle (later known as Mills) was hit
> seventy-five times for becoming too affectionate
> with an alleged lesbian.[37]
> The normal practice was for church notary
> publics to obtain signed permissions from par-
> ents and guardians before the public floggings
> . . . .
> Boxing matches were soon inaugurated for the
> children--almost as entertainment. Laughter and
> lightheartedness predominated as an errant child
> was pitted against a stronger opponent who was
> supposed to win. Some were as young as five.
> If the wrong child won, tougher opponents would

be called into the arena until the child was taught a lesson.

The next step was introducing adults to the matches. The brutality became severe as full-grown people donned gloves and began throwing punches seriously. Sometimes they knocked each other silly or bloodied each other. A person stupid enough to fight too hard would go toe to toe with bigger and better opponents until vanquished. But if he did not fight at all, he was ridiculed and hit anyway. Every punch carried the message: one cannot fight the "collective will." The will of Father.

The battling conditioned people to believe that they would win if they fought for the church and would lose if they fought against it. Jones justified his psycho-drama by saying that society was full of rough conditions, that people needed to be rugged and capable of self-defense. Yet it really was an extension of the catharsis sessions, with physical pain added to the psychological. Through corporal punishment, Jones could simultaneously strengthen internal order, mete out justice and indoctrinate . . . .

No one, not even Jim Jones and white elite, was exempted, technically speaking, from the punishments . . . .

Punishment was applied not just for deviation from policy but for serious cases of delinquency. In some instances the Temple was substituting its own punishment for an act that might well have led to a jail term on the outside: for example, there was the man whose penis was beaten with a hose after he was caught molesting a child. Another in this category was a fourteen-year-old boy who had karate-kicked his sister in the back, putting her in traction.[38]

The orientation of the Temple around sexuality had begun soon after Jones's visit to Father Divine, when, following the latter's example, he had encouraged members to maintain celibacy and adopt children.[39] As the years passed, Jones fluctuated between advocating celibacy and unselfish sex. In 1968,

He preached about physical love as well as emotional love--and encouraged his members to cast aside selfish, exclusive relationships and share their love with others. In essence, he urged

his congregation to have sex with different people, married or not, young or old, beautiful or
ugly. He talked about the uplifting experience
of free love.[40]

The advantages of celibacy continued to be preached,
however:

The dogma seesawed between sexual awareness and
total celibacy. Did not sex squander energy
that could be better applied to building socialism? Was it not elitist to continue marital
relations when so many Temple members had no
partner at all, selfish to make babies when so
many were starving? Good socialists ignored the
sex drive . . . .
Partly as a bonding ritual, partly as an
escape valve, the church did sanction some marriages and arranged others. Usually people
without real romantic feelings for each other
were asked to form a marriage of commitment to
the cause. Some lovers, especially interracial
couples, were asked to marry for the sake of
appearance.
Jones promoted interracial marriage, despite
his general condemnation of all one-on-one relationships as counterrevolutionary. Such marriages advanced the interracial lifestyle and
also served to tie the couples more closely to
the Temple, which remained a rare racially hos-
pitable environment.[41]

In addition to specific practices advocated by the Temple,
Jones promulgated certain ideologies about sexuality. In
1974 he began to preach

that he alone, among Temple men and women, was
the only true heterosexual. All the rest were
hiding their homosexuality, he declared: having
heterosexual relations was simply a masquerade.
Perhaps out of shame for homosexual tendencies
within himself, Jones made his members publicly
admit homosexual feelings or acts, past and
present, latent or overt. Planning commission[42] members were forced to list all the
sexual partners in their lives, male and female,
as well as type of sex. He had wives stand up
and complain about their husbands' lovemaking.
He had male children fill out questionnaires

that asked, among more doctrinaire matters, about their sexual feelings for Father.[43]   And he personally had sex with some men in his church, ostensibly to prove to them their own homosexuality.[44]

Jeannie Mills reports that "The first time Jim had talked like this, people were shocked, but like everything else he did, after a few times, it ceased to be shocking."[45]

The issues of sexuality and punishment were inter-related in that members were punished for sexual transgres-sions, as seen above, and that sex was sometimes used for other types of transgressions. For instance, Jeannie Mills reports one occasion in 1974 when a member, Clifford, was falling asleep in a Planning Commission meeting. When another member punched him in the arm to wake him up, he punched back. Jones decided to make a point of it, and, discovering from Clifford's wife that he was a "prude," decreed that Clifford should perform oral sex on a woman member as punishment. He chose a very shy woman, Alice, to participate, but

> Tami came to her rescue. She would do this for the Cause. "I'm on my period, Jim. I'll give Clifford a little bloody black pussy."
> Jim looked relieved at not having to make an issue of this with Alice. It was obvious that she couldn't go through with it. "Okay, Tami, thank you for your dedication to the Cause. I know this is a big sacrifice for you to make."

Clifford was extremely reluctant to accept this situation, and tried to talk his way out of it. Jones stated,

> "If you refuse to do as I have requested, you will have to leave the group."
> "Fine, I'll leave today."
> "Do you mean you are so prudish, and so racist, that you would leave your family, your job, and this group, just to save yourself the embarrassment of licking Tami's pussy?"
> Tami was still lying spread-eagled on the table and beginning to feel utterly foolish. "Oh, come on, Clifford," she called to him, "let's get it over with."
> "You racist, you racist pig!" The counsel-lors were shouting now, and Clifford's anger overcame his aversion to Tami. He strode over

to Tami, put his mouth between her legs and
licked, not gently, but with hostility and
rage. Tami was startled at his roughness, but
she did nothing. He continued to lick until Jim
realized that Clifford had lost control of himself and commanded him to stop.

Clifford stormed out of the room and Jim
allowed him to leave. Jim knew Clifford didn't
want to leave his wife and children and was sure
he'd be back. Tami was trembling. She stood
up, grabbed her underwear, and ran downstairs to
the restroom.

"Are you all right, Tami?" Jim called to
her.

"Yes, thank you, Father," she shouted from
the foot of the stairs.[46]

This incident, among the Planning Commission, is not really
reflective of what happened among the rank and file members. The story indicates the use of sex as punishment and
"consciousness raising" among the elite. Among the rank
and file membership (i.e., in general meetings), there was
much talk about sex but little acting out.[47]

Jones made policy from the pulpit, with a graph-
ic and witty style. He gave earthy commentaries
that made the audience howl. With a clever
sense of humor, he tossed off all pretensions of
piety, adopting the language, intonations and
vocabulary of his inner-city people and mixing
it with a vocabulary nearly as florid as his
mother's writing. The brew was spell-binding.
No subject grabbed his congregation like sex

Whereas an ordinary preacher might have been
uncomfortable with the subject, Jones spoke with
candor, giving off the sexual magnetism of a
crooner. Women of all ages adored the good-
looking preacher in dark glasses and satiny red
or blue religious robes from New York religious
suppliers, and men admired and envied his macho,
straight-talking manner. The bawdy words and
gestures provided vacarious thrills.[48]

At the same time that distinctive beliefs and practices began to develop within the Temple, Jones led in
increasing the power of the Temple through increasing membership and through using that membership as a political
force. In 1967, Jones was appointed Mendocino County grand
jury foreman, and also worked for the Legal Services Foun-

dation, where he met Timothy Stoen. The county counsel was to become one of Jones's most trusted and powerful advisors, and then later, one of his most bitter enemies. Jones began to control the Temple vote: in a town with two or three thousand registered voters, his three or four hundred followers, voting in unison, could exert considerable influence. Ultimately, however, Redwood Valley proved to be simply too small, and too conservative, for projects of the scope he envisioned. In 1972, Jones and his flock made yet another exodus, to Geary Street, in the Filmore District of San Francisco.

The ground had been well prepared for such a move. The Temple, with an 80% black membership, had already been holding services in the area for some time. It was merely a matter of solidifying the commitment of those who had been responding to handbills such as this:

> PASTOR JIM JONES ...Incredible!...Miraculous!... Amazing!... Unique Prophetic Healing Service You've Ever Witnessed!...Behold the Word Made Incarnate in Your Midst!
> God works as tumorous masses are passed in every service...Before your eyes, the crippled walk, the blind see!
> Scores are called out of the audience each service and told the intimate (but never embarrassing) details of their lives that only God could reveal!
> Christ is made real through the most precise revelations and the miraculous healings in the ministry of His servant, Jim Jones!
> This same spiritual healing ministry does not oppose medical science in any way. In fact, it is insisted that all regular members have yearly medical examinations and cooperate fully with their physicians.
> See God's Supra-Natural Works Now![49]

Naturally, Jones would not start out the services with the healings and the miracles; in fact, he would not even appear until things were well under Way.[50]

The services would start with singing, lots of singing--by the interracial choirs, by soloists, by the congregation. The songs were a mixture of civil rights songs ("We Shall Overcome" was sung half a dozen times during the course of an afternoon), songs borrowed from Father Divine, and songs written by Temple members for the

services. There were many talented musicians in the congregation, so all of this music was skillfully chosen,
written, arranged, and performed. Marceline's solo of
"Black Baby," about her adopted son, is said to have been
very moving.[51] The songs borrowed from Father Divine, of
course, were equally appropriate for Jones. These
included:

Minds and attention
Love and devotion
All directed to you
It's true
I've never thought I'd be living in
Heaven
Today
Living with God in the body
Who is ruling and reigning
and having his way[52]

and

Brotherhood is our religion
For democracy we stand
We love everybody
We need every hand
It's based on the Constitution
and certainly is God's command
These are the rights we adore —
LIBERTY - FRATERNITY - EQUALITY for all
These are the rights we stand for.[53]

Traditional Christian hymns were conspicuous by their
absence.[54]

Finally, when everyone was ready, Jones would appear. Wearing a red robe and sunglasses he would appear at
the back of the auditorium, sweep through the crowd, and
appear on stage.

At first he would just talk about how wonderful it
was for them all to be together, and the beauty of their
faces before him, white and black and brown and yellow.

He spoke about race and economics and nuclear
war. "The world will destroy itself. It will
happen," he warned. "Greed!" he shouted. And
he began to repeat the word until I thought he
would never stop. "Greed! Greed! Greed!
Greed!" It sounded ugly and terrible. I felt

ashamed.   "This imperialist hunger for success is destroying us!" he preached.

"It's a terrible thing," Jones said, "when a black man walks down the street with all those white eyes staring him down. It's an unjust world! It's an unmerciful world!"

"Yes! Yes!" People would shout back. "Yes, father!"

"I tell you there is mercy here in this room!" Jones shouted joyously and with power. "There is justice in this room! There is love here in this room!" And I knew he was telling the truth.   I could just feel the sincerity. There was love here.

Jones went on to talk about the current letter writing campaign, telling them "to get off their asses and turn off the television."

Jones looked to the left. The band broke into music. Once more, "We shall overcome." This time Jones held the microphone and sang it loudly. They repeated it over and over. People stood up. The lady in front of me started to cry. She was a big black woman. "Oh Father Jim," she cried. "Father Jim. How we love you, Father Jim."

The crowd was in a joyous frenzy now.

Some were clapping, some were jumping, some were dancing. My sisters and my mother mixed right in. I was ashamed of them all and quite turned off.

Jones himself was happy, jumping and dancing.   I couldn't believe it.   That man is excited. Eventually the band stopped. A bit breathless, everyone began to wind down.

"What a glorious day here in the Redwood Valley." Jones said. "You people don't know what a future you have in store for you. This is the cornerstone," he shouted.   "This is the cornerstone! You and I here tonight! They'll speak about us for years to come. These are historic days.   This is the beginning of real socialism, real equality! Aren't you glad? Isn't it exciting to be part of this?"

There were peaks and valleys throughout a Jim Jones performance. The crowd would be worked into a frenzy and then slowly relax only to be brought to their feet again with the thundering applause and shouts. It left one exhausted.[55]

It was only after the crowd was fully ready that
Jones would swing into the next phase of the service, the
healings and revelations which the handbills had promised.
Jones certainly produced what he promised.   So he could
tell people "the intimate (but never embarrassing) details
of their lives," he would have had members look around the
houses of people who were becoming interested in the
Temple. He had a regular crew of people who would visit
prospective members at home and look through the medicine
cabinet while using the bathroom, in order to find out what
medicines they used; look through windows if they weren't
home, to discover the color of the kitchen linoleum; or
sift through their trash, to find out what kind of mail
they got and what brand of breakfast cereal they ate.
Jones preferred the homey detail, the sort of thing beyond
a guess, but apparently impossible for him to know. The
healings were a mixture of the real and the fake; obviously
he could not guarantee that "tumerous masses are passed at
every service" without a little planning. Jones would call
an unsuspecting cancerous prospect out of the audience,
send them to the bathroom with his nurse-wife Marceline,
who would give them an enema or stick her finger down their
throat, and present a "cancer"--rotting chicken entrails-to
the person healed and to the congregation at large. There
were other fakes as well. Members would be costumed and
provided with canes so they could be cured, toss their cane
aside and race out of the auditorium. Casts would be set
on arms that were not broken.   And yet, at the same time,
there were many genuine cures. Jeannie Mills reported:

> I was in charge of the "testimony file," where
> we kept the affidavits from people all over the
> country who had claimed a miraculous healing
> through Jim's picture, prayer cloth, anointed
> oil, or simply his spoken word. Because I was
> also in carge [sic] of producing the monthly
> newsletter I often had occasion to call these
> people and ask for permission to use their
> testimony. In every case, the person I called
> was still totally convinced of a miracle--and
> often added even another miracle that they felt
> that had received, which they said we could use.
>
> . . . [M]iraculous things happened in our
> family. I am convinced now that they were
> simply a manifestation of my own total faith -
> or mind power. I do know that very impressive

things happened to thousands upon thousands of people through their faith in Jim -- and I know that he was a 100% fraud. It's a difficult puzzle to try to put together![56]

Having prepared the ground thoroughly, it was time for the collection:

"Okay, we want you to know we've got a lot of work to do," [Archie] Ijames said. "We've got these kids in Santa Rosa College. We need doctors and nurses for our medical missionary operation, and we need help in our drug rehabilitation program. We need money for stamps," he said.
Ah, the offering, I thought.
"We've got a lot of mail," he said. "We're sending out letters to congressmen. We have friends, we have mayors and legislators out there, but they need our letters. They believe in the socialist dream. They believe in us. They are on the front lines."
Now the people started cheering Ijames.
He had none of the charisma of Jones, and none of the macho-enthusiasm of [Jack] Beam. It seemed as if anybody could have excited the crowd. "We're going to do it!" they shouted back.
Archie Ijames nodded in the direction of Jones. "You don't know our father. You don't know how hard he works. He tries so hard." Ijames choked up tearfully. "He gets three hours of sleep some nights. He's trying to help." Ijames broke down for a few seconds. "He helps the poor," Ijames said. "He helps the sick. He raises the dead." . . .
"You aren't just giving," Archie said. "You are a part of this dynamic movement of truth. As the plates are passed back and forth we will sing that song once more."
It was "We Shall Overcome" and as they sang Jim Jones sat quietly with his head bowed in humility.[57]

The chrome buckets were passed not just once or twice, but coutless times over the period of an hour or two, while Jones and others harangued for more money. Each bucket would be taken to a counting room when full, so that a half dozen helpers could keep a running balance of receipts.

Someone would report the total to Jones, who would announce
a figure a half or a third or a tenth as high as the several thousand dollars they had, in fact, already collected.
People would start tossing in their rings, their watches,
their social security checks.

In addition to collections during services, Jones had
a variety of other methods for collecting money. Members
would sell their homes and, turning the profits over to the
Temple, move into Temple housing, where they paid rent.
Members would sell their cars, cash in their insurance
policies, and turn the proceeds and their bank accounts
over to the Temple, thousands of dollars at a time. Members would sign blank deeds, blank powers of attorney, and
hand them over to the Temple. They tithed 25 - 50% of
their income. Older members--"seniors"--regularly signed
over their social security checks. Welfare payments for
foster children[58] would also be handed over. There were
many artifacts for sale: Jones lockets, Jones prayer
cloths, bottles of oil annointed by Jones, Jones key chains
"for safety on the road," two-minute timers for the recom-
mended amount of prayer before turning on the car ignition,
and personalized Temple stationery (with a pen and a small
picture of Jones). Some members would stroll around services with trays slung from their necks like cigarette
girls, selling a variety of pictures of the pastor.[59]
Jones, ever legally canny, made no specific claims of
efficacy for these objects, though the suggestion was
clear. Preprinted testimony letters were provided to the
beneficiaries of miracles: forms complete with a space to
specify the amount of the "love offering."

The Temple's wealth is one of the main things that
outrages its opponents. Its net worth is estimated to be
in the neighborhood of $26 million;[60] even lower esti-
mates of $10 or $15 million,[61] however, are large enough
to be startling. At the suggestion of Tim Stoen, Temple
attorney, funds were spread around in a number of banks in
the Bay area and, later, throughout South America, and a
good deal of it was in Jonestown, in cash. Although Jones
had a real talent for raising money, it is not clear that
he had anything particular in mind to do with it. Between
1966 and 1978, they gave $1.1 million to the Disciples of
Christ, the denomination with which they were affiliated.[62] In addition, the cost of stocking the agricultural mission in Jonestown was given as $1 million per
year, and the "home church" budget was about $600,000 per
year.[63] These expenditures, however, scarcely made a
dent in the totals coming in. Jones was <u>not</u> using the

wealth himself:

> There were all these rumors about all the bucks
> Jones was pulling in. He was supposed to have
> had a garage in San Francisco with every kind of
> fancy car in it -- a Rolls, a Lamborghini -- but
> I didn't believe that. It would have been
> easier to understand if he had had some vacation
> retreat somewhere, and was off drinking pina
> coladas in the Bahamas.

> With all that income, with better direction,
> they really could have had something fantastic.
> It's amazing what they did do.[64]

What did they do with the money, then, other than
start their agricultural mission? Occasionally the Temple
would send a check for a few hundred or a few thousand
dollars, as they had in the early days, to protect freedom
of the press, to support neighborhood services, to reward
doers of good deeds, to support Dennis Banks, Angela Davis,
or the NAACP; but these, again, made no real dent in the
income. Some suggest that Jones had nothing at all in mind
for the money. Grace Stoen[65] says:

> If Jones really wanted to make money, he could
> have done a lot more . . . . It became almost a
> joke with him . . . . We used to wonder what to
> do with it all. But we never spent it on
> much.[66]

Perhaps this was simply a matter of power for him, asserting his symbolic as well as actual power over the members.
The latter, of course, was quite important; by depriving
the members of their possessions, Jones made it extremely
difficult to leave the group.

Jones clearly enjoyed power. His political activi-
ties--the Human Rights Commission in Indianapolis and in
Redwood Valley, and the honing of an active political bloc
in Redwood Valley--continued in San Francisco. Jones cour-
ted the local politicians as well as those on the state and
national levels. Mayor George Moscone, Sheriff Richard
Hongisto, District Attorney Joseph Freitas, and Assemblyman
Willie Brown, all of San Francisco, all visited the Temple,
although Congressman Leo Ryan never did. Governor Jerry
Brown and Lieutenant Governor Mervyn Dymally did as well.
Jones met with then-Vice President Walter Mondale on his
private jet on a campaign visit to San Francisco, and

provided a crowd for a rally at which Roselynn Carter appeared--a crowd which, embarrassingly, cheered far more loudly for him than for anyone else. Temple members would write letters, make phone calls, ring door bells, cheer at rallies. They were willing troops in support for the causes and candidates Jones endorsed. Moscone appointed Jones to the San Francisco Housing Commission in 1976 in gratitude for the Temple bloc of votes in a close election.[67] Some claim that he was able to tip the balance--a matter of a few thousand votes--by bussing in more than 500 members from the Los Angeles Temple and having them vote illegally.[68]

The services which these supportive politicians saw were, of course, carefully arranged; they were a more watered down version of the usual proceedings and did not include discipline or obviously phony healings. One day Moscone simply dropped by, and could not understand why he was kept waiting. They had to detain him for a moment while someone ran upstairs and told Jones he was there. Jones was in the middle of an exercise designed to break down people's hypocrisy: he was leading the entire congregation in yelling "Shit!   Shit!   Shit!" as loudly as they could.[69]

Language is one of the most basic components of social reality, and one would expect a group which is creating a new reality to use language to create and define that reality. Unlike certain of the new religions, however, which create their own vocabulary to describe experiences, states of being, or people because of the inadequacies of the larger vocabulary, or change and color the meanings of words in more general usage to give them a specific intra-group significance, the Temple did not develop its own distinctive vocabulary. At the same time, however, the Temple used everyday language in very distinctive ways, which served the same purpose. Imagine the scene above, for instance, for a genteel, elderly lady--one of the dozen or so who had come to Jones from the Peace Mission after Father Divine's Death, perhaps.[70] The purity of the language in the Peace Mission was so complete that they substituted "Peace" for "Hello" as the standard greeting, and when they went for a walk, it was down "Amster-bless Avenue." This woman is being exhorted by the man who had cured her physical and her spiritual ills:

"All you sanctimonious hypocrites, all you religious idiots who have gone your whole life believing in the Bible and Jesus Christ and God--

> I'm sick of your hypocrisy!   I want you to come
> down off your pedestals and learn about the gut
> level of life!
>   "Get down where it's really at.   Come on
> now--everybody say 'S--t!'"[71]

Jones was aware of the effect his language had on his
listeners, and deliberately punished those whom it really
offended by making them swear.[72]

The Temple developed a milieu in which the language
used was unusual in when and where it was used--"cursing"
in church. This served to help members understand that the
Temple was "not just like every other church," and served
to define the group as different from the larger society,
where its use was not appropriate. This led to some problems with the children. Jeannie Mills was called by her
daughter's teacher, who complained about Daphene's "nasty
mouth:"

> It was inevitable that this would happen. These
> small children listened to Jim for hours on end,
> and his speech was filled with crude words. How
> could I tell Daphene that she couldn't use the
> same words she heard Father using and still ask
> her to respect him as our leader?   The teacher
> threatened Daphene with suspension. I knew I
> had to do something. Al and I decided to let
> the counsellors handle it.   The church had
> created the problem, let them solve it.
>   That evening, Daphene went to talk to Don
> Beck, the children's counsellor. As we watched
> him talking with her, we could see a bit of a
> smile on the corners of his mouth.   Daphene was
> tiny for her age, and she looked so innocent.
> Don did a good job of explaining the situation
> to her.   "Daphene, sometimes Father uses certain
> words to help people understand a point he is
> making. When he says these words, it isn't like
> swearing.   But outsiders don't understand these
> things. If you use the same words or tell the
> same jokes at school, your teachers will get
> mad. You have to learn never to use those words
> at school."
>   Daphene promised she wouldn't swear at school
> again.   It had been Daphene's first experience
> with the council and she was still trembling as
> she got into our car.   "I was so scared, Mommy,"
> she said.[73]

This incident occurred in 1974, a year after Jones's decision to have everyone call him "Father." This was, perhaps, inevitable. Given the many techniques he had borrowed from Father Divine, in fact, it is rather surprising that he had waited this long to do so.[74] The congregation truly came to see Jones as their father, with all the power and all the authority that this implies. Jeanne Mills said:

> Up to that time we loved him. We would follow him because he was a really neat guy. He was our buddy. We would sit in his house with him and talk to him. You could joke with him then. He was a neat, neat person. But in 1973 he turned into 'Father' and you couldn't confront him anymore.[75]

Other things symptomatic of this change began to occur around this time. Calling Jones "Father," the emphasis on punishment of sometimes unusual sorts, and talk of the impending fascist takeover are all intimately interconnected.

This is the importance of understanding the Peoples Temple as an organization equally religious and political. Their shifting concerns—the Cold War in the 1950s, civil rights in the 1960s, and concern about impending fascism in the 1970s—start from a political concern but are framed in a religious context. We have already seen that the first hegira, from Indianapolis to Redwood Valley, was precipitated by Jones's vision of the destruction of Indianapolis. The context was the Cold War, but this was translated into a vision of the Temple as the Chosen People—chosen because of their racial integration—who would wait out the Holocaust in a big cave and then repopulate the earth.[76] This was gradually dropped,[77] though the emphasis remained on the Temple's significance as an interracial group. Throughout, however, the group's intention was to create a strong group which would be able to deal with whatever socio-political criticism would come their way. Jones became "Father" to clarify his role as the leader of the group. They were a family, and as their father, it was his role to discipline them and keep them in line:

> [I]n the early days the congregation spent many hours in preparing to survive the nuclear holocaust, and in the later days, to survive the jungle outpost they might soon inhabit. Tim Stoen explains the change in emphasis in the

early seventies. "Jones's teaching shifted from
the nuclear holocaust concern to a fascist
concern. Those were the years Jack Anderson was
writing that Nixon might call off the 1972
election. Jones would say, 'Maybe we err on the
side paranoia, but look what the Jews failed to
do when the handwriting on the wall in Germany
under Hitler. It is better to be prepared for
this than not.'"[78]

The punishments inflicted on various members of the
Temple were given in order to strengthen them, to prepare
them for the "New Land" to which Jones was going to lead
them. This vision only gradually focused on Guyana. The
first idea was Africa, perhaps Kenya--an understandable
choice in view of the predominantly black population of the
Temple. Then Chile was considered, but rejected because of
the shakiness of Allende's regime.[79]

The Temple considered moving because the first negative articles appeared in 1972. In September of that year,
the San Francisco Examiner published a series of articles
about Jones and the Temple written by the Rev. Lester Kinsolving (an Episcopal priest). In these articles, Kinsolving reported Tim Stoen's claim that Jones had raised more
than forty people from the dead, and described Temple services, including the presence of armed guards.[80] The
Temple responded by picketing the Examiner's offices,
claiming concern about "'negative and erroneous'" infer-
ences in the series. Their main concern was about Kinsolving's report of a suit brought against the Temple by an
Indianapolis couple. The couple claimed that their under-
aged daughter was married in a Temple service by Tim Stoen,
who, though having the title of "associate pastor," was not
ordained. The Temple protestors claimed that the woman was
"actually 20 or 21 years old at the time of the marriage,"
and that therefore the suit was unjustified. (They did not
deal with the question of Stoen's ordination.) The protestors also charged that the Examiner "quoted an unfavor-
able Indianapolis Star story about the Rev. Mr. Jones,[81]
but failed to mention that that newspaper also presented
him with an award for humanitarianism," an award which the
Star denied having made.[82]

On the second day of the two-day protest, Jones
appeared and was invited to be interviewed. In the course
of the interview (which took place the following day),
Jones reiterated his claim of having raised 43 people from

the dead (out of 43 attempts); claimed that the armed
guards[83] were there only at the request of the Temple's
Board (the 17 September article quotes Temple attorney
Eugene Chaiken's statement that they were armed at the
request of the Sheriff's Department, which the latter
denied); and denied profiting from his position.[84]

Two sections of the interview are of particular
interest. He answers a question on the "spiritual thrust"
of the Temple by saying:

> The thrust of our church has been built on my
> character, humanism, and others in the nucleus
> who founded it . . . .
>   I provoke thinking. They explain me as
> developing certain aspects of mind . . . .
>   We don't orientate around the furniture of
> heaven and the temperature of hell. Rewards and
> punishment are not our thing.
>   I'm probably serving all of mankind because I
> want a better world for my children.
>   I don't have this sense of being sent from
> another world with a sword of the spirit or
> power from the cosmos in my hand. I get my
> fulfillment out of serving mankind: you can
> quote it just like that.[85]

This point is stressed again later:

> Rev. Jones doesn't exactly like being called a
> prophet. Not that he denies he's got some
> powers along this line. It's just that to him
> the title seems sort of . . . unseemly. Some
> folks have said he brought his flock (of 165
> members) to Ukiah in 1964 because he prophesied
> the world was about to face nuclear holocaust
> and Ukiah looked like a safe place.
>   Rev. Jones: "I have never prophesied the end
> of the world. Where that came from I'd be
> interested in finding out . . . I'm not that
> fatalistic."
>   Q--Do you think we might one day blow it up?
>   Answer: "No, I'm a hopeless idealist.
> Things that are emerging in the international
> arena--understanding--even in a Republican
> administration . . . I have hope.
>   "If I had all the ESP I'd like to have, we
> wouldn't have all the problems we have in the
> world society, because I'd have been right there

warning people about them. . . .
"I project the positive. If I can't, I keep
my mouth shut. I wouldn't talk about the end of
the world. I might as well fold up--why should
I work so hard?"[86]

The Kinsolving articles are of special importance in
the evolution of the Temple's belief system. In the late
50s and early 60s, the primary context of their self-image
was the Cold War--the rest of America would be destroyed
but they would be saved through Jones's leadership. The
danger was from Russia, not because it was a Communist
nation, of course, but because it was at odds with their
own country. As the perception of imminent destruction
became less plausible through the 60s, the emphasis had to
change. Jones began to focus on more immediate dangers:
America's perceived movement toward fascism. Jones
emphasized the danger and threat of those directly around
the Temple more and more. He did this through, for
instance, staged attempts on his life and the posting of
guards.[87] It was only with the Kinsolving articles,
however, that the threat became objectively present and it
became necessary to lie to protect the truth. The point is
not that there had been no lying or secrecy before, but
that Kinsolving provided evidence that the lies were
necessary. It is also significant that serious concern
about the Temple did not arise until much, much later--in
the wake of the New West expose in August of 1977. Maria
Katsaris (Jones's last mistress) joined the church in 1973,
a year after this, when the public was still relatively
unworried about the Temple. Her brother Anthony says of
this period:

[My father's] reaction was basically the same,
that they were a good group and were getting
maligned, because of the social structure and
stuff. Neither of us really believed all the
rumors that were going around, we both thought
they were ok, mostly because of our faith in
Maria . . . .
Question--So when did you begin to get concerned?
Answer: I feel so stupid now. These things
that people were actually doing, and you'd hear
these wild rumors. But the people I knew--
Maria, Liz[88]--were so calm and mild mannered.
We were growing apart, but it didn't seem
ominous. But, looking back, knowing now how
these groups work, why didn't I know?

Question--So when <u>did</u> you begin to get
concerned? Was it the <u>New West</u> article?
Answer: I really don't know.   I had kind of
been concerned all along, 'cause I didn't like
Jones, and she's pouring all this energy into
the group . . . .
There was this air of secrecy, like, don't
mention this to anyone else, that she's in the
church, 'cause they wouldn't understand, with
all the prejudice.
And then she moved to Guyana, and the <u>New
West</u> article came out--at that point, the concern was real.

This concern could be delayed for five years because
Jones engineered an almost complete split between the
public and private faces of the Temple. The Kinsolving
articles were not actually detrimental to the Temple: no
members left; with the national publicity, they received
hundreds of letters asking about the church; and they
attracted several new members.[90]   The incident, however,
served to justify the maintenance of a secret, inside
Temple.   In 1971, the Temple had been closed to drop-in
visitors, requiring members to give name, address,
telephone number, and place of employment for potential
converts. Jones "explained that some agency or group was
trying to discredit him, so he had to careful who we let
in."[91]   The Kinsolving articles proved the necessity of
this caution.   Outsiders clearly did not understand the
Temple's beliefs and practices, and therefore must be kept
ignorant of the Temple's true nature.   Outsiders were
perceived as potential enemies of the church and its
ideals. This secrecy led to further cohesion of the group:
they gained strength and a sense of importance from the
secret they kept.

This is the context of punishment and abuse within
the Temple. Submission to and silence about the various
techniques Jones used were both seen in terms of definition
of oneself as a member of the group and in terms of solidifying one's commitment to it. There was a series of loyalty tests. The origins of these were in Redwood Valley,
although one could argue that the first test had been the
decision whether or not to be guided by Jones's vision of
nuclear holocaust in the first hegira from Indianapolis.
Presented as a series of hypothetical situations, the significance of each act increased. Members of the Planning
Commission, for instance, were told that if they really
believed, they would be willing to sign a piece of paper

with any of a number of absurd and not-so absurd "confessions" on them: that they had plotted to overthrow the
United States government, that they had molested their own
children, or that they had done any one of a number of
bizarre, illegal, or perverted things.   They would sign
over custody of their children, sign over power of attorney
to the Temple--they would sign a blank piece of paper that
Jones could fill in later as he wished. Tim Stoen signed a
piece of paper asserting that he had asked Jones to father
a child by his wife, Grace. This child, John Victor Stoen,
was to become the center of much controversy. Tim Stoen,
like the others, signed willingly. They had absolute faith
in Jones, and it seemed only reasonable to prove it.
Later, of course, the thought that they might be prosecuted
for crimes they had not actually committed was powerful
persuasion to remain in a situation which had become
difficult. Elmer and Deanna Mertle, two of the better
known defectors, had to change their names (to Al and
Jeannie Mills) on the advice of their lawyers, because of
the variety of documents they had signed for Jones.[92]

It was in 1973 that the idea of mass suicide came up
for the first time. Jones was troubled about the defection
of eight members.[93]

> Jim tried to sound confident, but then he shook
> his head in despair. "These eight people might
> cause our group to go down. They could say
> things that would discredit our group. This
> might be the time for all of us to make our
> translation together." He had mentioned the
> idea of a "translation" a few times before, but
> no one had ever taken it seriously. His idea
> was that all the counsellors[94] would take
> poison or kill themselves at the same time, and
> then he promised we would all be translated to a
> distant planet to live with him for eternity.
> The few who believed this fairytale said they'd
> be happy to do it anytime. Now, however, faced
> with death, it became obvious that there were
> many who didn't want to.

Jones dropped the idea, at least temporarily, when it was
pointed out that:

> "There is a possibility the public might think
> of us as the biggest fools of all time, instead
> of courageous revolutionaries."

Jim thought about [this] statement, and he
seemed to agree.   More than 100 bodies lying
dead in his church might indeed make him look
insane.   He dropped the subject for the time
being and settled for a debate of how to chase
the defectors.[95]

The distinction between the Planning Commission and the
rest of the Temple, who did not hear about these suicide
plans until after they were in Guyana (as Gerald Parks reports, see above p. 2), is an important one.   Jones tended
to test things out on this smaller group before taking them
to the Temple.   Although a few members did defect in the
aftermath of this first talk about suicide, most of them
stayed and adjusted to the idea.   Once the Counselors had
made the idea part of their conceptual framework, Jones was
ready for the next step, this suicide drills.   The first
one occurred on New Year's Day, 1976, when Jones had the
Planning Commission join him in having a glass of wine, a
treat usually denied them (because the whole world could
not have it).   After they had drunk it, Jones told them
that it was poison, and that they would all be dead in an
hour:

Mrs. [Grace] Stoen says that while she didn't
believe him, others did.   She recalls Walter
Jones, who was attending his first meeting as a
member of the Planning Commission, standing up
and saying that he just wanted to know "why
we're dying.   All I've been doing is working on
bus engines ever since I got here and I want to
know that I'm dying for something more than
being a mechanic working on all these buses."
Mrs. Sly . . . also believed Jones that
evening.   She remembers Jones telling the assem-
blage that the F.B.I. or the C.I.A. was closing
in and would kill everyone.   "I had so much
going through my mind that the 30 minutes was
like 20 hours."   After a while, Mrs. Sly reported, "Jones smiled and said, 'Well, it was a
good lesson.   I see you're not dead.'   He made
it sound like we needed the 30 minutes to do
very strong, introspective kind of thinking.   We
all felt very strongly dedicated, proud of ourselves."
Today Mrs. Sly . . . says she had not been
afraid of death that evening.   After all, she
says, Jones "taught that it would be a privilege

to die for what you believed in, which is exactly what I would have been doing."[96]

As was mentioned above, the main reason for moving the base of Temple operations to San Francisco was that Ukiah did not provide sufficient scope for Jones's ambitions. Apparently concerned about his ability to keep the public and private Temples separate, Jones began to make plans for an overseas colony--a place where the faithful could escape the coming descent into fascism in America. Guyana was chosen for a number of reasons: for one, Jones had visited it on his return from Brazil in 1964, and had thought the country charming and the people "receptive to his brand of 'spiritual healing.'" He also had a series of pragmatic reasons: the main language, and the official one, was English; like his congregation, most of the population was black; the country was relatively close to home, making the transportation of people and goods less expensive than it would be to Africa. The new government, for Guyana had only achieved independence in 1966, was socialist, though not strictly Marxist. Finally, since the country was so poor, it would be cheap to live in.[97] On its part,

Guyana was looking desperately for just such a respectable group of black homesteaders from overseas willing to set up on the remote interior of the country where local blacks refused to go. A multiracial colony would help defuse growing criticism of Guyana's racial problems. Guyana could see many showcase uses for the proposed settlement. The Guyanese cabinet was predisposed to the group. They had heard favorable comments about Jones . . . .

Guyana also saw the colony of Americans as an excellent buffer close to the Venezuelan border. . . . Guyana felt that the People's Temple members sounded so deeply committed they might well fight and die for their Socialist brothers and sisters. Or, more realistically, it was felt that they would at least make a lot of noise-maybe enough to have Washington tell Caracas to back off. Buying time is a major problem for a Third World Country.[98]

The deal was struck in December of 1973, and by the middle of 1974, a small colony at Jonestown had been started. At first there were fewer than 100 people there, but it was

described to them in glowing terms as a future home for all
of them:

> [O]f course everybody knew it was going to be a
> lot of work, a lot of hard work, and it was
> going to take a lot of money, and things like
> that, but at the time he promised, he said there
> wouldn't be any discipline rules to go by, he
> said "You'll be able to live comfortably, you'll
> have your own home, get a good school, college,
> swim, fish," just a regular little paradise, you
> know, the way he talked . . . .
>   [A]nd they had a group that stayed over there
> all the time and they acquired a lot of equip-
> ment--bulldozers and tractors and wagons and
> things like that--that they needed, and they
> started building these little cabins and things
> for people to live in. So then they began to
> send pictures, films, and things like that back
> to the States, and so we'd see these films . . .
> they'd show us just what they wanted us to see,
> a place where you could go fishing, and all the
> flowers, and how the people were being taken
> care of, and then people began to go over to
> work. And it sounded pretty good, and the films
> that you could view, you know, I said, "It
> sounds good."
>   Well, you've got your hectic pace here in the
> States to live by, really, and you thought, you
> begin to think in your own mind, "Now, if I, you
> know, sold my home and gave them the money I
> could go live in an area, a country like that,
> and you would build a city where you're not
> going to be taxed to death, you're not going to
> go around breathing pollution all the time and
> eating food with chemicals and things like that
> constantly."   And it began to sound pretty good
> to me. And you wouldn't have to worry about old
> age, you know, it was supposed to have become a
> self-sufficient city, and so it sounded pretty
> good. And so we began to think about it all,
> would it be worth doing something like that, and
> giving up what you have here and trying your
> life with nature.[99]

As another member said, "To me, my God, it was the greatest
privilege in the world to get to go to Guyana.   Gee whiz,
to be able to work to build paradise! Whooo!"[100]   Odell

Rhodes, the night he arrived,

> was so excited he forgot to sleep, and as he sat
> on the half-finished porch of the new cabin
> watching the stars fade into a spectacular
> jungle sunrise, he decided Jonestown was the
> most beautiful place he has ever seen.
> A few hours later, after breakfast, Rhodes
> and [Stanley] Clayton were both assigned to a
> work crew preparing a field to be planted with
> kasava [sic] roots. "It was," says Rhodes, "by
> about a million miles the hardest work I ever
> did, but it wasn't like you kept waiting for the
> day to end or anything like that. You were out
> there with all your friends and you knew you
> were doing it so people you loved would have
> food to eat--and I didn't mind at all. It felt
> good to me."[101]

It was just as well that the Temple was working on a
new home in another country, because in the summer of 1977,
the gap between the public and private sides of the Temple
began to narrow. Marshall Kilduff, a reporter for the San
Francisco Examiner, was eager to work on a story about
Jones and his followers, but they blitzed the paper with a
phone call and letter campaign and made a $4,000 contribu-
tion for a journalism scholarship, and the editors decided
against it. New West magazine--a then-recent arrival on
the west coast attempting to establish itself as a magazine
emphasizing investigative journalism as well as lifestyle
commentary--decided to go with the story, assigning one of
their contributing editors, Phil Tracy, to the story.

A good deal of pressure came down on the magazine
from a number of sources, including the American Civil
Liberties Union, but they stuck to their decision to pub-
lish. The publication of the story itself became a story,
with a number of articles appearing in mid-July describing
the pressures brought to bear on editors at New West re-
garding this story and pressures on reporters who had previously investigated--or attempted to investigate--the Temple.[102]. The Temple hired attorney Charles Garry, a
well-known attorney for various radical defendents (Huey
Newton and Bobby Seale, the Chicago Eight, The San Quentin
Six).

The story, featuring the stories of ten defectors,
including Al and Jeannie Mills (Elmer and Deanna Mertle)

and Grace Stoen, outlined most of the main points that were
to be made about Jones in future attacks. The Millses
talked about the use of physical discipline; Wayne Pietila
and Jim and Terri Cobb talked about the faked healings;
Micki Touchette, Walter Jones, and Laura Cornelious talked
about financial abuses; and Grace Stoen talked about
Jones's political aspirations.[103] Kilduff and Tracy con-
cluded that "life inside Peoples Temple was a mixture of
Spartan regimentation, fear, and self-imposed humiliation."[104]

New West followed up the 1 August article with
another on 15 August which described the mysterious deaths
of William Head and Maxine Harpe.[105] Again, the Temple
responded with outrage and denials. These denials were
supported by some, including Dr. Carlton B. Goodlett,
publisher of the Sun Reporter and a significant figure in
San Francisco's black community. Goodlett and Jones had
both won the Martin Luther King Jr. Humanitarian Award
(presented by Cecil Williams of Glide Memorial Church) in
January 1977. Goodlett published an editorial stating:

> In the article by Kilduff and Tracy these mal-
> contents, psychoneurotics, and, in some instan-
> ces, provocateurs--probably establishment
> agents--have found willing ears and consummate
> skill to organize fragmented gossip into a
> cloak-and-dagger mosaic that portrays Jim Jones
> and Peoples Temple as a malevolent instrument
> destroying human personalities, robbing the
> poor, and engaged in a conspiracy against the
> established social and political order . . . .
> We have from time to time investigated the
> complaints that persons have lodged against
> Peoples Temples [sic]. On the basis of repeated
> in-depth investigations, we say, as one with
> strong commitments to the role of religion in
> the lives of men: We have found no fault with
> Jim Jones's religious philosophy or the activi-
> ties of the Peoples Temples [sic].[106]

Herb Caen, well-known columnist for the San Francisco
Chronicle, was another defender. He had first met Jones in
1972, and had put a number of favorable items about the
Temple in his column over the years. In retrospect, the
"reaction [to these items] was unnerving, to say the
least," (he received many letters "obviously . . . ordered
by Jones and their contents dictated"),[107] but he used

his column on five occasions in 1977[108] to scoff at the charges brought against Jones.   The Berkeley Barb was the only paper to run favorable stories without this personal bond that both Goodlett and Caen had. Apparently taken by the figure of Charles Garry, they asked, "Are Investigators Trying to Destroy A Progressive Church?" (23-29 September 1977).

    A number of investigations were launched after the New West articles. Kilduff wrote a series of articles for the Chronicle outlining more charges.   Not surprisingly, the papers which followed the story most intently were those in the Bay Area (San Francisco's Examiner, Chronicle, and the Oakland Tribune, in addition to the Berkeley Barb) and Mendocino County (the Santa Rosa Press Democrat, the Ukiah Daily Journal, and the Willits News), though the Indianapolis Star picked up the story on the local boy. It did eventually reach a national audience with a story in Newsweek Magazine on 15 August and one in the New York Times on 1 September. Most of the coverage was effectively a series of charges and counter-charges. Although San Francisco District Attorney Joseph Freitas did begin an investigation,

> The final report to the district attorney placed the Peoples Temple inquiry on "inactive status," although the Temple Leadership's practices were "at least unsavory" and raised "substantial" moral questions.[109]

    One development which was to turn out to be of significance was the formation of the "Concerned Relatives" group in the fall of 1977. Consisting of ex-members (Al and Jeannie Mills, Grace and Tim Stoen, et al) and families of members (Steven Katsaris, et al), they were an informally organized group determined to get their relatives out of Jonestown and to stop Jones.

    Virtually the entire Temple had moved to Guyana by this time. This was done in response to the New West article. The Temple denied that it was making the move:

> Press reports that Peoples Temple is moving to Guyana in a "mass exodus" of its membership represent a continuation of the biased and sensationalistic reporting that has characterized recent coverage of the Temple.
> For the last two years we have provided our

members with the opportunity to reside at our
agricultural project. Even though there are
nearly a thousand there now, and more want to
go, we are absolutely not pulling out of San
Francisco or California. With nearly 9,000[110]
members in the local area, we couldn't afford to
relocate everybody, even if we wanted to. However, we are trying to make it possible for
those of our members who wish to live in a
setting of peace, safety, and natural beauty to
do so--regardless of what they have or have not
contributed to the church.

San Francisco will continue to remain our
"home base" and we are determined that Peoples
Temple will continue to be a strong force here
in the struggle against racism and oppression.

Peoples Temple and Rev. Jim Jones are the
targets of a politically-motivated, neo-McCar-
thyite smear campaign against their socialistic
beliefs and their activism in successfully
fighting injustices inflicted upon poor people.[111]

Despite the strains put on the project by the massive
influx of people--some thirty to forty were arriving every
week--the summer and fall were happy and optimistic times
in Jonestown. Odell Rhodes reports a typical incident
during this period:

Late [one] afternoon, after an eight-hour shift
in the fields, Rhodes's crew was called to form
part of a bucket brigade laboriously watering
one of the experimental gardens. Jones himself
took a turn in the line, and after about an
hour, as Rhodes remembers it:

"There was this big commotion down the line.
Turned out Jones had emptied a bucket of water
over somebody's head, and then somebody got him,
and all of a sudden there was one hell of a
water fight going on. Most people couldn't wait
to get into it, but there was this one, kind of
older man who was bitching about getting his
clothes wet--hell, you were already soaked with
sweat--and Jones just took out after him laugh-
ing and shouting about how he hoped he never got
so old and sour he couldn't have fun like a kid
every once in a while. It was fun--and damned
if that water didn't feel just like what you
needed."

When the water fight finally ended, Rhodes wrung out his shirt and went off to dinner marveling at Jones's ability to turn work into something more than work. "It's like he knew just how far he could push people, and when you had to let off some steam--and how to make you feel everybody, including him, was all in it together."[112]

Rhodes had been enthusiastic about the community all along. Stanley Clayton had come down expecting a paradise of leisure, and originally shocked by the hard work and discipline. However,

Pioneer spirit--or whatever it was--eventually even Stanley Clayton caught it. "You just couldn't be there," Clayton admits, "and not want to be part of building it." In fact, after a few weeks in the fields Clayton volunteered for the jungle clearing crew, the most demanding and difficult work at the settlement. Jonestown's master plan called for clearing a mile of jungle in every direction from the Central Pavillion--2,500 acres. Although less than a third of the planned total actually was cleared, even 800-odd acres was an achievement, the largest successful jungle reclamation in the country, in fact; and Clayton's clearing crew managed it; with no machinery more sophisticated than chainsaws and hand axes. "You just cut for a while," Clayton shrugs, "then you chop for a while. Chopping is fun. It's the damn stumps that drive you crazy."[113]

Conditions deteriorated during the year as Jones became more preoccupied with the activities in San Francisco. It is ironic that a group which had always defined themselves in terms of the forces against them should founder only when this external reaction to the Temple became real. The Concerned Relatives were active in California, and Jones became more and more absorbed in controlling them, the Guyanese government, the American government, or anyone else who might be interested in investigating the Temple, getting members to leave, or in any way threatening his position.

Part of the control was over life in Jonestown, of course. Working hours became longer, food became less plentiful, and meetings lasting all night were held at the central pavillion. Punishments were severe for those who indicated disagreement with any aspect of life there or for those who said they wanted to go home:

> [T]he beatings were all over there with very minor infractions of the rules. People would be humiliated in front of the crowd at these meet-ings, invariably somebody would be breaking the rules, and Jones would sit there and just smile. You could not ever say anything about wanting to come back to the States, you couldn't say anything against what Jones was doing over there, you couldn't say anything negative, what they would call negative, or if someone heard you, you could be turned in. A lot of people that he had their minds controlled, he would tell them if they'd say anything negative, that they in turn would get sick or something would happen to them, or something like that, and so a lot of people were afraid to really say any-thing, even though they thought, because they believed in Jones, they still believed he was God, so, and they still believed that he could heal their bodies when they was sick, or what-ever, so . . . .[114]

Jones cut off all communication with the States early in 1978:

> Communards were told that Los Angeles had been abandoned because of severe drought. They were led to believe that the Ku Klux Klan was march-ing in the open throughout San Francisco streets and that race wars had broken out across the country.[115]

In addition, he stressed that there was no means of leaving:

> There was people who tried to escape, and they didn't make it. And there was a couple, I guess, that did, and they came back to the States. But he would tell everybody that the Guyanese people, who were black, and they were hostile to whites and that they'd kill you and they lived in jungle, so we didn't know, we had no way of knowing, if this was true or not. He

also said he had friends in the State Department
and Georgetown if we made it there, we wouldn't
be able to make it back to the States, they'd
send us right back to Jonestown. And so, he
said, if you _was_ lucky enough to make it through
the jungle, and it was very dangerous, black
cats and snakes and swamp, and it was a dangerous jungle to be in, and there's no way any of
us who didn't know the jungle could have made it
through the jungle to Georgetown, that was about
a hundred and fifty miles.[116]

At the same time, it is important to stress that
there were many for whom the decision to stay was positive,
and not merely resignation to the difficulties of leaving
and the lack of any place to go. Odell Rhodes reports:

"To most people Jonestown was home and they
weren't about to run away from home just because
things weren't perfect. Besides, no matter how
bad it was getting, I think most people still
felt it was better than where they came from. I
know I did. I knew things were getting pretty
bad in a lot of ways, but to me, I never stopped
feeling like I was doing a lot better than I
would have been doing someplace else. I mean
where the hell was I going to go--back to the
streets?" . . . .

Whatever they felt had gone wrong, Rhodes,
Clayton and most of the rest of the community
were inclined to place most of the blame on the
enemies they heard so much about--and not to
look any farther (or nearer) for other reasons.
If they had questions about Jones, they were
questions about his health, perhaps even his
mental health, but never about his motives.

"Besides, you have to remember," Odell Rhodes
says, "I wasn't sitting around thinking about
what was wrong with Jonestown. I might have had
those kinds of thoughts, but I didn't sit around
trying to have them. Most of the time, I was
with the kids, or with my friends, or working at
night, or listening to the band rehearsing--or
whatever. And when I did start thinking about
how bad things were, I'd say to myself: "Damn,
I've seen this place when it works. I know it
can work, so I can put up with it for another
day. I can hold out until we get through all

this bullshit and get things moving in the right
direction again."[117]

There were visitors from the outside. These visitors
did not, however, provide any information which would
contradict the understanding of the communards that they
were, in fact, a beleaguered minority:

> [Temple attorney Mark] Lane used the com-
> pound's public address system to warn members
> that the FBI and CIA were their worst enemies;
> that the agencies would torture them all if the
> members ever talked to them.   This incident,
> ex-members insist, succeeded in silencing the
> few moderating voices in Jones's inner circle.
> That an outside observer, non-member and well-
> known lawyer, confirmed their worst fears was
> taken as a fateful confirmation of what Jones
> had been claiming all along--that they would
> always be hounded and harrassed by agents com-
> missioned to destroy their humanitarian move-
> ment.[118]

Other visitors did not have to reinforce this, though they
were carefully chosen so that they would not say anything
in basic disagreement with it. Not all relatives of members were kept out--only those who were clearly aligned
with the Concerned Relatives. The Rev. John Moore and his
wife Barbara, visited their daughters Annie and Carolyn:[119]

> We walked the thin line of compromise. We ques-
> tioned aspects of Peoples Temple with our daugh-
> ters and Jim Jones.   We chose not to criticize
> publicly. I did commend publicly specific pro-
> grams of Peoples Temple.[120]

In the fall of 1978 Maria Katsaris begged her brother to
come down for a visit.   He said he couldn't but then the
trip with Ryan came up and he decided to go. When he told
her this,

> [I]t was the same thing, only reversed: I'm com-
> ing down, you can't come down, I'm coming down,
> you can't come down, I'm coming down, you can't
> come down. She was like this robot who had to
> get the message out, no matter what I was say-
> ing.[121]

The only visitors allowed were those for whom the public/-private split could be maintained. A number of Guyanese officials visited, and the Embassy in Georgetown came out periodically to both talk to specific individuals and keep a general eye on things. Mervyn Dymally, Lieutenant Governor of California, was the only official visitor from the States; he, too, pronounced it good. Due to the isolation of the commune, it was impossible for people to drop by casually, as Moscone had that one time in San Francisco. There was always enough time to get out the good clothes, fix a special meal, and allow the band to practice. Work hours would be cut for the day, and members instructed to tell any who asked how much they loved Jonestown.

It was important to have these sympathetic visitors, because the Concerned Relatives group was becoming an important oppositional force. On 10 May 1978 they filed two petitions, one to Secretary of State Cyrus Vance and one to Guyanese Prime Minister Forbes Burnham, entreating them for protection of the human rights of the residents of "Jonestown" (quotation marks theirs). Among the Concerned Relatives were Tim and Grace Stoen, whose child John, was in Jonestown. As mentioned above, Tim Stoen had earlier signed a statement that he had asked Jones to impregnate his wife because he "wanted [his] child to be fathered, if not by [him], by the most compassionate, honest, and courageous human being the world contained."[122] When still attorney for the Temple, Stoen had advocated the choice of Guyana as site for the agricultural project because the extradition laws there would favor the Temple if enemies had tried to get members to return to the States. Now, ironically, Stoen was in a position of trying to do just that. On 22 November 1977 a California court assigned custody of John Victor to Grace and Tim, but Jones was not going to budge. Deborah Layton Blakey's affidavit (123) described his reaction:

> 13.   In September, 1977, an event which Rev. Jones regarded as a major crisis occurred. Through listening to coded radio broadcasts and conversations with other members of the Temple staff, I learned that an attorney for former Temple member Grace Stoen had arrived in Guyana, seeking the return of her son, John Victor Stoen.
> 14.   Rev. Jones has expressed particular bitterness toward Grace Stoen. She had been Chief Counselor, a position of great responsi-

bility within the Temple. Her personal quali-
ties of generosity and compassion made her very
popular with the membership. Her departure
posed a threat to Rev. Jones's absolute control
Rev. Jones delivered a number of public tirades
against her. He said that her kindness was
faked and that she was a C.I.A. agent. He swore
that he would never return her son to her.

15. I am informed that Rev. Jones believed
that he would be able to stop Timothy Stoen
. . . from speaking against the Temple as long
as the child was being held in Guyana. Timothy
Stoen . . . had been one of Rev. Jones' most
trusted advisors. It was rumored that Stoen was
critical of the use of physical force and other
forms of intimidation against Temple members. I
am further informed that Rev. Jones believed
that a public statement by Timothy Stoen would
increase the tarnish on his public image.

16. When the Temple lost track of Timothy
Stoen, I was assigned to track him down and
offer him a large sum of money in return for his
silence. Initially, I was to offer him $5,000.
I was authorized to pay him up to $10,000. I
was not able to locate him and did not see him
again until on or about October 6, 1977. On
that date, the Temple received information that
he would be joining Grace in a San Francisco
Superior Court action to determine the custody
of John. I was one of a group of Temple members
assigned to meet him outside the court and
attempt to intimidate him to prevent him from
going inside.

17. The September, 1977 crisis concerning
John Stoen reached major proportions. The radio
messages from Guyana were frenzied and hysteri-
cal. One morning, Terry J. Buford, public relations advisor to Rev. Jones and myself were
instructed to place a telephone call to a high-
ranking Guyanese official who was visiting the
United States and deliver the following threat:
unless the government of Guyana took immediate
steps to stall the Guyanese court action regard-
ing John Stoen's custody, the entire population
of Jonestown would extinguish itself in a mass
suicide by 5:30 PM that day. I was later informed that Temple members in Guyana placed
similar calls to other Guyanese officials.

18. We later received radio communication to the effect that the court case had been stalled and that the suicide threat was called off.

After describing the wretched conditions at Jonestown, the financial situation, and Jones's health and state of mind, she goes on to say:

29. There was constant talk of death. In the early days of the People's Temple, general rhetoric about dying for principles was sometimes heard. In Jonestown, the concept of mass suicide for socialism arose. Because our lives were so wretched anyway and because we were so afraid to contradict Rev. Jones, the concept was not challenged . . . .

31. At least once a week, Rev. Jones would declare a "white night", or state of emergency. The entire population of Jonestown would be awakened by blaring sirens. Designated persons, approximately fifty in number, would arm themselves with rifles, move from cabin to cabin, and make certain that all members were responding. A mass meeting would ensue. Frequently during these crises, we would be told that the jungle was swarming with mercenaries and that death could be expected at any minute.

32. During one "white night", we were informed that our situation had become hopeless and that the only course of action open to us was mass suicide for the glory of socialism. We were told that we would be tortured by mercenaries if we were taken alive. Everyone, including the children, were told to line up. As we passed through the line, we were given a small glass of red liquid to drink. We were told that the liquid contained poison and that we would die within 45 minutes. We all did as we were told. When the time came when we should have dropped dead, Rev. Jones explained that the poison was not real and that we had just been through a loyalty test. He warned us that the time was not far off when it would become necessary for us to die by our own hands.

33. Life at Jonestown was so miserable and physical pain of exhaustion was so great that this event was not traumatic for me. I had become indifferent as to whether I lived or died.[124]

For others, the question was not exhaustion but the degree
of identification with Jones. If there was no way out for
Jones, there was no way out for the Temple. And, quite
simply, despite attempts in October of 1977 to sound out
other countries[125] for yet another hegira, Jones felt
trapped.   In the fourteen months between the September
seige over the Stoen case and the final days of the Temple,
Jones left Jonestown only once because of his fear of
arrest.   (The trip out was to Port Kaituma, the nearby
town, where he felt sufficiently confident of the protection of the local police.[126])   Gerald Parks[127] summed
up the situation in this way:

> [T]here was a lot of people that were loyal to
> him over there, and they thought, you know, they
> had plans built for this city, where the grocery
> store was going to be, and things like that.
> But there, Jones always, in these meetings,
> there was always something going on, there'd be
> CIA or mercenaries out in the jungle. You'd
> hear gunshots and things like that, I knew
> they'd stage it for our benefit, but . . . .
> Most, a lot, of the people were loyal to him,
> they were the people on the inside, and other
> people really thought these were really going
> on. He had them scared to the point, you know,
> nobody could go back to the States if they were
> worried that they'd be picked up by the FBI,
> CIA, because what we believed in, you know, was
> socialist, uncorrupted, and he talked about the
> socialist doctrine. And Jones never could have
> come back because he'd really get put in jail
> because he kept people over there against his
> will, including this boy that he wouldn't return
> [John Stoen] . . . . Jones had things really
> tied up, really sewed up good, with these
> threats of suicide, mass suicide.   Go through
> these suicide drills, I suppose we went through
> about five or six of them in the course of seven
> and a half months we were there.   And we were
> asked would you be willing to die? Commit sui-
> cide, if you knew they was coming to get you,
> kill you, or whatever? Scare tactics he used on
> people.   And what we had, when we would have
> these drills, these white nights, in the pavil-
> lion, we would be surrounded by guards, you
> know, as if there was anybody out there they was
> going to protect us, but actually, in essence it

was the other way around, none of us was going
to get out to anywhere else, we really was being
guarded with the guns. Jones figured we were
too stupid to know, and a lot of them
didn't.[128]

This, then, was the situation at Jonestown when Congressman
Leo Ryan came down to investigate in November, 1978.

Ryan had heard a number of stories about the Temple
from a variety of sources. His constituency was San Mateo
County (due south of and adjacent to the city of San Francisco), from which many Temple members came. He began to
hear certain stories over and over again, about mysterious
deaths and horrible punishments, loyalty tests and bizarre
behavior. An activist politician--something of a maverick,
according to his colleagues; a publicity hound, according
to his detractors--Ryan had personally investigated the
state prison system, inner-city schools, and seal slaugh-
ters in Newfoundland. He was actively involved with the
anti-cult movement.[129] Accompanied by Concerned Relatives, and reporters, he was stalled in Georgetown for
several days before being permitted to go to Jonestown.

When Ryan, four of the Concerned Relatives, and the
reporters arrived in Jonestown, they were greeted warmly by
Marcie Jones. Charles Krause of the _Washington Post_ said:

> Everything seemed to be going well. People in
> our party were doing exactly what they had come
> to do: the relatives were talking, Ryan was
> talking, Lane and Garry were counseling, and the
> newsmen were interviewing. Considering all the
> problems we had had getting here, the Jonestown
> people seemed quite hospitable. I couldn't
> understand why there had been such a fuss; the
> buildings were impressive, the people seemed
> healthy, rational, and friendly. If any of the
> awful things we had been told were true, they
> weren't apparent. I was, on the whole, im-
> pressed.[130]

Not everyone was so accepting of the situation. Anthony
Katsaris became more and more concerned after his initial
cold greeting from his sister:

> I tried [to talk to her] but I was too dispiri-
> ted . . . . I was partly relieved, though.

What do I say to her? She was like a stranger.

They brought dinner, and she starts saying, aren't you afraid we're trying to poison you, this might be human stew, and I'm just like "Hunh?" And she's talking about all the things you read about us in the paper. And I said, "You're not that important, you're not in the paper all the time." Now, of course, knowing how Jones controlled everything they knew, but then, I was just flabbergasted, what are you talking about, there's more on the public's mind than Jonestown . . . .

[I]t was like talking to a robot.

We were talking, and we were saying something at the same time, and I grabbed her arm, like "hey," and she freaked out and started calling for help. So I backed off, and I started crying and she started to pretend like she was so concerned. She put her arms around me, but she was like a wooden Indian. She starts saying how open and supportive we are in Jonestown, and how it's ok to let out your emotions, but with this wooden pat on my shoulder, like it's supposed to be meaningful.

I just didn't know what to think. It was like there was nobody behind it, no feelings at all.[131]

So, again, there was this public/private split. The reporters were impressed, as was Ryan, but the Concerned Relatives were very concerned.

Some members of the Temple began slipping notes to the reporters and the Congressman, asking to leave with the party. All told fourteen members of the Temple wanted to leave. Jones was quite upset at the prospect: he had Marceline talk to Gerald Parks to try to talk him out of allowing his family to leave. Publicly, he said merely that he wanted to hug them all before they left.[132]

At the last moment, Larry Layton joined the group of defectors who were leaving with the Congressman. The other defectors were concerned, but Ryan insisted that everyone who said they wanted to leave be allowed to do so. When the truck arrived at the airstrip, Layton led the ambush in which Ryan, three reporters, and Patricia Parks were killed and most of the others in the party injured. In Jonestown, Jones called for a White Night; the Temple's final White Night.

It all started as they all started, with Jones talking calmly, smoothly, about enemies without and traitors
within.   He told them that Ryan and his party were dead,
that their plane had crashed and the GDF, Guyanese Defense
Force, would be there soon. "It was said by the greatest
prophets from time immemorial: No man takes my life from
me. I lay down my life . . . . If we can't live in peace,
then let's die in peace."[133]

The tub was brought out, with a special mixture of
fruit flavored punch drink, sedatives (thorazine, halio-
parael, largatil), a painkiller (demarol), and a substance
that makes the bloodstream absorb substances quickly, in
addition to the cyanide.   Dr. Larry Schacht, trained at
Temple expense, had carefully calculated the formula months
before--including sedatives to ease death, sedatives that
would take effect some fifteen minutes after the cyanide
had done so.

They started with the babies, squirting the mixture
deep in their throats so they wouldn't spit it back up.
"Don't tell the children they are dying. Don't tell them
it's painful. To die in revolutionary suicide is to live
forever! We must die with dignity! We must all die!"[134]
Christine Miller protested.   She was shouted down. "We'll
all die tonight," said one member, speaking for all, "but
Father will raise us from the dead tomorrow."[135]

I'll see you in the next life," said Jones. "I'm
going to my rest. We'll finally be at peace.

"Mother, mother, mother, mother, mother . . . "
There were three shots, and then silence.[136]

FOOTNOTES

[1]George Klineman, Sherman Butler, and David Conn, The Cult That Died (New York: G.P. Putman's Sons, 1980), pp. 39-40.

[2]Richmond (Indiana) Palladium-Item, 15 March 1953.

[3]C. William Fisher, Why I Am A Nazarene (Kansas City, Missouri: Nazarene Publishing House, 1958), p. 21.

[4]Richmond Palladium-Item, 29 June 1976.

[5]Marshall Kilduff & Ron Javers, The Suicide Cult (New York: Bantam Books, 1978), p. 10.

[6]Interestingly enough, Phil Kerns, who was brought into the Temple by his mother in 1967 (when Kerns was 15), describes much the same sort of phenomenon. The first time he saw Jones, he was struck by the fact that animals "were very much relaxed around him--even attracted by him. It was magical and strange . . . . The horse and chickens plodded along with the people, following the man with the jet black hair. It looked stupid and yet it was so remarkable, so uncanny, something that only happened on Sunday morning cartoons. 'See,' Carol said, 'even the animals love him.'" (Phil Kerns with Doug Wead, People's Temple: People Tomb [Plainfield, NJ: Logos International, 1979], p. 37). Cf. stories told about Sun Myung Moon, whose followers "were told that whenever he went to the zoo, all the animals would run over to that part of the zoo. When he visited a fish pond, all the fish would swim over to him. He had dominion over creation . . . ." (Ronald Enroth, Youth, Brainwashing, and the Extremists Cults, [Grand Rapids, Mich: Zondervan, 1977], p. 108).

[7]Kilduff and Javers, p. 12.

[8]Richmond Palladium-Item, 15 March 1953.

[9]Kilduff and Javers, p. 14.

[10]Richmond Palladium-Item, 15 March 1953.

[11]John Maguire and Mary Lee Dunn, Hold Hands and Die (New York: Dale Books, 1978), p. 65.

[12]Reprinted from the _Georgetown_ (Guyana) _Chronicle_ of 6 December 1978 by _Accuracy in Media Report_ (hereafter, AIM Report), 2 February 1979, p. 3, elisions in original.

[13]For instance, there is the story of the young girl who is involved in a cancer passing incident when she is asked to testify that her father's breath smells different before and after the passing of the "cancer": "She didn't notice anything different about [her father's] breath, nothing at all, but she knew she had a choice: she could tell them what she smelled, or she could go along with the program." Klineman takes her decision to go along with the program as an early test of loyalty (p. 61).

[14]Quoted, ibid., pp. 52-54.

[15]Quoted, ibid., p. 54.

[16]Ibid., pp. 57-58.

[17]Quoted, Kilduff and Javers, p. 19.

[18]Klineman, p. 58.

[19]AIM Report, p. 3, elisions in original.

[20]_Indianapolis Star_, 11 December 1971, punctuated as in original.

[21]AIM Report, p. 3, elisions in original.

[22]Klineman, p. 64.

[23]Caroline Bird, "Nine Places to Hide," _Esquire_, January 1962.

[24]Ross Case, letter dated 12 April 1979.

[25]Bonnie Theilmann with Dean Merrill, _The Broken God_ (Elgin, Illinois: David C. Cook Publishing Co., 1979).

[26]Ibid., p. 7. Reiterman doubts that the picture was of Castro, because "the bearded figure in fatigues standing beside Jones . . . was too short . . . ." Tim Reiterman with John Jacobs, _Raven_. (New York: E.P. Dutton, Inc., 1982), p. 62.

[27]Thielmann, p. 29.

[28]Cf. comments by his college rommate, Kenneth Lemmons, who "found Jim's religious views incongruous and his knowledge of scripture full of holes . . . [Jones] seemed blind to sophisticated points of theology." Reiterman, p. 35.

[29]Thielmann, p. 29.

[30]Ibid., p. 51.

[31]Which was to become Guyana in 1966.

[32]I heard two radio editorials while in Ukiah doing research (June, 1981) which I am told accurately reflect local sentiment. One endorsed Phyllis Schafley's charge that women who are the victims of sexual harrassment are "asking for it"; the other concerned the educational system in this country, and decried the fact that it is in the hands of intellectuals who are out of touch with the needs and desires of their true constituency and who ignore the need for strong moral instruction. I do not recall if the intellectuals were called "pointy-headed" or if the phrase "secular humanism" was used, but both would be consonant with the general tone.

[33]Ross Case, letter dated 12 April 1979.

[34]See below, p. 76 .

[35]Cf. Father Divine.

[36]Jeannie Mills, Six Years With God (New York: A&W Publishers, 1979), p. 130.

[37]This incident will be discussed below (pp. 152-153).

[38]Reiterman, pp. 259-260.

[39]Ibid., p. 59.

[40]Ibid., p. 119.

[41]Ibid., pp. 173-174 (Cf. arranged marriages in the Unification Church).

[42]The ruling body of the Temple.

[43]"Sandy Rozynko Mills was only fourteen when she

received a questionnaire from Jones, addressed to the youth
of the Temple, asking, 'Do you fantasize about Father
sexually?' She said, 'Here I was, fourteen years old, and
I was thinking "What . . . ?" But we all knew we were supposed to answer yes, so I said yes.'" Mel White, Deceived,
(Old Tappan, NJ: Fleming H. Revell/Spire Books, 1979), p.
131, emphasis In original.

[44]Reiterman, p. 173.

[45]Mills, p. 257.

[46]Mills, pp. 252-253.

[47]This will be discussed more thoroughly in Chapter
Three.

[48]Reiterman, pp. 175-176.

[49]Quoted, Kilduff and Javers, p. 33.

[50]This account by Phil Kerns of a service in Redwood Valley in the late 1960s seems to be reliable, despite
his role as "apostate" (see Introduction p. 4). Other
accounts indicate that all services followed this same
pattern, though the Redwood Valley meetings could become
much more rigorous than the more public meetings in San
Francisco or Los Angeles. Thielmann, p. 81.

[51]Thielmann, p. 74.

[52]Cited by Maguire and Dunn, p. 89.

[53]Ross Case, 4/12/79.

[54]Thielmann, p. 46.

[55]Kerns, pp. 42-44.

[56]Jeannie Mills, letter dated 17 April 1979.

[57]Kerns, pp. 52-53. Ijames and Beam were assistant
pastors.

[58]Usually the offspring of one member being brought
up by another to loosen the biological tie and make the
Temple the focus of family feeling. This is connected with
the encouragement of celibacy discussed above.

[59]Kilduff and Javers, p. 86.

[60]San Francisco Examiner, 7 January 1979.

[61]Pete Axthelm, et al, "The Emperor Jones," in Newsweek, 4 December 1978, p. 60; "Messiah from the Midwest" in Time, 4 December, 1978, p. 27.

[62]Klineman, p. 250.

[63]Kilduff and Javers, p. 86.

[64]Anthony Katsaris, telephone interview, 24 September 1981.

[65]Tim Stoen's (ex) wife and a significant defector.

[66]Quoted, Kilduff and Javers, p. 82.

[67]People Forum, the Temple newsletter, carried an article in November 1976 in which Jones was interviewed about this appointment (p. 3). At the bottom of the page was a one-line "space filler" stating: "FOR YOUR INFORMATION: Peoples Temple makes no endorsement of political candidates."

[68]John Peer Nugent, White Night (New York: Rawson, Wade, 1979), pp. 41-42.

[69]Thielmann, pp. 77-78 is only one of several similar versions of this story.

[70]According to Reiterman, despite Jones's strenuous efforts to recuit among members of the Peace Mission, only about a dozen joined the Temple (pp. 139-141).

[71]Thielmann, p. 77.

[72]White, p. 115.

[73]Mills, pp. 255-256.

[74]He started claiming Divine as one of his previous personae soon after the latter's death in 1965, in part as an effort to lure members of the Peace Mission into joining the Temple.

[75]Quoted, White, p. 58.

[76]Cf. The Manson Family's Helter Skelter, where the Chosen People (the Family) would wait out the holocaust in a big cave. Their holocaust, however, was to be caused by a race war--indicating the change in mood between the late 1950s and the late 1960s.

[77]Mills, pp. 206-207.

[78]Quoted, White, p. 70.

[79]Mills, pp. 220-221, 229-230.

[80]San Francisco Examiner, 17-18-19-20 September, 1972.

[81]The story concerned the investigation by the Indiana State Board of Psychology Examiners into Jones's claims to heal and raise the dead. The Board took no action because Jones hadn't called himself a psychologist. San Francisco Examiner, 19 September 1972, p. 8.

[82]San Francisco Examiner, 20 September 1972.

[83]According to Reiterman, "By the mid-1970s, all the military elements were in place. The church had stockpiled almost two hundred guns; a security squad of a few dozen people had been trained; Jones traveled everywhere with body-guards; there were procedures for searching all who entered Temple services; and Temple buses had armed escorts" (p. 200).

[84]San Francisco Examiner, 20 September 1972.

[85]Quoted, ibid., elisions in original.

[86]Ibid., elisions in original (except between "warning people about them" and "I project the positive").

[87]Cf. The letter writing campaigns against Jones in Indianapolis (see above, p. 22). It seems clear that Jones was aware of the benefits of a feeling of persecution for enhancing a feeling of community; and, in the absence of such persecution by outsiders, was capable of arranging for it himself.

[88]Liz Foreman, the woman who got Maria involved.

[89]Anthony Katsaris, 9/24/81.

90Mills, p. 183.

91Ibid, p. 148.

92Marshall Kilduff and Phil Tracy, "Inside Peoples Temple," New West, 1 August 1977, p. 34.

93See Reiterman, pp. 219-229, for full description of this incident.

94The lowest level of the leadership hierarchy.

95Mills, pp. 231-232.

96Carey Winfrey, "Why 900 Died in Guyana," New York Times Magazine, 25 February 1979, p. 42.

97Kilduff and Javers, p. 92.

98Nugent, pp. 77-78.

99Gerald Parks, interview, Ukiah, California, 26 June 1981.

100Neva Sly, quoted by Winfrey, p. 46.

101Ethan Feinsod, Awake in a Nightmare (New York: W. W. Norton, 1981), p. 114. Odell Rhodes was one of two men to leave Jonestown during the suicides.

102San Francisco Examiner, 11 June 1977 (page 3); San Francisco Examiner and Chronicle, 17 July 1977 (page 4f).

103Kilduff and Tracy, p. 34.

104Ibid.

105Head died on 19 October 1975, approximately a month after giving the Temple $10,000 he had received from an insurance settlement. Although the Los Angeles Coroner declared the death a suicide, Head's mother noted "serious discrepancies" in the report, such as "the report claims the boy's body bore no scars or surgical wounds. Mrs. Head claims, however, that her son had 300 stitches as a result of the motorcycle accident" for which the insurance settlement was made (p. 19). Harpe died on 28 March 1970 and was found hanging from a rafter in her garage. Her death was

considered questionable because it occurred a week after
she gave the Temple $1,000 and because her house was ran-
sacked before the police came. It was said that "temple
[sic] members went through the dead woman's belongings 'to
remove anything that would identify her with the temple.'
At the time, the attorney general's office looked into the
matter, but did not discover anything unusual." (ibid.)
See Klinemann, pp. 212 ff, for a fuller version of these
stories.

106_The Sun Reporter_, 21 July 1977, p. 7. According
to Goodlett, this article, like all articles about the
Temple in _The Sun Reporter_, was written by Temple members
(interview, Cascais, Portugal, 5 August 1982.)

107Kilduff and Javers, p. 195.

10820 July, 8 and 18 August, 1 and 9 September.

109Kilduff and Javers, p. 89.

110A greatly exaggerated figure.

111Peoples Temple press release, 17 August 1977.

112Feinsod, pp. 114-115.

113Ibid., p. 116. Clayton was the other person to
leave during the final White Night.

114Parks, 6/26/81.

115Kerns, p. 191.

116Parks, 6/26/81.

117Feinsod, pp. 155-156.

118Nugent, p. 163.

119Carolyn was one of Jones's main mistresses and
the ex-wife of Larry Layton, who instigated the airstrip
ambush.

120John V. Moore, "Jonestown: Personal Reflections," _Circuit Rider_, May, 1981, p. 4, used with permission.

[121]Katsaris, 9/24/81.

[122]Affidavit quoted in entirety, Nugent, pp. 31-32.

[123]Blakey had been in the ruling elite of the Temple, and thus her defection and testimony were additional sources of concern to Jones. Her brother Larry instigated the ambush at the airstrip.

[124]Charles A. Krause, et al, Guyana Massacre (New York: Berkley, 1978), Appendix D, pp. 187-194.

[125]An unidentified Temple member wrote to about 18 countries, including Albania, North Korea, Finland, Sweden, Mozambique, Angola, Bangladesh, Turkey, and the United Arab Emirates, as well as the Soviet Union. Reston states that "the inquiries were posed through the simple-hearted method of asking the U.S. State Department about the possibilities." James Reston, Jr., Our Father Who Art in Hell, (New York: Times Books, 1981), pp. 196-170.

[126]Ibid., p. 137.

[127]Parks and his family left with the Congressman on the last day. His wife Patricia was killed in the ambush at the airstrip.

[128]Gerald Parks, 6/26/81.

[129]Anson D. Shupe, Jr. and David G. Bromley, The New Vigilantes, (Beverly Hills: Sage Library of Social Research, 1980), pp. 212-213.

[130]Krause, p. 44.

[131]Katsaris, 9/24/81.

[132]Parks, 6/26/81; Kilduff and Javers, p. 166.

[133]Reston, p. 323.

[134]Kerns, p. 194.

[135]Ibid.

[136]Kilduff and Javers, p. 179.

CHAPTER TWO

THE FORMATION OF THE PEOPLES TEMPLE

Underlying this attempt to discuss the development of the Peoples Temple in terms of normal sociological processes is a sociology of knowledge approach. As was suggested in the Introduction, to layer other schools of sociology on top of this basic paradigm need not be contradictory. Although exchange theory, which is generally considered to be a functionalist approach, may seem to be in conflict with the more non-evaluative phenomenology of the sociology of knowledge, just such an approach is necessary to explain the formation of the group before the processes of social reality construction can begin.

Peter Berger and Thomas Luckmann simply do not tackle this problem in The Social Construction of Reality.[1]   In Part II, "Society as Objective Reality," they posit a randomly chosen group of people in the proverbial desert island to suggest the ways in which a reality would be created de novo, which of course is impossible, for we are born onto a merry-go-round already in progress. In Part III, "Society as Subjective Reality," they examine the ways in which an alternative reality is maintained through the resocialization of the members of the group. They do not explain how this group might be created. Their focus on secondary socialization as a process necessitated by "the division of labor and the concomitant social distribution of knowledge"[2] is highly significant, for such subgroups are an integral part of our society. They are thus tacitly acknowledging that there is no way to explain the creation of a group around an alternate vision (i.e., a "non-essential" subgroup) if one remains strictly within a sociology of knowledge framework. Their case-point of religious conversion[3] stresses the necessity of a religious community for the maintenance of the shift in plausibility structures experienced in conversion:

> Alternation . . . involves a reorganization of the conversational apparatus. The partners in significant conversation change. And in conversation with the new significant others subjective reality is transformed. It is maintained by continuing conversation with them, or within

the community they represent. Put simply, this means that one must now be very careful with whom one talks. People and ideas that are discrepant with the new definitions of reality are systematically avoided.[4]

This is all very true, but does not confront the issue of exactly where this group comes from.

Despite the importance of subjective self-consciousness in their schema, Berger and Luckmann are unable to talk about the process of the formation of the group because it is necessary to place the subjective experience in a functional context in order to do so. A group—especially a religious and/or political group—will form around the vision, the subjective vision, of an individual who gathers the group to share in this vision. In the mature stages of the group, we can again begin to talk in pure sociology of knowledge terms, but in the early stages, we are trying to discover the means through which a new social "language" can be developed.

The group forms (institutionalizes) around the visionary, and individuals join the group because the vision and the group meet needs of these individuals that are not being met in the larger society.[5] It will be argued in this chapter that the origin of the group, and of any individual's commitment to it, are necessarily framed in the "language" of the larger society, and that through various "commitment mechanisms"[6] a group is formed that is in a position to develop a new "language."

In other words, a functionalist approach is necessary to fill a gap which cannot be filled if remaining in a sociology of knowledge context. "Commitment mechanisms" are the specific means by which the process of the development of the new language is achieved. Individuals become attracted to the group for any of a number of reasons, and then become committed to the group by means of certain mechanisms. These mechanisms are used to form the structures within which a group can create a new reality.

The sociology of knowledge approach cannot deal with this question for two reasons. First, it is focussed too exclusively on the cognitive aspects of an individual's interaction with reality: it ignores the affective and the functional. Second, it does not have a way of talking about the means which the nascent society must provide for individuals both to break their ties to the larger society and solidify commitment to the smaller society. Before we can talk about the ways in which the Peoples Temple created and maintained a new reality, it is necessary to find out how the Peoples Temple came to be a group. The sociology of knowledge provides no tools with which to do so.

In this chapter, two forms of exchange theory will be used. The exchanges begin in the "coin" ("language") of the dominant reality, and then a new "coinage" ("language") in which exchanges would be made is gradually developed. Exchange theory provides a means of explaining the formation of the group which complements the underlying sociology of knowledge approach.[7]

Exchange theory, in its simplest form, argues that all human behavior involves a calculation of the costs and benefits resulting from any particular action. People tend to do things that are rewarding, and to avoid things that are not. Naturally, not even George Homans, the founder of the school, would be satisfied with as bald a statement as this, and those who followed him tended to make the theory more and more precise, and more and more accurate. The following analysis is based on two second generation exchange theorists: James Downton and Rosabeth Moss Kanter.[8]

Exchange theory need not posit the conscious weighing of alternatives; rather, it merely rests on the assumption that any activity which does not "pay off" on any of a number of possible levels (affective, cognitive, practical, etc.) will tend not to be repeated. This is as true of a cat or a dog as it is of a human being. The human is capable of conscious calculation in addition to stimulus-response behavior, and not just instead of it.

In this section, we will begin by looking at the appeals of the Peoples Temple (i.e., what the "pay offs" were), and then examine the process through which the exchanges take place. The end result, of course, is a new group, a new society, whose dynamics we will then analyze in terms of the sociology of knowledge (the creation of this group's new reality) in Chapter Five.

The central appeal of the Temple was healing. This includes, most obviously, physical healing, which was one of Jones's main drawing cards, as we have seen; but it also includes emotional and socio-political healing. There were

other, additional kinds of appeal, but all of them cluster
around the concept of healing--the healing of individual
personal ills, whether they be physical, spiritual, or
emotional; the healing of small groups, most importantly,
families;[9] and the healing of society through eradication
of racial injustice and economic inequality.

As mentioned in the previous chapter, Jones was, as a
young man, undecided about whether to devote his life to
medicine or ministry.   He began his healing, however, not
in an attempt to combine the two, but as an instrumental
means of attracting followers. Regardless of his intentions, he did perform actual healings.   This point cannot
be stressed strongly enough, although how it occurred is
beyond the scope of the current discussion.   The faked
healings were perhaps only manipulative; they were seen as
such both by Jones and by the inside ruling elite.[10]   It
seems likely that most of the rank and file members of the
Temple were either unaware of the faking or unsure about
it. Gerald Parks says of Jones's psychic abilities:

> I never knew for sure whether he could or
> whether he couldn't, but he put on a lot of good
> demonstrations--if he wasn't able to, he was
> sure putting on good demonstrations . . . .
> [A]fter I got back [from Jonestown], I talked to
> some of the people that worked with him that had
> left the church before we did, and they told me
> how he set these things up, and things like
> that, so . . . .
> And there was one time that he called out my
> wife in the service and told her that something
> would happen to her health-wise in a certain
> month. Just about that time she did have a
> hysterectomy, and I talked to her about surgery,
> [but] the surgeon told me [later] that there
> wasn't anything, anything there, you know, the
> hysterectomy was over and so I don't know, you
> know, how much of it was real and how much of it
> was false.   I couldn't decide, I have no way of
> knowing if he could heal, but I'd prefer in my
> own mind to disbelieve it all as far as he was
> concerned.[11]

Parks still isn't sure; he can only say that he "would prefer to disbelieve it all."

It is probably safe to discount Jones's claims to be
able to raise the dead, but his ability to heal drew hun-

dreds to the church.   Even those who had no specific ail-
ment to be cured found safety in his protection.   Jones
claimed to be able to foresee and prevent accidents. Gerald Parks says:

> [T]o the kids, grownups too, for that matter, he
> did become God to them, because he was supposed
> to have had special protection.   You were to
> start out on an automobile trip, he's have you
> to meditate for two minutes . . . . And there's
> a lot of people attested to near accidents, and
> accidents, that were—supposedly [they] couldn't
> get a way out of them, but [they] came out of
> them, and I'm sure as I'm sitting here that the
> biggest percentage, if not all of them, were
> lying at the time, but I didn't know that
> then.[12]

On the other hand, Gerald's son Dale:

> was not a believer, but even [he] wonders about
> the times he drove Jones over the steep, winding
> two lane mountain roads   around Redwood Valley.
> It was standard procedure for Jones to tell Dale
> when he could pass another car blindly in the
> lane of oncoming traffic.   "I don't believe in
> ESP; I don't even believe in astrology, but I
> drove those damn roads with him a hundred times,
> and whatever it was, nobody will ever convince
> me it was pure, dumb luck."[13]

The Temple also provided a positive alternative for
individuals whose lives were being wasted on the streets.
Odell Rhodes was trying to break his heroin addiction. He
had done so physically, but knew that he had to stop his
old street habits to do so fully:

> For Rhodes, the Temple could hardly have come at
> a better time.   The opportunity the Temple pro-
> vided to escape the streets, to escape Detroit
> altogether, was exactly what he was looking
> for.   "Man, I was so tired, so tired of hust-
> ling, so tired of looking over my shoulder all
> the time, that I might have gone with just about
> anybody."[14]

He worried about what the Temple would want from him in
return, but, unable to figure it out, he put his questions
to one side. Upon their arrival in San Francisco,

Rhodes was shown to a free bed on the balcony of
the Temple auditorium, fed a free breakfast,
introduced around, and left to rest up from the
trip. That night, after dinner, Marie Lawrence
borrowed a Temple car and began showing Rhodes
the sights of San Francisco . . . . Between
excursions, he was introduced to the Temple's
version of social services: an appointment with
a specialist to check his chronically inflamed
leg; another specialist to check his eyes; a
trip to the dentist. He was given money to buy
a special orthopedic shoe, new eyeglasses, and
new clothes. "I couldn't believe it," Rhodes
remembers, "anything you needed, all you had to
do was ask for it. It wasn't just that you
didn't have to pay, it was the difference between trying to get something out of welfare,
standing in lines and filling out forms, and
just asking for what you needed."[15]

The Temple's appeals included the healing of family
units. This was important to Jeannie Mills, whose second
marriage, to Al Mills, did not seem to be answering her
needs for this kind of wholeness. Despite her (admitted)
latent racism, she was touched by the sight and sound of
the interracial children's choir:

The sight of these black and white children
smiling and holding hands was strangely
satisfying. I had never before witnessed the
warmth and love I was seeing in this totally
integrated group, and their songs were sweet and
simple. This made a strong impression on me.
Our children were so wrapped up in their own
problems that they could think only of themselves. Here were children learning about
social justice and singing songs about love and
freedom. Their radiant faces conveyed the
message of the songs as eloquently as their
voices . . . .
[O]ur children loved every minute of it. We
were happy to see them smiling and associating
with wholesome-looking friends. Each time we
looked over to where they were sitting, we saw
them looking at Jim with rapt attention. Their
new-found friends answered all their questions
and begged them to come back again, often. My
thoughts meandered back to my own childhood. In
all the years I attended church, I never felt

the warmth and friendliness that our family was
being shown here as visitors . . . .
    All the way home our children were bubbling
over with enthusiasm about the wonderful time
they'd had.[16]

More importantly than the healing of individual
family units, however, the Temple itself became a family
for its members, healing the breaches of modern alienated
society. Ethan Feinsod suggests that this emphasis on the
Temple as family was an integral part of the ideology:

[F]amily pathology was a persistent feature of
the lives of Temple members, especially, but not
exclusively, the poorer, black members. In 1970
the decadal national census showed that a third
of all non-white children were growing up in
fatherless homes. Jones, who was well aware of
these statistics--and well aware that broken
homes were the rule within the Temple--openly
advertised the Temple as a surrogate family. In
fact, he even liked to claim that the breakdown
of the American family was a blessing in dis-
guise. In Jones's view, old-fashioned nuclear
families were a species of social dinosaur, outmoded relics of a dying society which oppressed
poor people by isolating them from those with
whom they had common cause. The wave of the
future, according to Jones, was for poor people
to join together in an entirely new kind of
family, a broad extended network of associations
not based upon the narrow, accidental bonds of
biology, but upon the utopian idea of the brotherhood of mankind.[17]

The personal and familiar healing segues almost
imperceptibly into the social and political healing Jones
promised. The immediate appeal was on a personal level,
but

Jones told the congregation that he had the answers to the world's problems. If each of his
members would follow him in complete faith, the
church could end poverty, racism, political
oppression, hunger, and even death.[18]

Even personal problems were explained in a socio-political
context. The Temple prohibited its members' use of alcohol, drugs, and tobacco: their "objection was on the

grounds that mind-altering substances were means by which
the ruling class controlled and exploited the poor."[19]
The Temple proposed to help the individuals make themselves
better people as a first step in making society better.
Jones would heal individuals so the Temple could heal
society. For many, however, this emphasis on making the
world a better place was the primary appeal of the church.
This was especially true of the members of the elite.

The Temple, in its early days, had framed this in
terms of concrete activist Christianity. Ross Case reports
that social activism and religion was

> actually . . . what drew me to Peoples Temple.
> It had bothered me considerably that eleven
> o'clock Sunday morning was the most segregated
> hour in America. I felt that if Christians were
> to be so committed as to lay down our lives for
> one another, that it was unacceptable that
> Christians of different races couldn't sit to-
> gether in church. I wanted to see the gospel do
> the same thing in our culture that it did in the
> segregated society of the first century when it
> broke down "the middle wall of partition (or
> segregation) and made one new man so making
> peace," and I felt that if Christ's words, "In-
> asmuch as ye have done it unto one of the least
> of these my brethren, ye have done it unto me"
> were to be applied in this area, that those who
> segregated themselves from fellow-believers of
> another color, would be judged for segregating
> themselves from Christ.[20]

Case is talking about his perception of the group's
ideology of the early 1960s. By the end of the decade,
Christianity was no longer seen as a means of combatting
racism, but rather as a means of its continuance:

> "The King James Bible is full of contradictions
> and errors," [Jones] said angrily. "The slave
> owners forced black people to take the King
> James religion and forsake their own beautiful
> African beliefs. Any black person who still
> believes in the Bible is a sellout."[21]

> Jones would . . . throw the Bible on the floor,
> making sure to remind the congregation that the
> King James whose name graces the classic English
> translation of the Bible was none other than the

same King James who brought the slave trade to
the New World. "Are you gonna sit there and read
this garbage?" Jones would demand. "Are you
gonna sit there and read this slave Bible?"[22]

Thus, by the 1970s religion was being downplayed as the
Temple moved away from the trappings of traditional Christianity.[23] This is a further example of the public/pri-
vate split discussed in the previous chapter, for although
the Bible was denounced, the Temple continued to call itself a church and continued to affiliate with the Disciples
of Christ.

A similar phenomenon can be discerned with regard to
the Temple's political ideology. They presented themselves
to the outside world as a non-political group, keeping the
details of their beliefs to themselves. Even within the
Temple, however, there was some differentiation as to how
the ideology was explained. Socialism was regarded suspi-
ciously by most of the lower and middle-class rank and file
members. Jones knew this, and would distinguish between
Communism and communalism. Jeannie Mills reports that he
told her:

> "Some people confuse our communal way of life
> with communism. Actually it has nothing to do
> with politics. If everyone would live as we do
> here, there would be no need to fear a communist
> takeover in our country. Our church could be
> this country's answer to fight communism."
> Either Jim had a psychic ability or he was one
> of the most sensitive persons I had ever met.
> He seemed to sense that this was one of the
> things that bothered me most. I relaxed. As
> long as I knew that Jim wasn't trying to threa-
> ten the democracy I loved, I would listen to
> whatever else he had to say.[24]

The political was there, of course, but it was a level of
interpretation given to the facts of social and racial
injustice which the Temple was combatting:

> Although Rhodes had never spent much mental
> energy thinking about capitalism or the social-
> ist revolution, the more he listened to Jones,
> the more he felt as if Jones was expressing his
> own feelings, feelings he had never been able to
> put into words. When Jones vented his rage at
> the racism of white America, Rhodes remembered

[his experiences in] Alabama, and, when Jones jabbed his finger in the air and told the congregation that "This system is the reason you are where you are," Rhodes nodded his head as if there was nothing more that needed to be said. "He'd say," Rhodes remembers, "that slavery had never really ended. It just painted up its face, but in its heart, it had never really changed . . . .

"Even if it hadn't been Jones saying it--no matter who might have said it--you don't have to try very hard to convince black people they're still treated like slaves. I mean, when he said living in this country is like living in hell, believe me, you sure as hell didn't see anybody stand up and start waving a flag."[25]

The interracial mix of the Temple was one of its most appealing aspects. For blacks, who made up approximately 80% of the Temple's membership, Jones personally seems to have been the appeal. He was a white man, therefore powerful, but one who was working on sharing the power with them. In addition, he claimed to have been part Cherokee, although apparently his dark coloring was traceable to his Welsh ancestors. The effect, however, was to lessen the racial distance between him and his followers.[26] Outside the ruling elite, where the whites seem to have been politically motivated, Diane Johnson suggests:

It appears that the whites that were most attracted to the idea of nonracism were those whites who under other circumstances might be most fearful of blacks, status-deprived, threatened economically by them, living in neighborhoods undergoing integration, or, in the case of younger whites, tense about integration in ways unknown to older whites.[27]

This might also be true of some of the older black women, for whom the black militancy of the 1960s might seem threatening. An organization which presented itself to the public as religious, and which was working to provide concrete social reforms--"working within the system"--would probably seem an attractive refuge in a world where racism was being attacked by a variety of radical groups proposing radical solutions.

One final aspect of healing and safety offered by the Temple was Jones's promise to protect his followers in nuclear war by leading them to a big cave to wait out the holocaust. Jeannie Mills recalls Jones saying in the first service she attended:

> I have seen by divine revelation the total anni-
> hilation of this country and many other parts of
> the world. San Francisco will be flattened. The
> only survivors will be those people who are
> hidden in the cave that I have been shown in a
> vision. Those who go into this cave with me
> will be saved from the poisonous radio-active
> fallout that will follow the nuclear bomb
> attack. This cave is what lead our church to
> migrate to this little valley from Indianapolis,
> Indiana. I have been shown that this cave goes
> deep into the earth. All the members of my
> church will stay in it until it is safe to come
> out. We have gathered in Redwood Valley for
> protection, and after the war is over we will be
> the only survivors. It will be up to our group
> to begin life anew on this continent. Then we
> will begin a truly ideal society just as you see
> it here in this room today. People will care
> about one another. Elderly people will be made
> to feel needed and will be allowed to be produc-
> tive. People's needs will be met because they
> are loved, and not because they have money.
> This church family is an example of what society
> will eventually be like all over the world.
> There will at last be peace on earth. I have
> seen this all by divine revelation." . . .
> My logical, rational mind didn't want to
> believe any of this nonsense, but in November
> 1969 talk about bombs and war was very preva-
> lent . . . . The war in Vietnam was in the news
> every day, and we all lived one day at a time,
> never knowing when some power-crazed leader
> would take all our lives into his own hands to
> prove that his country was stronger than any
> other country.[28]

Jones's healing was about his attempt to provide answers for the things his followers--or potential fol-
lowers--most feared. These were social and political as
well as personal. People fear sickness and death--Jones
would heal them, and, if need be, raise them from the dead.
People fear racial strife--Jones would bring whites and
blacks together. People fear an unfeeling society--the
Temple cared. People fear nuclear war--Jones would lead
them to safety.

Before going on to discuss the commitment process,
let us pause to consider some of the ways in which the
individuals who went through that process and became
involved with the Peoples Temple can be distinguished from
followers in the new religions (e.g., the Unification
Church, Scientology, the Divine Light Mission). The
members of the Temple, with one or two significant
exceptions, do not fit the profile of the "typical cult
member."[29]

Ronald Enroth, an adherent of the anticult movement
(ACM) ideology, describes the "typical cult member":

> The majority of people who join new-age cults
> are between eighteen and twenty-two years old at
> the time of first contact. In other words, the
> immediate post-high school period is when a
> potential joiner is most vulnerable, although
> persons as young as fourteen have become vic-
> tims. A profile of the typical cult member
> reveals that he or she is white, middle or
> upper-middle class, with at least some college
> education and a nominally religious upbringing.
> In short, the typical cult prospect fits the
> image of the All-American boy or girl next
> door . . . .
>   Most have grown up in average American homes,
> and many have experienced varying degrees of
> communication problems with their par-
> ents . . . .
>   Perhaps more than anything else, the young
> people pursuing cults today are involved in a
> search for identity and a quest for spiritual
> reality that provides clear-cut answers to their
> questions.[30]

With two very obvious exceptions--Maria Katsaris and
Deborah Layton Blakey--most members of the Temple simply
did not fit this profile. And, significantly, these two
important exceptions were both members of the ruling elite.

Deborah Layton Blakey (who did join with other members of her family: her brother Larry, who was the first to
join; her mother Lisa; her husband Philip; and her two
sisters-in-law, Karen and Carolyn) opens her "Affidavit . . . Re the Threat and Possibility of Mass Suicide by
Members of the People's Temple":

> I was 18 years old when I joined the Peoples Temple. I had grown up in affluent circumstances in the permissive atmosphere of Berkeley, California. By joining the People's Temple, I hoped to help others and in the process bring structure and self-discipline to my own life.[31]

Although—or perhaps because—her upper-middle-class background fits the profile, she was a member of the ruling elite and cannot be seen as a "typical" member. Nor can Maria Katsaris. She is usually portrayed as a young woman so traumatized by her revered father's second marriage that she was swept into the Temple.[32] What makes her case so interesting, however, is that she is one of the few members who brought no other members of her family into the Temple. Her brother Anthony was interested, and in fact talked with some members in 1974:

> I was originally positive about the group, and was trying to decide, maybe I should join, too.
> Maria came by with a couple of people from the Temple and we went down to Ukiah, to this coffee shop, to talk. It was just like a job interview. I was pretty naive, trying to say what they wanted to hear, like about trying to make the world a better place, and working to end injustice in our society, junk like that. But I was wrong—they didn't see things as getting better. They were already so negative, so pessimistic—they didn't seem to see any hope for the world.
> I dunno, it was strange—it was just like a job interview, and I didn't get the job.[33]

Anthony's failure to "get the job" is interesting, because one of the most striking features of the Temple is its recruitment of entire families. This is one of the most fundamental differences between the Temple, a marginal religion or cult, and the new religions. Because new religions recruit primarily among young adults, the possibility of further recruitment of the convert's family is limited to the same age cohort. This focus on the recruitment of young adults by the new religions and their concomitant separation from their families is one of the central concerns of the anticult movement.[34] Thus, despite the significance of the family of the Unification Church, it has been relatively unsuccessful in bringing whole families into the fold. Like other new religions,

the Unification Church stresses the replacement of the
biological family with the group, which is to serve as the
new family.

The Temple, on the other hand, recruited families.
It was not unusual for three generations—and several
branches—of a family to belong at the same time. This
resulted from the Temple's attempts to proselytize with
family groups. Thus, although the Temple was to become the
family, as suggested above, this did not preclude the pro-
selytization to other members of the convert's biological
family.

This was possible, from the potential convert's point
of view, because Peoples Temple presented itself as an
intergenerational group which encouraged people to bring
their loved ones into the Temple to share in the healing
and other benefits Jones offered. Another factor was that
the Temple was publicly perceived as a legitimate church,
affiliated with the Disciples of Christ, whose pastor was
endorsed by public figures. The new religions simply do
not share this public legitimacy.[35]

There are a number of possible reasons why the Temple
would have recruited whole families. Most obviously, it
was an easy means of increasing membership with less effort. For another, it brought individuals into the group
with existing affective bonds which could then be trans-
ferred to the group. In addition, Jeannie Mills suggests
that there were more pragmatic, long-range reasons for the
recruitment of seniors along with their children and
grandchildren. She reports that Jones told the Planning
Commission that:

> They serve several functions that will be very
> helpful to us in the future. First, if we are
> ever trying to escape into another country the
> border guards will see all our old people and
> assume that we are a humanitarian group. Also,
> no border guard would want to detain buses that
> are loaded with elderly people who might have
> heart attacks or strokes. But more importantly,
> if we are ever to relocate in another country
> these people's Social Security and pension
> checks would follow them. In a communal situa-
> tion in another country, where the cost of liv-
> ing is lower, our entire group might be able to
> survive on these checks until we are able to
> find other means of making money.[36]

The Parks family's experience seems to be fairly
typical of the ways in which family ties led to increasing
involvement with the Temple. In each of the hegiras (first
from Indianapolis to California, then from California to
Guyana), there was a tendency to move members in family
groups. Gerald Parks reports:

> I knew Jones, he was in Indianapolis. I'd heard
> of him, he'd held meetings in Cincinnati, Ohio,
> Columbus, some places like that. And when I was
> younger I went to a few of his meetings he had
> in Cincinnati, but it was nothing like later,
> like after we got here. He was more in the
> realm of the church area then, you know . . . .
> Basically I [just] come to California, but
> since I had some relatives in this area at the
> time, that come out here when Jones came out, I
> decided to come here, 'cause there was a couple
> of jobs available in my line of work. So that's
> the reason I settled here in Ukiah per se, not
> just because of Jones. Anyway. But we started
> right into his church, which was a little bit
> out of the ordinary at that time. . . .[37]

Family ties were used more consciously in the move to
Guyana. The Temple would have families go down a few
members at a time and have them report back to the others,
urging them to join them. As Gerald Parks reports,

> My son [Dale] who was in the church at the
> beginning had left . . . he was a little more
> involved than we were. He was in the medical
> field at the time, and still is. And he held
> down a full-time job, and worked around the
> church up here and helped in the meetings and
> things. So, you know, it was just—to him it
> just—he'd been in it since he was 14 years old,
> and it really wasn't what he wanted any more, so
> he just left. And he was gone for about six
> months where he didn't even tell them, you know,
> where he was at. But they finally tracked him
> down. Marceline, Jim Jones' wife, talked him
> into going over, because they wanted him in
> their medical area over there, and they said,
> well, he says he wants to. So, "If you're
> interested," she said, "If you'll go over," she
> said, "We'll give you a round trip ticket, just
> to go look at it, you can come back." All the
> time, once they got him in there, he wasn't

going anywhere. And so he thought about it, and
decided to go check it out, and so he went. And
then once you get over there, once they've got
one of your family there, they force them to
write to the rest of the family and tell them
how nice it is, beautiful. And they'd tell you
it's about 70 and 80 degrees over there and it's
about a hundred and thirty, and [they'd say]
there's beaches right on the grounds. So he
wrote us a letter, finally; . . . there was
nothing else he could do, he had to write us and
tell us how nice it was over there, they forced
him to write. So we got the letter, you know,
so we thought about it, so we put up our home
for sale and decided to go. With much reluctance, I might add. Even the last day we were
leaving I knew that something was kind of wierd,
telling me I was making a big mistake. But you
think, you know, well, when you sell your home
and your furniture and everything you've had for
years, it's a big step, you know. It's really a
big change, and I thought that's really what it
was . . . .

The poverty of Georgetown bothered Parks, and caused him to
have second thoughts:

So I talked it over with my wife, and, I dunno--
my oldest daughter and her boyfriend and my
mother was on their way, so I think we better
radio them and tell them not to come. So we was
gonna talk it over with Marceline Jones and two
or three of the others, so we did sit down and I
told her how I felt. I said, I don't want to
go, that I'd rather go back, and Marcie said--
told me the same thing she'd told my son--she
says, "If you want to go back, you can go
back." She said, "We'll call the kids and tell
them whatever you want to tell them." And she
said, "Just go out and try it." She said, "Just
go out and look around at things there and if
you won't want to stay, you come back and go
home." Well, ok, so we'll do that.[38]

Many families were moved down in a similar manner, a few
members at a time. In this way, the ties of the family
intertwined with the ties of the Temple membership in general and gave the group a cohesiveness the new religions
lack.

The various sources of the Temple's appeal can be left to one side in considering the commitment process itself. James Downton suggests that the process of committing oneself to a revolutionary group involves a process of increasing investment:

> If individual choices can be conceived as products of a cost-rewards calculation, then commitments (which develop through decision making) must be understood as behavior that has become more consistent because it becomes more gratifying than costly.[39]

In other words, the preliminary motivations lose their sociological, though not personal, relevance once the initial commitment is made, because the neophyte then becomes involved in the unwinding of a sociological process with its own logic and dynamics. This is why exchange theorists argue that _why_ something is valued is unimportant. They start at the point where we are now, accepting the values as given. The intention of the following section is to uncover the ways in which the values of the old society are exchanged for the values of the sub-society.

Downton posits four stages in the process of commitment to a "deviant" socio-political point of view: personal tension; availability to move into a new social role; the opportunity to act (i.e., the "deviant" group will provide opportunities not available in the larger society); and high profit accompanied by rising investments and sacrifices.[40] In this typology, Downton is focussing on the steps involved in embracing a new perspective: later we will turn to Kanter to discern the actual mechanisms involved in the process of becoming committed to this perspective.

The first stage is the existence of personal tension. Downton frames this in terms of the fulfillment of one or more of the sets of needs that Abraham Maslow has argued are basic to human development: biological; safety; affection and belongingness; self-esteem; and self-realization. The motives for joining the Peoples Temple span primarily the middle three terms of this progression, with one or another dominating for different individuals. As each of these sets of needs is taken care of, the individual moves on to the next. Part of Jones's power arose from the fact that membership in the Temple could fulfill such a variety of needs. In this way, membership would continue to satisfy the same individual in different ways as he or she passed through this progression.[41]

Downton points out that the exchange necessarily involves giving up something that one has as well as getting what one wants or needs:

> Certainly, it is true that the revolutionary life increases the tension in some areas of life while it satisfies others. Sacrifices of physical necessities and increasing insecurity in social relations can be compensated for by increasing comradeship, pride, and purpose.[42]

Naturally, this compensation takes place in terms of the values that the individual holds. Eric Hoffer insists that the prime characteristic of the "true believer" is an undervaluation—or a complete non-valuation—of the self. He sees the true believer as happiest when the first exchange is made and the self can be shed:

> [A] mass movement, particularly in its active, revivalist phase, appeals not to those intent on bolstering and advancing a cherished self, but to those who crave to be rid of an unwanted self . . . . Anything undertaken under the auspices of the self seems to them foredoomed. Nothing that has its roots and reasons in the self can be good and noble. The innermost craving is for a new life—a rebirth—or, failing this, a chance to acquire new elements of pride, confidence, hope, a sense of purpose and worth by identification with a holy cause.[43]

Exchange theory, however, necessarily posits the continuance of the self: the individual seeks involvement in a larger whole, but must retain enough of self to be gratified by that involvement. Thus, when behavior is described as altruistic, it is usually because the person so describing the behavior is not aware of other factors which may be motivating the actor, or because the appearance of altruism is valuable to the actor for other purposes. Even the experience which genuinely transcends self, such as mystical experience, should be seen as a temporary interlude which legitimates the self in other ways (e.g., as proof of holiness, satisfaction at having communed with the Godhead, a mark of favor to distinguish oneself from one's peers). The search for, and occasional attainment of, an experience outside the self arises in and for the self. Thus, from

the point of view of the exchange theorist, Hoffer is wrong
in positing that extinction of the self is the goal of the
true believer. Downton, for instance, suggests:

> [I]t is the increase of personal tension fol-
> lowed by decreasing opportunities for the grati-
> fication of needs that lead some . . . to consi-
> der revolution seriously. In this sense, a
> revolutionary organization should be understood
> as the member experiences it: as an opportunity
> to solve personal problems that cannot be solved
> elsewhere, even though these problems are con-
> nected ideologically with a set of larger social
> issues that depersonalize his claim on so-
> ciety.[44]

In addition to the existence of personal tension
(deprivation), the individuals must be in a position where
they are free to revolt. This means, on the one hand, that
they will be in a transition period between an outmoded and
a new activity. Examples of this state of transition would
be elderly people left at loose ends by Father Divine's
death and who came to the Temple from the Peace Mission, or
Odell Rhodes, who was trying to get off the streets.[45]
On the other hand, Downton is also referring to the disrup-
tions in individual lives caused by larger social currents. The civil rights movement disturbed the automati-
city of the lives of some by changing the expectations and
possibilities within the larger society. This latter kind
of uncertainty is more important for prospective members of
the Temple, who, as was pointed out above, tend to be older
than the members of the new religions.[46] The middle aged
and elderly lower and middle class members of the Temple
found themselves displaced by the social currents of the
1960s, and found refuge in the Temple.

The individuals in this "transitional" group Downton
describes still have various options in the actual choice
of alternative activity. These choices will be affected by
three factors: conscience, resource capacity, and countervailing forces. The fact that the Peoples Temple was
affiliated with the Disciples of Christ helped in terms of
the first of these. It gave the group a legitimacy which
other groups operating in the 1960s did not necessarily
have. This very legitimacy, however, meant that some considering joining the Temple would reject it as an option in
favor of other, more radical, groups, such as the Black
Panthers or the Nation of Islam. By resource availability,
Downton means such simple things as time, energy, and

money. These resources were to become more and more mono-
polized as involvement in the Temple deepened, but in the
beginning phase being considered here, it would involve an
afternoon and an evening in church every week, for instance, and a financial donation (not necessarily large)
during the collection. Countervailing forces refer to the
reaction of friends, family, and associates to one's involvement. This was generally not that important in the
case of the Temple, especially since members tended to join
in family blocs. In addition, the maintenance of the pub-
lic/private split was designed to lessen the possibility of
negative feedback which might discourage potential converts, among other functions.

The individuals experiencing personal tension and
finding themselves in a state of transition, whether
because of the stage of life in which they are or because
of broader social currents, must find a niche in which to
pursue their goals. As Downton says,

> [W]e have to consider whether the roles and
> statuses for which a person is available are
> open to him . . . . If opportunities are limited
> and restricted . . . , the disadvantaged can
> turn to new organizations or develop their own
> organizational base.[47]

This is precisely what we see the Temple doing. They
offered the disadvantaged an opportunity to actively
participate in the creation of a new order.[48]

It is only with the fourth stage that the exchange
process _per se_ begins. During the first three, it is a
matter of weighing alternatives and dealing with possible
conflicts, choosing a course of action and preparing to
embark upon it. In the fourth stage, the choice is made
and the process of commitment begins. It is a period
characterized by high profit accompanied by rising investments and sacrifices.[49] Once the first concrete commitment if made, the individual's involvement in the Temple
will be, generally speaking, a gradually increasing process:

> At each step in the commitment process a person
> increases his investments, providing a base for
> making choices involving even heavier sacrifices
> . . . . By the time a person has become firmly
> committed to a protest organization, when his
> activity consistently adheres to the norms of

the movement, he has usually invested considerable time, energy and money. The changes are
that corresponding sacrifices have been made
also, for instance, loss of leisure, possibly
failing health, the termination of socialities,
and diminished economic solvency.[50]

In addition, once the commitment has been made, other
dynamics than the individual's exchanges come into play:

[T]he politically deviant activity is considered
attractive by the person (a pulling force) while
simultaneously action by societal agencies is
pushing him further into deviance (a pushing
force).

This societal pushing is usually achieved through language;
the deviant group is stigmatized:

This "negative" identity, as seen from the perspective of societal agents, assumes a positive
character for the deviant, who finds it easier
to solve his problems in the deviant sub-culture
than in "legitimate" society.[51]

This usually leads to a double stigmatization, where the
rebel also denigrates the non-rebel as hypocritical or
shallow. In other words, the rebels receive an additional
benefit (pay-off) through this redefinition: a better self-
image for being aligned with the "right side."

Let us examine these exchanges and commitments a bit
more concretely. Rosabeth Moss Kanter suggests that there
are a number of different means for attaining a sense of
unity in Utopian communities. She examined various
experimental communities of the nineteenth century, but her
findings are, at least to some extent,[52] applicable to
alternative communities in general, including the Peoples
Temple. She sees two types of processes involved, the
associative and the dissociative. Both are at work in the
specific mechanisms in the six-part typology she develops.
She arranges the mechanisms into those involving commitment
to roles: sacrifice (dissociative) and investment
(associative); those involving commitment to relationships:
renunciation (dissociative) and communion (associative);
and those involving commitment to norms: mortification
(dissociative) and surrender (associative).[53]   (see
Figure 1)

FIGURE 1

Mode	Direction	
	Dissociative	Associative
Roles (cognitive)	Sacrifice	Investment
Relationships (affective)	Renunciation	Communion
Norms (moral)	Mortification	Surrender

Kanter argues that if many of these mechanisms are used in a group (obviously, no single group will manifest all of them), it will tend to bind the group and make it stable enough to continue.[54] Her thesis is that:

> When people are committed to social orders, structure and phenomenology are mutually reinforcing, and maintenance of the social system is intimately linked with maintenance of the self.
> The proposition follows, then, that groups whose existence is dependent on the commitment of their participants should be more successfully maintained if they utilize social arrangements which promote commitments of all three types.[55]

Her first set of mechanisms is grouped around the concept of sacrifice, which she subdivides into abstinence and austerity. Membership in the Peoples Temple involved both of these. Jones required that members forswear any number of pleasures until "the whole world could enjoy them";[56] these included everything from wine to decent food.   There was a ban on drugs, alcohol, and tobacco. Members of the group were encouraged to be celibate. Life at Jonestown in the final year, was nothing if not austere, the diet consisted of rice, vegetables, and gravy, three times a day;[57] workdays were long; and they lived in crowded huts.   Kanter suggests that, "Once members have agreed to make the 'sacrifices,' their motivation to remain participants increases.   Membership becomes more valuable and meaningful."[58]

She bases this assertion on Festinger's work on cognitive consistency: once the sacrifice has been made, the indi-

vidual needs to value the result in order to justify the
"expense" and remain self-consistent.[59] This sort of
rationalization is central to exchange mechanisms,
especially when they involve commitment to "deviant" per-
spectives.

The second group of mechanisms involves investment.
These are of two main types: physical (e.g., living communally in the States and going to live in Jonestown) and
financial. The financial includes both the investment
itself (Temple members signed over virtually everything
they had to the church upon admission, and continued to
contribute what they received as members), and the irrever-
sibility of the investment. It is this second type which,
especially in today's society, makes it so difficult to
renege on the commitment. Most defectors cite their financial situation as one of the things that kept them in the
group so long.[60]

Renunciation mechanisms involve the creation of a
distinction between the community and the society at large.
Kanter includes isolation, cross-boundary control, dyadic
renunciation, and renunciation of the family in this group.
The Temple employed many of these. Jonestown, as a community, took to an extreme the idea of physical isolation;
it ws not just an enclave in San Francisco, it was in the
middle of a jungle on another continent. There was also an
almost absolute "cross-boundary control," or what Downton
calls "gatekeeping."[61] This involves control of information, both in-coming and out-going. This was facilitated
by their jungle isolation; Jones was able to convince the
members that the United States was in a complete state of
anarchy. He had also been able to control the public's
knowledge of the Temple. This is evidenced by the line of
politicians who endorsed Jones and his work, and by his
ability to escape prosecution even when he was investigated.

Dyadic renunciation refers both to free love and to
celibacy: both were involved at different times, because
they each serve to weaken monogamous bonds. As for renunciation of the family, although families did tend to join
in blocs, as we have seen, there was an attempt to break
down those families once in the Temple, primarily through
shuffling children around among foster families:

> The example of Jones's seven adopted children
> did more than present the happy image of a
> caring minister for a father. It served by

example to break down the bonds of parenthood
within the Temple and made it easier for Jones
to reshuffle families. Parents were encouraged
to move into communal homes and leave their
children grouped in other Temple facilities.
Cutting personal ties enhanced the role of Jones
as the only major figure in a member's life.[62]

At the same time, the erosion of personal ties tended to
strengthen family feelings within the group at least as
much as it may have weakened individual family bonds--and
the strengthening of the ties to the group may have been
even more significant. Jeanne Mills, for instance, says
that her bonds to her foster children, whom she would not
have been able to take with her if she left the Temple,
were a factor in her staying, although she did ultimately
leave.[63]

Homogeneity, communal sharing, communal labor, regularized group contact, ritual, and persecution experience
are the attributes of communion mechanisms. For instance,
Kanter suggests that similarity of religious background is
a strengthening feature, and many of the members, both
black and white, were from fundamentalist backgrounds.[64]
In addition, members shared a similar economic and educational status. Jonestown was, of course, a self-declared
commune, so naturally most of the property was owned, and

labor performed, in common. Group contact was regularized;
there was communal living, communal dining; little place or
opportunity for privacy; more than two-thirds of the day
was spent with other people; and there were regular or
daily group meetings, as Kanter suggests. The "White
Night" suicide drills can surely be considered a community
ritual, and the Temple did experience what they perceived
as persecution. In fact, of the 26 specific criteria
grouped by Kanter as communion mechanisms,[65] the Peoples
Temple manifested 24: common ethnic background and prior
acquaintance of members are lacking. Thus, in addition to
actual deterrents to leaving, the Temple provided many
structures encouraging group orientation and loyalty.

Kanter suggests that mortification mechanisms enhance
a feeling of commitment by imposing the standards of the
group on the individual:

One intended consequence of mortification
processes in these settings has been to strip
away aspects of an individual's identity, to
make him dependent on authority for direction,

and to place him in a position of uncertainty
with respect to his role behavior until he
learns and comes to accept the norms of the
group.[66]

The Temple shows many of the mechanisms she suggests, such
as confession and mutual criticism, mortifying sanctions,
deindividuating mechanisms, and "spiritual" differentiation
(distinguishing "members on the basis of their living up to
group standards and taking on the community identity").[67]
Mortification--the harsh punishments given transgressors of
the many rules of the Temple--was one of the aspects of
life in the Temple which most appalled outsiders when they
heard about it.[68]   It is interesting that it is just this
that many members who later defected remember as one of the
most positive benefits of their time in the Temple:

> Although Jones's followers . . . hated the ver-
> bal and physical cruelty sometimes meted out at
> catharsis meetings at the Temple, most of them
> agreed that there was also benefit in having a
> place where they could share their sins and
> receive forgiveness and discipline from the
> community.   An amazing number of defectors even
> . . . [said] that the discipline they received
> in the Temple was a turning place in their
> lives, causing them to "go in the right direc-
> tion."[69]

This may, of course, be just another example of the attempt
to maintain cognitive consistency. On the other hand,

> When demands made by the system are evaluated as
> right, moral, just, or expressing one's own
> values, obedience to these demands becomes a
> normative necessity, and sanctioning by the
> system is regarded as appropriate.[70]

The sixth and last set of criteria involve surrender
mechanisms.   Among these are institutionalized awe, both
ideological and structural; programming; ideological
conversion; and tradition. The first of these are the ones
most strikingly present in Jonestown. "Institutionalized
awe," Kanter says,

> requires an ideological and structural system
> that orders and gives meaning to the individ-
> ual's life and which attaches this order and
> meaning to the organization . . . . Such systems

with great ordering power not only satisfy the individual's need for meaning, but they also provide a sense of rightness, certainty, and conviction that promotes transcendence and surrender to the source of power.[71]

This was achieved by means of several of the techniques she lists, such as relating the community to figures of historical importance (Jones claimed to be the reincarnation of Lenin, as well as Ikhnaton, the Buddha, Jesus, and Father Divine). It is more apparent in the power and authority structures, which she suggests as the other subdivision of the institutionalization of awe. Jones (and, to a lesser degree, the members of the elite) had special prerogatives, special immunities, a special residence (and a special diet), a special form of address--and the Temple surely exhibited an irrational basis for decisions. These mechanisms, like all the others, are both associative and dissociative. When individuals give up things they would have in the larger group (dissociative mechanisms), they gain a firmer place in the smaller group (associative).

Throughout the process which brought those who joined into a firmer and more concrete state of commitment, there were also many others who were exposed to the group but did not join. Tim Stoen, Temple attorney,

estimates that, in ten years, somewhere between 50,000 and 100,000 people came to hear Jones speak. But, he says, despite Jones's boasts of 20,000 members, the actual membership never exceeded 3,000.[72]

In addition, there were those who joined the group but later defected, usually at a point when the stakes were raised substantially. There were defections when Jones instituted disciplinary committees; when the group moved from Indianapolis to Redwood Valley; when Jones declared mandatory celibacy; and when he began to talk about mass revolutionary suicide. Each of these "defection points" was followed by a time when the membership was smaller but more committed. Thus, those who made the final move to Guyana were winnowed from a larger group, during a ten or fifteen year process of separating the genuinely committed from the merely curious. The very fact that it took about four months to become a full member, during which time even the simplest investments, such as time spent at services,

increased gradually, served as the first winnowing of pros-
pects.   Because the process was so gradual, it was not
difficult for the neophyte to make whatever psychic adjust-
ments were necessary (e.g., in terms of self-perceived consistency) before progressing to the next stage.

     In this way, the group had been prepared by small
degrees for the decision to go through with the suicides.
The idea was first mentioned in the Planning Commission,
and was rejected.   Then, after it was accepted in prin-
ciple, ritualistic drills were conducted among the elite.
Only gradually did the idea filter down to the rank and
file members. The suicides were not imposed on an unprepared group of people. The members were self-chosen in
terms of their commitment to the cause.   They had been
asked many times, in many ways, how important the cause was
to them.   Which was more important, the cause or smoking
cigarettes? The cause or drinking wine?   The cause or
sleeping with their spouse?   The cause or their checking
account? The cause or a private home? When the answer was
not "the cause," the individual would leave the Temple.

     Each of these questions, however, was asked in a
sub-society whose answers would not necessarily be the same
as the answers of the larger society. Thus, for instance,
the decision to give up cigarettes would be easier when it
was understood that they were not only an addictive, expensive habit leading to cancer--which every smoker knows--but
"mind-altering substances . . . by which the ruling class
controlled and exploited the poor."[73]   In this way, each
of these questions was asked only after Jones was fairly
certain that the answer would be "the cause."[74]

     We see, then, that these questions were asked in
terms both of commitment and of meaning. It was because of
these two mutually reinforcing aspects that many members
continued to answer "the cause" to the increasingly significant series of questions, up until the point when the
question became, which is more important, your life or the
cause?

     At the same time, however, it was possible--though
obviously very difficult--to join the Temple and yet not
become fully committed. The Parks family, who left with
the Congressman on the last day, did so.   Gerald talks
about some factors involved in their withholding or
commitment:

     [M]yself and my family, we weren't in it that

much. We would attend meetings once a week or
something like that, after they moved to the
city [San Francisco]. But we were not in any
communal homes or anything like that because I
wouldn't live that way.   Life would be despis-
able.   And everything in me was contrary to
that, and they knew it, so they didn't bug me in
that area, or my family. But a lot of people
worked here, lived communally, no paycheck, and
everything was provided for them.   It wasn't my
way of life at all . . . .[75]

The Parks family managed to remain somewhat emotionally
aloof from the Temple.   They did this in part by maintaining the biological family ties:

The area that I worked in was in the "L" area,
they had a warehouse about a mile and a half
from the compound.   And I took care of the
warehouse.   I was supposed to keep an inventory
of it, which was just a stupid-ass job, but at
least I didn't have to work all that hard. So,
while I was down there, . . . [I would think] If
I could just get out of here, if I could make it
to Georgetown and to the State Department, get
my family out of here somehow, constantly just
thinking about [that].
My youngest daughter--the warehouse I worked
in, they had some Koolaid in there, and some
canned milk, that was about all the food that
was edible that was in the warehouse.   So she,
on Sundays, she would come down and stay with me
for part of the day, if she could get permission.   They tried to keep families separated,
they separated us as soon as we got there, the
children from the parents.   And so I would
actually steal this Koolaid, and they had sugar
in the warehouse, and make Koolaid for her,
every Sunday.   There was canned milk and a
little water and she could have that, and things
like that.   So actually, what we would steal
food if we could get it.   My son worked in the
medical department, which was close to the
kitchen, he'd come back late at night [with] a
peanut butter sandwich or something.   My wife
would be in a cot in this one cottage and that
was the extent of our living area.   He would
bring a sandwich or something, you know, and
talk to us--whisper, so   nobody could hear us.

> But there was sixteen people in that cabin. Anyway, we'd talk about getting out of there, how nice it would be to have a Pepsi again, or a milkshake or something like that. So we tried to help each other, talking . . . .[76]

Although there were no kidnappings or deprogrammings of Temple members by non-member families, (due primarily to the socio-economic class of most of the members, which precluded both the resources and the mind-set of the anti-cult groups), Parks did effectively "deprogram" his youngest daughter, Tracey, who was nine or ten at the time.

> She believed in Jones, she was raised--we came out here when she was six weeks old, so she was raised in it, you know. Most of the kids really believed in him, thought he was fantastic. And she did, she believed that he had this gift, and I had to convince her over there that he didn't have. 'Cause after being raised in that, and conditioned, her mind conditioned to it, she thought, you know, if we said anything about him . . . it'd come back to us, or he'd found it out, or whatever. And so I, you know, talking to her and convinced her that he had no gift, he had no way of knowing what you were thinking or what you were doing. He was an evil person, there was nothing about him to be concerned about at all. So she finally saw that, so she hates him to this day. Because even though the security guards pulled the triggers at the airstrip, Jim Jones was the one who done it, killed her mother and the rest of the people.[77]

Let us conclude by considering the implications of Kanter's work. She is correct in pointing out that the individual needs to turn away from the old group and become bound to the new group on emotional, intellectual, and moral levels. We have seen that the People's Temple, by using many of the same mechanisms as Kanter's "successful" groups, created a highly committed group of followers.

The question, which is one that Kanter asks herself, is what is meant by "successful"? To call a group "successful" that extinguishes itself because of the members' commitment to its vision of the nature of reality cannot be done without some qualification. Kanter uses longevity as

the criterion for success because it is easily quantifiable
as well as one which is interconnected with other possible
criteria.[78]   She points out, however, that although these
various mechanisms may bring about a long-lived group, it
may not be "successful" in terms of the individual lives of
members:

> It is possible that there can be a surfeit of
> commitment mechanisms.   That is, up to a point
> the greater the number of commitment mechanisms
> the group uses, the stronger the commitment of
> its members. But past that number, commitment
> mechanisms may become dysfunctional for the
> group; they may be perceived as oppressive and
> may stifle the person's autonomy to the extent
> that he become less rather than more commit-
> ted . . . .
> [M]ost of the successful nineteenth century
> groups retained some private space. All of them
> had enough land and buildings to provide a sense
> of movement around community territories; mem-
> bers were not tightly enclosed in a small
> space.   There were many options about places to
> be within the community, even if these places
> were not always totally private. In fact, it
> was the unsuccessful rather than the successful
> groups that more frequently developed communal
> households in which all members lived together
> in one space, this being the only instance in
> which a higher proportion of unsuccessful groups
> utilized a commitment mechanism.   In the suc-
> cessful groups, even if members spent most of
> their time with other people, they often had a
> spot where they could retire to be alone or
> visit with just a few.[79]

To call Peoples Temple "successful" is to say that it
succeeded in creating a highly committed band of followers.
Its success lay not in its longevity--Jonestown lasted four
years from its founding, a year and a half from the massive
influx in the summer of 1977--but rather in the creation of
a new group which gradually shifted the basis of exchange
from that of the old group (the original appeals discussed
above) to its own, where membership in the group per se
became an appeal. The coinage shifted from the instrumental (e.g., the opportunity to be healed) to the affective
(feeling good about creating the new society). It was only
when the "language"/"coinage" shift had occurred for each
individual that the individual could begin to participate

in the groups's creation and maintenance of its own reality. In other words, the mechanisms that Kanter suggests
will lead to a successful group were, in fact, success-
ful--they led to a group which was so internally consistent
that it collectively chose to self-destruct.   As Feinsod
observes:

> Despite his fears and the sense of failure that
> had led him to conclude that life was not worth
> living, the ironic and incredible truth was that
> in a perverse and horrible way Jim Jones had
> actually succeeded; he had managed the most im-
> probable--and perhaps the rarest--feat a leader
> of human beings can attempt: he had fused an
> entire community into a single organism. What-
> ever one felt, all felt; whatever happened to
> one, happened to all. He had convinced nearly a
> thousand human beings that they lived only for
> each other.   And, whatever the morality of the
> enterprise, that was exactly what he had set out
> to do.[80]

FOOTNOTES

[1] Garden City, N.Y.: Doubleday Anchor, 1967.

[2] Ibid., p. 138.

[3] Ibid., pp. 158ff.

[4] Ibid., p. 159.

[5] Thus in a sense Berger and Luckmann are correct in their focus on the occupational (i.e., functional) groups.

[6] The term is Rosabeth Moss Kanter's. Committment and Community, (Cambridge, Mass.: Harvard University Press, 1972).

[7] NB: This is not necessarily the only possible way of bridging the theoretical gap. Since, however, most of the groups for which formation is a critical issue are "deviant," this might well prove to be the most useful insofar as it deals with the issues of splitting and the mutual definition of the larger and smaller groups.

[8] Kanter, op. cit.; James V. Downton, Jr., Rebel Leadership (New York: The Free Press, 1972/1973). Downton cites Homans in his bibliography though Kanter does not. It is clear from her language, however, that she should be included in the exchange school.

[9] The fact that a large percentage of the membership joined in family groups is highly significant, and will be discussed below.

[10] Anthony Katsaris discussed them with his sister, Maris, who explained them in this way: "I said it seems so phony. She gave me some line about these people healing themselves, healing with their minds. I thought it could have been done with more class than these people running around throwing up, and she said 'Yeah, but we're trying to approach people on a level they could understand, until they could see what we're really about and grow beyond that.'" Telephone interview, 24 September 1981.

[11] Gerald Parks, interview, Ukiah, California, 26 June 1981.

[12]Ibid.

[13]Ethan Feinsod, <u>Awake in a Nightmare</u> (New York: W. W. Norton and Co., 1981), p. 96.

[14]Ibid., pp. 86-87.

[15]Ibid., p. 89.

[16]Jeannie Mills, <u>Six Years With God</u> (New York: A&W Publishers, Inc., 1979), pp. 117, 128-129.

[17]Feinsod, pp. 36-37.

[18]Mills, p. 128.

[19]Feinsod, p. 90.

[20]Ross Case, letter dated 3 April 1979.

[21]Mills, p. 121.

[22]Feinsod, p. 93.

[23]NB: Religion as defined in the Introduction (the search for truth and transcendence) remained central to the motivation of the Temple.

[24]Mills, p. 128.

[25]Feinsod, pp. 92-93.

[26]See next chapter for a more thorough discussion of the leadership of the Temple.

[27]Diane Johnson, "The Heart of Darkness," <u>New York Review of Books</u>, 19 April 1979, p. 9.

[28]Mills, p. 122.   It is interesting that this originally Cold War-inspired vision could still be kept viable a decade later.

[29]James T. Richardson lists this as one of the eight differences between the Peoples Temple and the new religions in "People's Temple and Jonestown: A Corrective Comparison and Critique," in <u>Journal for the Scientific Study of Religion</u>, September 1980, pp. 239-255.   Reprinted in slightly different form in <u>Violence and Religious</u>

Commitment, edited by Ken Levi, (University Park, Pa.: Pennsylvania State University Press, 1982), pp. 21-34.

[30]Ronald Enroth, Youth, Brainwashing, and the Extremist Cults, (Grand Rapids, Mich.: Zondervan, 1977), pp. 149-150.

[31]Charles A. Krause, et al, Guyana Massacre: The Eyewitness Account (New York: Berkley Publishing Corp., 1978), Appendix D., p. 187.

[32]See especially Bella Stumbo, "Maria Katsaris: Jones Follower All The Way To The End," Los Angeles Times, 9 March 1979, part 1, pp. 3, 28-29. Anthony Katsaris says of this article: "My mother . . . just doesn't see any point in dragging it all up. We've been burned a couple of times. There was this woman from the Times--I was very impressed by her, and got Mom to talk to her. She really buttered us up and made a lot of promises about letting us see the article before it was published--which she didn't. And the article was not at all what she'd said. It put us in a very bad light. It wasn't so much that she lied, but we just didn't look very good." Telephone, 9/24/81.

[33]Anthony Katsaris, 9/24/81.

[34]See, e.g., Enroth, Chapter Ten, "The Plight of the Parents"; Caroll Stoner and Jo Anne Parke, All God's Children (New York: Penguin Books, 1977), Part Three, "Coping with the Crisis." In addition, Anson Shupe and David Bromley provide an excellent analysis of the dynamics of family reactions in The New Vigilantes (Beverly Hills: Sage, 1980), pp. 38-47.

[35]The problems connected with the lack of legitimacy are shared by both the cults and the new religions. See David Bromley and Anson Shupe, Moonies" in America (Beverly Hills: Sage, 1979), Chapter 6, for a description of the Unification Church's attempts to develop visibility and legitimacy. They point out that "Because world-transforming movements inevitably violate some social norms . . . , in general the greater the visibility such a movement achieves the lower its legitimacy." (pp. 166-167, italicized in original) Thus the Temple's "built-in" legitimacy gave it an enormous advantage in gaining new converts in that it was not perceived as a cult (or a new religion).

[36]Quoted, Mills, p. 178.

[37]Parks, 6/26/81.

[38]Ibid.

[39]Downton, p. 61.

[40]Ibid., pp. 61-70.

[41]Presumably those who reached the stage of seeking self-realization were those who ultimately defected. Since self-realization is a stage of autonomy, self-satisfaction, independence, etc., a "total commitment" such as was involved in Temple membership would allow little opportunity for attaining it, except for members of the elite.

[42]Downton, p. 62.

[43]Eric Hoffer, The True Believer (New York: Harper and Row, 1951), p. 12.

[44]Downton, p. 63. Downton is cited on this point to maintain theoretical consistency. See also Anthony F. C. Wallace, "Revitalization Movements," American Anthropologist, April, 1956, pp. 264-279.

[45]On this point, the Peoples Temple and other marginal religions are similar to the new religions, because both kinds of groups are alternatives to mainline institutions. (Cf. the quote from Enroth, above, p. 85 concerning the "typical cult member.") As J. Gordon Melton and Robert Moore point out, "Such persons are at points where society deems it proper to make the crucial decisions about career, marriage, and faith commitments." The Cult Experience (New York: Pilgrim Press, 1982), p. 29.

[46]This is not to say that this latter aspect is not a factor in joining the new religions. See, e.g., Robert N. Bellah, "New Religious Consciousness and the Crisis in Modernity," in The New Religious Consciousness, edited by Charles Y. Glock and Robert N. Bellah (Berkeley: University of California Press, 1976), pp. 333-352.

[47]Downton, p. 66.

[48]Again, this is also the situation with the new religions, although it is not generally stressed. Melton and Moore, for instance, list the appeals of the new religions as being genuine spiritual immediacy, group intimacy,

remythologizing of life, a therapeutic dimension, and joining as the first act of asserting adulthood (pp. 31-35).
Stoner and Parke, however, emphasize the effect of the
coming of age of the members of the "baby boom," with the
glutting of the labor market, so that "44 percent of the
country's seventeen-year-olds aspire to professional jobs
despite the fact that the Labor Department classifies only
14 percent of the national employment slots as 'professional'" (p. 125). Thus, the desired roles and statuses
are not available, and individuals turn instead to groups
which involve "assuming a very diffuse role requiring few
specialized skills . . . . [C]ommunal solidarity, rather
than developing the requisites for conventional careers,
was the preeminant UM [Unificationist Movement] concern,
and the UM's socialization process offered virtually no
preparation for integration into the contemporary American
economic system" New Vigilantes, pp. 39-40.

49Downton, p. 67.

50Ibid., p. 68.

51Ibid., p. 70.

52The qualification is necessary because of the
greater complexity of our society, especially in terms of
the ease of transportation and communication, which make it
more difficult to isolate a group.

53Kanter, pp. 72-74.

54Only one of the groups defined as successful in
terms of this typology lasted less than 33 years; no successful group lasted more than 16 years, but the average
was less than two. Kanter, p. 64.

55Rosabeth Moss Kanter, "Commitment and Social
Organization: A Study of Commitment Mechanisms in Utopian
Communities," American Sociological Review, August 1968,
pp. 501-502.

56See, e.g., Mel White, Deceived (Old Tappan, N.J.:
Fleming H. Revell, 1979), pp. 80, 113.

57Approximately a year before the suicides, "Jonestown's food, formerly one of its glories, . . . became a
bland, monotonous medly of rice and vegetables. Jonestown
never really had even approached agricultural sufficiency,

a goal that even under the best of circumstances may have been impossible given the problems of jungle farming and the fact that well over half the population was either too young or too old to be productive at farming or much of anything else; but until January, what it did produce had been supplemented regularly with fish, meat, and staples like rice and flour. By early spring, only the staples and an occasional shark or swordfish, caught by local fishermen, found their way to the Jonestown dinner table." Feinsod, p. 131.

[58]Kanter, _Commitment and Community_, p. 76.

[59]Ibid.

[60]See, e.g., White, pp. 172-174.

[61]Downton, p. 34.

[62]Marshall Kilduff and Ron Javers, _The Suicide Cult_ (New York: Bantam Books, 1978), p. 57.

[63]Mills, p. 299.

[64]It might seem impossible for Jones to convert Fundamentalists, who believe in Biblical inerrancy, to his perception of the Bible as racist, contradictory, and filled with erros. Jeannie Mills reports her first reactions to his teaching:

> [Jones] was . . . shouting about the errors in the Bible, and he began to throw in a few spicy swear words to make his point perfectly clear. I was shocked and offended. "How can he say things like that about God's Holy Word and get away with it?" I asked Al in a whisper.
> As if he had heard my words, Jim smiled and said, "If there were a God in Heaven, do you think he would let me say these things about His Holy Word?" and looking up toward the ceiling, he shook his fist violently and challenged, "If there is a God in Heaven, let Him strike me dead!"
> I waited. I'd had a fundamentalist upbringing, and I visualized Jim clutching his throat, unable to breathe, writhing in pain all over the floor of his podium. I was certain a bolt of lightning would come out of heaven and strike

> him, but nothing happened. The room became
> silent as Jim grinned and said, "Someone in this
> room is waiting," and the entire audience, with
> the exception of a few of the visitors, burst
> into laughter. My faith took a sharp nose dive
> and I braced myself for what was still to come
> (p. 121).

She later went on to write a booklet entitled "The Letter
Killeth but the Spirit Giveth LIFE," "that Jim sold to his
members to help wean them away from the Bible" (letter
dated 17 April 1979). In addition, Fundamentalism developed in opposition to the Social Gospel Movement in the
early part of the century, so the Temple's activism, too,
would involve a conceptual shift on the part of the members.

[65]Kanter lists 12 specific criteria in the areas of
communal sharing (i.e., property ownership) and communal
labor (p. 104).

[66]Kanter, <u>Commitment and Community</u>, p. 103.

[67]Ibid., p. 108.

[68]See, for instance, the 1 August 1977 <u>New West</u>
article ("Inside Peoples Temple" by Marshall Kilduff and
Phil Tracy). The <u>San Francisco Examiner</u> articles by Lester
Kinsolving (17, 18, 19, 20, and 24 September 1972) mention
only the armed guards and the rumors of intimidation.

[69]White, pp. 119-120.

[70]Kanter, <u>Commitment and Community</u>, p. 69.

[71]Ibid., pp. 113-114.

[72]Carey Winfrey, "Why 900 Died in Guyana," <u>New York
Times Magazine</u>, 26 February 1979, p. 45.

[73]Feinsod, p. 90.

[74]See Chapter Four for a more thorough discussion
of the question of meaning in the Temple.

[75]Gerald Parks, 6/26/81.

[76]Ibid.

[77]Ibid.

[78]Kanter, <u>Commitment and Community</u>, p. 128.

[79]Ibid., p. 132. This overly public aspect of life at Jonestown resulted, at least in part, from the sheer mechanics of the 1977 hegira.

[80]Feinsod, p. 214.

CHAPTER THREE

THE LEADERSHIP OF THE PEOPLES TEMPLE

In the previous chapter, the sources of the Temple's
appeal--the things that Jones offered potential members
both on concrete and ideological levels--were discussed.
Through use of Kanter's typology, we have seen some of the
ways the organization was oriented to obtain the commitment
of followers. In this chapter, the focus will be on the
organization of the Temple itself: the power structure and
the effects this had on the ultimate fate of the Temple.
Breaking these foci down to be considered separately does
not mean that one of them is prior to the other, for indeed
they arose out of dialogue with each other. The structure
influenced the process of commitment, and the process of
commitment influenced the structure. It is important to
realize, however, that the argument in the previous chapter
is focussed on individuals: on the ways in which they
gradually became committed through the use of specific
mechanisms that would pull them away from the old society
and draw them into the new, instrumentally, affectively,
and morally. It is time to look more concretely at the
structural arrangement of the organization. The structure
is heavily influenced by the means of commitment--for
instance, an organization that is created through the moral
mechanisms of mortification and transcendence, as the Temple was, will, almost necessarily, lack certain democratic
elements--but there is leeway within the use of these mechanisms for the structure to take certain directions. The
choice of the specific path the Temple took is perhaps the
most important factor in the determination of the fate of
its members.

The center of the Temple was, of course, the Reverend
Mr. Jones himself. He was not only the founder, but also
the leader--the charismatic leader--of the Peoples Temple.
As Max Weber defines charisma:

> Charisma knows only inner determination and in-
> ner restraint. The holder of charisma seizes
> the task that is adequate for him and demands
> obedience and a following by virtue of his mis-

113

sion. His success determines whether he finds
them. His charismatic claim breaks down if
his mission is not recognized by those to whom
he feels he has been sent. If they recognize
him, he is their master--so long as he knows how
to maintain recognition through "proving" himself. But he does not derive his "right" from
their will, in the manner of an election.
Rather, the reverse holds; it is the <u>duty</u> of
those to whom he addresses his mission to recognize him as their charismatically qualified
leader.[1]

Jones obtained this recognition from his followers. Gerald
Parks says of him:

Jones was supposed to have had a gift. I don't
know what kind of a gift you'd call it, maybe he
could see the future, or call him psychic, or he
was supposedly supposed to read people's minds
and things like that. I never knew for sure
whether he could or whether he couldn't, but he
put on a lot of good demonstrations . . . .
I--I was always a little skeptical in that
area anyway--I had a hard time believing that.
I don't mean to say that Jones wasn't--he did
seem like something, someone different, I have
to say that. His basic philosophy, his basic
message was fantastic, but somehow he got
screwed up with his, I dunno, way of life, the
way he looked at things, the way he would work
things around. And I really didn't realize it
at the time here in the States, because he would
speak out against things like the Viet Nam war,
a lot of injustices that were going on right
here in the States, you know, the minorities especially and things in that area that you knew
were true, that they were well-founded on the
basis of truth. And he had a good message, you
know, in that area, and he could draw crowds, he
just had the charisma. There did seem to be
something different and unusual about him, you'd
have to be around him to know what I meant . . .
[H]e had a way about him that would
soon convince you that what he was saying was
right. So basically, I, I wasn't religious, and
I didn't, you know, follow him for that
side of it, but his message on brotherhood,

on equality, social equality, economic equality,
and the whole thing was great for that, in that
area. That's basically why I followed the man
. . . .[2]

Anthony Katsaris saw him in the early 1970s, soon after his
sister became involved in the Temple, and talks about the
fear he felt in Jones's presence. At the end of our interview, when talking about my theories, he said:

Yeah, the people made Jones their leader, but--
He was really burned out at the end, but he
was really charismatic in the beginning. That
time when I saw him at the fairground, I was
only there for about half an hour and had to
leave, I was so threatened by his power. I was
really scared going to Jonestown, scared to see
him again, but his power was gone, he was
wasted. He was ruling on brute fear.[3]

I have chosen these two examples from my own interviewing
because I know in both cases I did not myself suggest the
word "charisma." The word has become devalued through
overuse in our society--everyone from baseball players to
TV stars to politicians is called "charismatic" without
hesitation, usually to indicate an engaging personality or
sex appeal. These two men, however, are describing Jones
as charismatic not because they found him attractive
(Katsaris was scared, perhaps merely the other side of
attraction), or because women found him attractive, but
because there was "something different and unusual about
him, you'd have to be around him to know what I meant."
Katsaris said, when asked in what way Jones scared him,

I don't know, it's really hard to pin down.
He'd wear those sunglasses all the time, to cut
down on distractions, they said. Somebody told
me, I can't remember who, that he wore them because his gaze was too powerful--he wore them to
shield others from his gaze.
I dunno, it was just a feeling, it wasn't
some well thought out thing, it was a gut reaction.[4]

In the previous chapter, the appeals of the Temple
were discussed, but the importance of the fact that it was
Jones himself who was offering the healing and providing
the language, Jones himself who was going to lead the

faithful into the cave to wait out the holocaust, was not
emphasized. The point is important.   It was not so much
that Jones was personally charming or attractive—Jones had
a power, a force, that demanded acknowledgment:

> Never did the Temple operate on the personal
> charm of Jim Jones. He had very little of that.
> Many in Jonestown disliked him personally and
> thought him authoritarian and had felt that way
> for years. But he was the leader and must lead,
> and the overbearing quality of his personality
> did not mean that the follower could be "anar-
> chistic" in response.[5]

His followers having bestowed power and authority
upon him, it was up to Jones to create the leadership
structures of the Temple. Although the Planning Commission
(P.C.) was nominally the ruling body, in actual fact most
of the power rested in the hands of an unofficial elite.
The composition of this elite changed significantly over
the years.

In Indianapolis, the elite consisted of the four
assistant ministers: Russell Winberg, Ross Case, and Jack
Beam, who were white, and Archie Ijames, who was black. As
Reiterman describes this period:

> As fellow crusaders and friends, they grew
> close, intertwining their social, religious and
> personal lives. They asked favors of each
> other, and called each other "Brother." . . .
> They talked for hours on end about the
> church, race relations, the Bible and practical
> Christianity. Sometimes they dined together
> with their wives, and the Cases once attended an
> outdoor concert with the Joneses. The true fra-
> ternizing occurred among the men alone, often in
> a car, driving aimlessly, as Jones liked to do,
> or heading to a service somewhere.[6]

This was the situation until the time of Jones's trip to
Brazil in 1962-3. During this period, the four assistant
ministers maintained the Temple in Indianapolis, though
Beam and his family went to Brazil for about six months.
Around the time of Jones's return, Winberg left the church,
apparently because his Pentecostalism was coming into

conflict with the aims of the church; Case left for Eureka, California (one of the "nine places to hide" from nuclear holocaust), though his final break with the Temple was not to occur for another couple years; Beam also left for California, apparently on Jones's instructions;[7] and Ijames was left holding the fort.

After Jones's return from Brazil, he recruited his first female member of the elite, Patty Cartmell:

> [H]e recruited her to gather information for his revelations, by spying and subterfuge. She helped him with his cheap magician's tricks, perhaps out of love, or belief in Jones. When Patty Cartmell said, "He's the only God you'll ever see," she did not necessarily mean that Jones was a heavenly God; she meant that there was no God except the force of goodness and love in each person. And she would believe to the end that Jim Jones was filled with more love than any living being.[8]

This was the direction in which Jones was to move throughout the rest of the history of the Temple. By the time of the suicides, virtually all of the members of the elite were women, and, for the most part, young, attractive, white women.[9] Maria Katsaris, Carolyn Moore Layton, Karen Tow Layton, Annie Moore, Grace Stoen and Deborah Layton Blakey (who both defected), Paula Adams, Patty Cartmell, Sharon (Linda) Amos, and Terri Buford[10] became members of the elite not only because of their abilities, but also because of their loyalty to the cause and their intense personal loyalty to Jones. For the most part, this personal loyalty was very much connected with the fact that they were, or had been, Jones's lovers.

Blakey's rise to the elite, for instance, was literally consumated by three sexual encounters with Jones. Although this is described in the Layton family biography as an "act of humiliation and entrapment,"[11] others on the staff carried on long-term affairs with Jones. As Reiterman describes it,

> Though some were unsatisfied or found him clumsy and rough, many a woman came away in a blush, feeling she was his favorite. But those who nursed such delusions for long found themselves called elitists. The competition and rivalry

was particularly bitter within Jones's own staff;
some who had regular or multiple sexual contacts
with Jones became possessive. Some fell in love
with him and went through all stages of a love
affair, from infatuation to seduction to letdown,
to the realization that Jones was community property and that they better accept the bittersweet
role of sometimes lover. In a much shorter
time span, they repeated Marceline's [Jones's
wife's] experiences. And like Marceline, most
remained loyal church members.[12]

It is clear that the female members of the elite were
divided by sexual jealousy, division encouraged by Jones,
who urged them to keep tabs on each other. For instance,
when Blakey was in Georgetown prior to her move to Jonestown, she, with other members of the elite, attended a
reception for a group of Cubans doing volunteer work in
Guyana. The purpose was:

to propagandize the Cubans about their cause. A
young Cuban doctor took a fancy to Debbie and
asked her to dance. She hesitated, because she
hadn't danced in years, and furthermore it was
against Temple rules. But Paula [Adams] gave her
the cue that she'd better do it--that was what
they were there for.
    Once out on the dance floor with the handsome
Cuban, Debbie found that she was enjoying herself
very much. After several long dances, she felt
herself drawn to him; he made her feel pretty.
Suddenly she realized, actually for the first
time in her life, that she was pretty. She
wasn't fat and dumpy anymore, she was thin-and
she was attractive to men.
    On the way back to the house in the Temple
van, however, it became clear that her enjoyment
had drawn resentment from the others, especially
Paula and Sharon [Amos]. She thought maybe they
were jealous because they hadn't been asked to
dance as much as she had. The tension was so bad
that she knew they were going to write her up--
report her to Jones. So she wrote the incident
up herself, changing only her reaction to what
happened. As she described it, this Cuban doctor
wouldn't leave her alone, and she was nice to him
out of her sense of duty and loyalty to the Temple, because that's what she thought she was
supposed to do. But actually, she reported to
Jones, it was an ordeal.[13]

We can see how this rivalry and tale-telling operated by Blakey's reception at Jonestown. As soon as she arrived,

> Debbie went up to the radio room to report to Jones and to hand over to Carolyn Layton the ten thousand dollars they [Blakey and her mother] had carried in. Jones was not particularly friendly. He said "Good to see you" and turned away. As they chatted in the radio room, Debbie sensed a coldness and reserve on the part of Carolyn and Maria Katsaris, which made her feel uncomfortable. She soon learned that a class structure had developed in Jonestown, based partly on how close a person was to Jones and partly on how long a person had been in Guyana.[14]

Thus the rank distinctions which had been there implicitly in Redwood Valley and San Francisco were finally explicit.

There were some male members of the elite as well. Assistant Pastor Jack Beam, Temple attorneys Eugene Chaiken and Tim Stoen, and Temple public relations person Michael Prokes were most significant among them. Jack Beam was, as mentioned above, a follower since the very beginning of the Temple, a loyalist through and through. Archie Ijames, the only black member ever to function as a member of the elite, was eased out by Jones in 1974.[15] Although the women members of the elite were "initiated" through sexual encounters with Jones, there is no evidence as to whether or not any of these men had sex with Jones. Stoen and Layton both publicly "confessed" their homosexuality,[16] though without mentioning Jones by name. For both of these men, however, an actual sexual encounter would be unnecessary, because Jones had achieved effectively the same end by coopting their wives.

Larry was the first member of the Layton family to join the Temple. He brought with him his wife, Carolyn Moore Layton, with whom Jones became enamored. He began an affair with her, ultimately telling Larry that he would have to divorce his wife and arranging for him to marry Karen Tow instead. Karen, too, was to become Jones's mistress, though she was never to reach the heights of favor that Carolyn did.[17] As the Layton family biography puts it, "the result was the addition of another loyal eunuch to Jones' palace guard."[18]

Tim Stoen, main Temple attorney, joined in 1970. He and Grace Grech were married in a Temple service about six months later. Tim was very important to the operation of the Temple, acting both for the Temple as a whole and providing advice to individual members. In 1971, Grace became pregnant. Despite pressure to abort the child, she was permitted to carry the child to term.[19] John Victor Stoen, the object of the custody battle which was the cause for the first suicide drills in Guyana,[20] was born on 25 January 1972. After his birth, Grace, too, gradually rose in the Temple, eventually reaching the position of head counselor in the Planning Commission. Tim and Grace gradually grew apart, ceasing to live together. As Feinsod puts it,

> As far as Grace could tell, if Tim was married to anybody, it was to Jim Jones. In terms of time spent together, emotional closeness and shared experience, Tim and Jones were far closer to each other than either was to Grace.[21]

Ultimately, however, Jones failed in his efforts to divide the Stoens and bind each, separately, to him. First Grace defected, in July of 1976, beginning a custody battle in February, 1977, after John Victor was taken to Guyana in November 1976. When Stoen left the Temple in the summer of 1977, he joined Grace in the fight for custody of John Victor.

These stories serve to indicate the importance of sex in the Temple. Jones "used his body to discipline, elevate and reward as well as to assert his own superiority and to humiliate."[22]   Jones created the elite of the Temple by making them his "property," or by taking the "property" of his male followers. He marked out his property by having sex with selected individuals. In this regard, Susan Brownmiller's work on rape is helpful. She points out that "the laws of rape . . . never shook free of their initial concept--that the violation was first and foremost a violation of male rights of possession, based on male requirements of virginity, chastity and consent to private access as the female bargain in the marriage contract."[23]   In other words, our society's laws reflect basic assumptions about the husband "owning" the wife's body, so that violation of the woman is somehow seen as an assault on the property of the husband.

Now whether or not Jones's sexual encounters should

be considered rape is somewhat problematical. Brownmiller
would define rape in these terms: "If a woman chooses not
to have intercourse with a specific man and the man chooses
to proceed against her will, that is a criminal act of
rape."[24] Under this definition, some of Jones's encounters were clearly rape. Deborah Layton Blakey, as we have
seen, found Jones "awkward" and the experience unpleasant:
she felt "diseased."[25] She was forced to testify to his
prowess, however:

> We all knew what we were supposed to say because
> we had seen it all before. We were supposed to
> say that we had approached him; that he had
> helped us psychologically; that he had the big-
> gest penis we had ever seen; that he could screw
> longer than anybody; and that we had never had
> an orgasm until we had sex with him. Until that
> moment I had always believed that what all the
> others previous to me had said was true; now I
> knew differently.[26]

This prowess was one of the tenets of the church, and
served Jones in gaining new lovers. Brownmiller would
classify this as an example

> of what men would call seduction since the
> sexual goal [is] accomplished without the use,
> or even the threat, of physical force, but the
> imposition of sex by an authority figure is
> hardly consensual or "equal."
> Coercion can take many forms, economic and
> emotional coercion are among them, and not only
> is the rape victim afraid to resist, but after
> the fact, she is seldom believed. Rape by an
> authority figure can befuddle a victim who has
> been trained to respect authority so that she
> believes herself complicitous. Authority
> figures emanate an aura of rightness; their
> actions cannot easily by challenged. What else
> can the victim be but "wrong"?[27]

The fact of the matter is that a sexual relationship with
Jones--whether rape or not--may have appealed to the women
because it gave them access to power, power unobtainable in
any other way. Once Jones's "property," they could be
trusted with the intimate secrets of the Temple--secrets
that the Planning Commission was unaware of--and trusted to
do the "dirty work" of Temple operations. The elite were

the ones doing "research" for Jones's revelations and helping with the healings, and they were the ones handling the financial and practical business of the Temple.

A good example of this is Maria Katsaris. She was a woman of 25 who had not finished college, and she was in a position of incredible power. Her brother ruminates on this:

> On the one hand, it's easy to see her as a victim, in the wrong place at the wrong time, just sucked under by the whole thing. On the other hand, I read in Reston's book that she was the one who was on the radio to Lamaha Gardens, that told them to use the knife.[28]
> I knew she was high up, but it's hard to imagine, it's hard to see her, some of the things I read and hear--
> Was she a power-crazed demon of the sort Jones was, that she would do something like that? When she was there, was she like that because she was up for hours and hours while they grilled her and left her emotionally battered? Or was she like that because that's the way she wanted to be? At that point there's not much difference between the two, because the effect of what she did to people was the same.
> She was responsible for a lot of the banking --going around South America to all these different banks. That bothered me. It seems really shabby. I mean, her motivating force in getting into it was social concern. It's not like some white liberal from the suburbs, "Good cause, let's work with the black folks." The feeling ran deep in her, and then to see her sell out like that.
> People were eating poorly. She's taking these vast sums and depositing them when people were hungry.
> Was she brainwashed? God, yes. But at what point do you say that there's no personal responsibility? . . . She went into it for a lot of good reasons, but she had to put those behind. She stayed though there were lots of bad things going on.[29]

These members of the elite had power, a great deal of power--and they split themselves off almost completely from the needs, from the lives, of the greater mass of the members in their use of that power.

This was perhaps made easier for them by virtue of the fact that they were not representative of that greater mass of the membership. The Temple was about 80% black and two-thirds female. The elite was white, and, although it was predominantly female, these white women were hardly representative of the membership. In fact, these are the women whom were excepted in the generalization about members of the Temple not being typical of the followers of most new religions. Most of the members were similar to those attracted to the traditional "cults" (e.g., Jehovah's Witnesses, Christian Scientists, Father Divine's Peace Mission) in that they were marginal to society in terms of age, class, race, and/or sex. These members of the elite, however, were the young, white, upper-middle-class individuals more typical of the membership of the new religions. This led to extreme dichotomization of the Temple. In a sense, the elite belonged to a new religion, and the followers belonged to a cult. The needs and intentions of the two groups were very different. The elite tended to be more politically motivated, more sophisticated, and less traditionally religious. This led to a separation of the interests of the individuals in the elite--in power, for instance--from the interests of those they presumably led, as we see in Anthony Katsaris's comments above. This separation was recognized both by the elite and by the rank and file members:

> [T]he staff was isolated. Scorned as elitists in an egalitarian organization, they were seen as a villainous secret police. Sometimes they were blamed for the unpopular deeds and policies of Jones, which is just what he wanted . . . .
> In the eyes of the rank and file, staff members were treated to special privileges. For instance, their special membership cards allowed them to enter the church without a body search or inspection of their ever-present suitcases. They had a special locked room for their files. Some members thought them snobbish and standoffish, too closemouthed about their precious duties, too close to Jim. Members begrudged them their cars and their freedom of movement. And some blacks resented the rapid rise of college-educated whites, especially bossy or bitchy women.

The resentment cut both ways. Staff members
felt they were doing the unglamorous, exhausting
and dangerous tasks. Bradshaw and perhaps some
others believed that men were excluded from
staff because they would not do the humiliating
dirty work. They saw themselves as unsung
heroines, commandos in the people's army, armed
with wiles and disguises.[30]

The Planning Commission (P.C.) was the third layer in the
hierarchy. The composition of the P.C. was somewhat more
representative of the Temple as a whole. It was originally
predominantly white, like the elite. In 1975, however,

One of the young black women in the church . . .
felt it was time for a change to be made. She
started a rumor among the black members that
Father didn't think black people were qualified
for leadership. The rumor got back to Jim that
the entire church was asking why there weren't
more black faces on the Planning Commission. He
knew he had to make a major change.
The following week he made a startling an-
nouncement. "All the counsellors in Los Angeles
and San Francicso will be added to the Planning
Commission." Since many of these counsellors
were black it meant that the racial balance of
the P.C. would be assured.[31]

Nominally the decision-makers for the Temple, the
P.C. was not in fact all that powerful. During their
meetings,

Hours and hours were spent discussing the people
in the church, from their work habits to their
sex lives. Meetings also covered less intimate
matters--organizing and expanding the church,
purchasing buses and other equipment, upcoming
events, travel, projects and political difficulties in the community. Everything was talked
about--from getting Mrs. Smith's rent paid, to
upcoming elections, to flirtations, to guardian-
ships, to the legality of selling guns collected
from members. Debate went on interminably.
Sometimes Jones would say nothing at all until
the others settled on a decision. Then he would

offer his opinion, stating his reasons so con-
vincingly that the others could see their own
faulty reasoning.[32]

Most of the meetings, however, were devoted to catharsis,
the confrontations of individual members about their various shortcomings.

The residual effects of the larger society
needed to be ripped away like dead skin, maintained Jones. It took repetition and confronta-
tion to crush ego problems and jealously games,
to excise the ugly scar tissue of racism and
sexism, agism, classism, and to replace it with
the healthy muscle of egalitarianism.[33]

Jeannie Mills was not impressed with her first Planning
Commission meeting. During this meeting, Jeannie was confronted about the fact that she did not want to have sex
with Jones, and her husband, Al, for saying that punishments were unfair. Jeannie's reaction was, "This was the
great P.C.? Where was all the planning?"[34]

The P.C. had two primary functions: first, its
members did most of the managerial level work of the Temple, and second, they served as testing ground for various
theories and practices Jones was working on. The first
suicide drills, in 1973, were held in the P.C.: the rank
and file did not begin to participate until after the move
to Guyana. In addition, Jones's homosexual relationships
and his teaching that everyone in the Temple except himself
was homosexual were first tested in the P.C.[35]

Although Jones had sex with many members of the Planning Commission, both male and female, sex did not play the
same role there that it did among the elite. Instead,
loyalty was ensured through the use of self-incriminating
"confessions."[36] The members of the P.C. would write up
confessions of various illegal or immoral activities, such
as conspiracy against the United States or its president,
having sex with family members, or blowing up banks or
trains. Jeannie Mills recalls that

Each time we were instructed to write another
letter, he would assure us of how much this made
him trust us. "You all know I wouldn't use any
of these letters against you. It's just that if
one person here were to leave this group and

threaten us, we could use these statements to convince that person to leave us alone . . . .

The members of the P.C. had already progressed through the commitment process outlined in the previous chapter and were already very much involved in the group. To some extent, achieving membership in the Planning Commission involved starting the commitment process again, at a higher level: members had attained a new level of involvement in the group, and needed to become committed to the P.C. in addition to their commitment to the Temple. The appeal of embarking upon this commitment process was not the healing in all its varieties which led them to join the Temple in the first place; now members were attracted by the prestige of being trusted by Jones with (some of) the secrets of Temple business and of being trusted to do the many organizational tasks of the Temple. This indicates, again, the extent to which there were two groups operating in the Temple: the elite and the P.C. on the one hand and the rank and file on the other.

Compared with the elite, the P.C. had fewer special privileges and was therefore less resented by the rank and file membership. There was, however, a clear separation between the two groups, the leaders and the led, and even at this level the important features of Temple leadership can be discerned. First, the leadership was comprised of people with strong personal bonds to Jones.[38] Second, it was not truly representative of the membership of the Temple. Third, it could be affected by the membership at large only indirectly, through the spreading of rumors which Jones would see as threatening to his leadership.

This clear separation between the two groups, as suggested above, can be interpreted by classifying the leadership as members of a new religion and the followers as members of a cult. At the same time, however, both groups were following a single leader. It is as though there were two circles, moving in opposite directions, rotating around a single center (See Figure 2). The elite

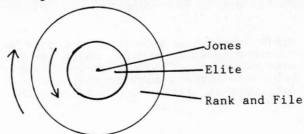

Figure 2.

and P.C. were following Jones because he offered them power in a very concrete sense. The rank and file, too, followed Jones because he gave them power, though in a very different sense.

        Jones and his elite were white: 80% of the members of the Temple were black.   Despite Jones's claims to lead an interracial congregation, there were virtually no Hispanic, Oriental, or Amerind members.   Thus, Jones's personal effectiveness arose from a combination of his personal charisma with the very fact that he was a white man leading blacks.   This point is important in terms of the specific social gestalt in which the Temple developed. C. Eric Lincoln, in The Black Church Since Frazier, talks about the nature of the black congregation's relationship to the white power structure in a way which may serve to illuminate this point:

> The Black Church's traditional reluctance to place itself in opposition to the white power structure grew partly out of lessons learned from actual experience and partly from the vicarious understandings communicated through the projections of actual experience. The fundamental beliefs contributing to this reluctance were (1) the absolute invulnerability of the white man, and (2) the absolute vulnerability of all Black people and all Black institutions. These two convictions, formidable in themselves, were usually buttressed by (3) feelings of contingency and dependence—the recognition that, ultimately, life itself depended on the white man's good will, his charitableness, or at the very least his passivity . . . .
> A fourth conviction had to do with the unreliability of Black leadership. Since all Blacks were equal in their equality, i.e., their social distance from whites, to trust any Black leader was to assume the miraculous . . . .[39]

Lincoln's observations serve to suggest some of the reasons why a white leader would appeal to a black congregation. As a white man, Jones was in a position of power which his followers could tap into (points 1 and 2). He did share these powers with his followers, through healing, primarily, but also in the provision of concrete social services (point 3), and not just in a passive way. His leadership, coming out of his whiteness, was reliable (point 4). In other words, the Temple offered a means of opposing the white power structure by using the very power of the whites whom they opposed. Lincoln offers one final point in his analysis--there

> was the question of "unfaithfulness" to white supporters who in times past were relied upon for such favors as they chose to deliver--charity, philanthropic intercession, advice and counsel, etc. Tradition has it that Black people never forget a favor and never remember a wrong . . . . [T]he concern of the sensibilities of "white friends" has undoubtedly been important in the structuring of strategy and the selection (or rejection) of leadership in the Black community.[40]

It seems likely that the Temple offered blacks a means of assuaging these feelings of unfaithfulness through working with the whites in the interracial congregation. Although Jones claimed to have Cherokee blood, in order to mediate the distance between white and black, he was perceived to be a white man rather than a black man. Identification with the leader, racially, was not the issue--being able to follow a man of power who would share his power with them was. In this way, the gestalt Lincoln talks about combines with other traditions of the black church, such as social and political service and participatory worship, to make for a bond which became completely focused on the person of Jim Jones.

This description of the power structure of the Temple makes it clear that it mirrored the power structure of the larger society: the educated whites led the uneducated blacks, and women would only achieve power through the good graces of their men. Thus, despite the Temple's claims to be founding the new society, the same racial and sexual imbalances were being perpetuated.

It is difficult to ascertain how the members felt about this. Most of the rank and file members died in Jonestown,[41] and it does not seem to have preoccupied the white leaders overmuch.[42] In the day-to-day operation of the Temple, racial tensions were not a real problem until the final days of the Temple, when

Internal division and racial bitterness tainted both California temples. Blacks were angry that whites alone controlled the pursestrings, made the day-to-day decisions and consulted more often with Jones on the radio. Some whites, in turn, thought blacks were themselves to blame for their isolation from the power positions because they refused tedious work such as radio room duty.[43]

In general, however, the Temple seems to have perceived itself as an interracial congregation, and the power distribution within that congregation only "right." This "rightness" in some ways arose out of the similarities to the structures within which all members--black and white, male and female--grew up. The Temple's perceptions of right and wrong were heavily influenced by Jones's teachings. Racism was bad; they were very clear about that, but Jones did not teach that it was therefore wrong for whites to continue to lead blacks. The consciousness raising within the Temple--a process conducive to, if not necessary for, the perception of systemic injustice--was slanted in very specific directions. With regard to the women's issue, for instance, Jones instituted women's meetings, led by Linda Amos, who was "chosen . . . since she had proven her ability to abstain from sex." She

> began the first meeting by saying, "I never enjoyed having sex with men, but I felt that it was something I had to do in order to keep a husband. Since Father helped me to become liberated, I know I don't need to have a man in my life. I have become free. No man will ever again be able to rule over me."[44]

We see, then, that the path to feminine emancipation was through Jones--and thus his bestowal of power would continue to be perceived as right. In a similar fashion, the implicit message of the Temple as a whole was that racism could be eradicated--or at least escaped--only through Jones.

We thus return to the point with which we began this chapter: the charismatic figure of Jim Jones. As suggested above, the "charismatic claim breaks down if [the leader's] mission is not recognized by those to whom he

130   MAKING SENSE OF THE JONESTOWN SUICIDES

feels he has been sent."[45] The Temple's power structures, as developed by Jones, were accepted by the membership as a function of their recognition of Jones's charismatic claim. It was necessary, therefore, for Jones to
maintain that claim.

> By its very nature, the existence of charismatic
> authority is specifically unstable. The holder
> may forego his charisma; . . . he may prove to
> his followers that "virtue is gone out of him."
> It is then that his mission is extinguished, and
> hope waits and searches for a new holder of
> charisma. The charismatic holder is deserted by
> his following, however, (only) because pure
> charisma does not know any "legitimacy" other
> than that flowing from personal strength, that
> is, one which is constantly being proved. . . .
> The charismatic leader gains and maintains
> authority solely by proving his strength in
> life. If he wants to be a prophet, he must
> perform miracles; if he wants to be a war lord,
> he must perform heroic deeds. Above all, how-
> ever, his divine mission must "prove" itself in
> that those who faithfully surrender to him must
> fare well. If they do not fare well, he is ob-
> viously not the master sent by the gods . . . .
> The subjects may extend a more active or pas-
> sive "recognition" to the personal mission of
> the charismatic master. His power rests upon
> this purely factual recognition and springs from
> faithful devotion. It is devotion to the extra-
> ordinary and unheard-of, to what is strange to
> all rule and tradition and which therefore is
> viewed as divine. It is a devotion born of dis-
> tress and enthusiasm.[46]

This, then, is the significance of Jones's healings and
revelations: they were not only his means of attracting
followers, but of maintaining his authority.

It cannot be overstressed that Jones had genuine
abilities in this area. Odell Rhodes, for instance,
recalls his reactions to a personal experience of this:

> A week or so after [a] meeting in which he
> praised Rhodes from the pulpit, Jones stopped
> Rhodes in the hall, threw an arm around his
> shoulder, and thanked him again for working with

the children. Then he pulled Rhodes aside and in a low, comforting voice, told Rhodes not to worry because the children were calling him "Dad." "I'm their 'Dad,'" Jones told him, "but I can't be everywhere--so you have to stand in for me."

The incident, his first personal contact with Jim Jones, chilled Rhodes to the bone. "It was true, those kids I was taking care of, they were calling me Dad sometimes. Well, I knew the only person in the Temple you called 'Dad' was Jones, so I didn't know what to do about it. I didn't want to tell anybody it was bothering me, because I was still thinking about whether I wanted to tell anybody. So, even if somebody heard the kids calling me 'Dad' and told Jones about it, there was no way in hell he could have known it was bothering me. No way in hell--and all of a sudden, there's Jones and he's telling me he knows its bothering me and not worry. I damned near thought I must have been talking to the devil."

"Maybe," says Odell Rhodes, "he was just so tuned into people, he could look at you, and he'd always have a pretty good idea of what you were up to, so maybe he could just guess about what was likely to be bothering you. I don't know, but if that wasn't it, I'd hate to think what the hell else it could have been."[47]

Jones, however, did not rely solely on his genuine abilities. From the very beginning, he ensured the continuing proof of his charisma by fakery. The real and the fake intertwined. As Jones himself recalls the early days, "People [started] passing growths and then by sleight of hand I'd started doing it, and that would trigger others to get healed . . . ."[48] Jeannie Mills, who was in charge of the testimony file, says that many apparently genuine healings were reported, and that she herself experienced Jones's power in her own life.[49]

Jones's revelations, too, were a mixture of the fake and the genuine. Although he had members of the elite out combing garbage cans and peering through windows for information, "[Sandy] Bradshaw saw him time and time again correct mistakes on the cards, made by his staff in gathering information or typing--mistakes he seemingly could not have picked up without some 'psychic' powers."[50]

The members' perception of these miracles varied significantly. Gerald Parks says that he was not aware of any fakery until after his return from Guyana.[51]   On the other hand, Odell Rhodes, another rank and file member,

> watched [Jones's] faith healing miracles in
> utter fascination, not because he believed in
> miracles, but because as a fellow professional,
> Rhodes recognized a class act when he saw it.
> For the small-time street hustler from Detroit,
> watching Jones cure cancer and bring the dead
> back to life was like Knuckles O'Toole watching
> Horowitz play the piano. "He was," Rhodes says
> flatly, "the best con man I ever saw--and I've
> seen quite a few. I knew guys who could talk
> you out of anything in your pocket and Jones
> would have taken any of them to the cleaners. I
> mean, he just got done telling them what a crock
> the Bible was, and then he'd turn around and
> pull off a miracle they wouldn't dare put in the
> Bible, it was so outrageous.   And he'd have
> people eating out of his hand."[52]

Among the upper echelons, reactions were likewise mixed. Jeannie Mills, although aware of the fake, acknowledged the genuine. For others, they were seen on a completely different level:

> Such "spiritual" theatrics won the devotion of
> many poor blacks, but they also raised the
> eyebrows of the liberal middle-class whites
> committed to the church's humanitarian works.
> This conflict was easily resolved once Jones let
> some of the congregation's white leadership in
> on a little secret. The poor were overly reli-
> gious and susceptible to such hokum. The per-
> formances were merely a means to an end, a
> vehicle to get their attention and secure their
> faith in Jim Jones. Once that was accomplished,
> he would guide them to a better life. When he
> told the poor, uneducated masses that he was the
> reincarnation of Jesus Christ, and when they
> believed that he was God, it was for their own
> good.[53]

Or, as Maria Katsaris told her brother, "[W]e're trying to approach people on a level they could understand, until they could see what we're really about and grow beyond

that."[54] Even those with the inside knowledge, however,
saw proof of Jones's ability, as Sandy Bradshaw's comments
indicate.

Jones used his gift to attract followers, and, despite his statements to the bemused elite, never led the
rank and file beyond their "primitive" understanding--for
to do so would undercut his authority. Aware of the need
to maintain this authority, he buttressed his gifts with
fakery, so that he could continue the leadership on the
same terms as it was granted. Not only the structure, but
the style of his leadership were predicated on its charismatic basis. As Weber states,

> Genuine charismatic domination . . . knows of no
> abstract legal codes and statues and of no "for-
> mal" way of adjudication.   Its "objective" law
> emanates concretely from the highly personal
> experience of heavenly grace and from the
> godlike strength of the hero.   Charismatic
> domination means a rejection of all ties to any
> external order in favor of the exclusive
> glorification of the genuine mentality of the
> prophet and hero.   Hence, its attitude is
> revolutionary and transvalues everything; it
> makes a sovereign break with all traditional or
> rational norms: "it is written, but I say unto
> you."[55]

In other words, Jones's charismatic claim to leadership
underlay every important facet both of leadership and
discipline in the Temple.[56]

Given the concentration of ultimate power and authority in Jones's hands, the question of a Temple apart from
him needs to be considered. According to one report,

> In late 1974, a few of the more mature new mem-
> bers actually approached Jones about retiring.
> They used the argument that he would be more
> effective if he dropped out of sight. They
> cited other cults where the disappearance of the
> guru made the movement all the more sought
> after. There's nothing like an absent God, they
> told him.   But Jones did not care about the
> movement: he was the movement.   It could fall

apart   without   him   as   far   as   he   was   concerned.[57]

Jones did, however, recognize his own mortality:

> Sometimes   with   John   [Collins],   Jones   would
> reveal   his   own   anxieties   and   fears.   Jones
> worried   about   growing   old,   showing   weakness.
> "He was rather   defensive   about   dyeing his hair
> or not wanting to move around when   his   leg hurt
> and   have   people   see him limp.   He's say, 'Now,
> people   out   there,   show   them   any   sign   you're
> growing   older   and   they'll   desert   you.   They'll
> leave.   You always   have to be   aware   of   that.
> There's   an   old   saying: 'He who rides the tiger
> dare not dismount.'"[58]

Gradually,   Jones seems to   have   focussed   on   John Victor
Stoen as his   successor.   "To most [members], . . . he was a
living tribute   to   progressive,   interracial   child   rearing.
Among P.C. members, John V. Stoen was   almost   a   reincarnation   of   Father as a   child   and was to be   loved in the   same
way."[59]   Tim   Stoen,   before   his defection and the custody
fight,   "said John was destined for   leadership role not just
in   the   church   but   in the world.   It was   as   though   the
five-year-old were heir to a throne."[60]

It is   interesting   that   Jones   would   focus on John as
successor,   since   he   already   had two natural   sons   whose
paternity was not in question: Stephan,   son   of   his   wife
Marceline,   and   Kimo,   son of Carolyn Moore Layton.   John's
paternity was   very much in   question.[61]   It   seems   possible, however,   that   he   would   reject Stephan as too sympathetic   to   his   mother,   and   to   avoid   the   same   thing
happening   with   Kimo,   chose a son whose mother was   out   of
the group and who   could   not   deflect   the   son's   loyalty.
John   was   seen   as central to the future of the Temple,   at
least by Jones.   This   is   the   significance   of the suicide
threat   in   response   to   the   custody   battle (see   above,
pp.   57-59).   We   see   the limits of this, however, in the
final White Night.   Christine   Miller,   the   only   member   to
protest   the   suicides,   ended   her pleas for reconsideration
by asking if Jones wanted   to see John die too.   He replied,
"Do you think I'd put John's   life   above   the   others? . . .
He's just one of my children.   I   don't   prefer   one above the
other."[62]   The   way to save John was the way to   save   all
the children: by helping them step over.

> [W]hen they [the Guyanese army] start parachut-
> ing out of the air, they'll seek some of our
> innocent babies.   I'm not--I don't want . . . .
> They've got to shoot me to get through to some
> of these people. I'm not telling them take your
> child. Can you let them take your child? . . .
>   I know there's no point--there's no point to
> this. We are born before our time. They won't
> accept us.   And I don't think we should sit here
> and take any more time for our children to be
> endangered; because if they come after our
> children, we give them our children, then our
> children will suffer forever . . . .
>   Ain't nobody gonna take Ejar [John Stoen].
> I'm not lettin' 'em take Ejar.[63]

The fate of the Temple was tied up in Jones's leadership
and in the limits of his commitment to his decision to pass
that leadership on to a small child.

People joined the Temple because of Jim Jones:
because of his healing, his protection, his message of
peace, justice, hope, and equality. Since Jones was the
source of the benefits of the Temple, it is understandable
that he should also be the leader of the Temple.   His followers bestowed authority upon him in recognition of his
power.   Once this authority had been bestowed upon him,
however, it was Jones's prerogative to use it, and to share
it, as he saw fit.

We have seen that Jones began by sharing his power
with four assistant ministers in a structure similar to
that found in many churches.   As the Temple's beliefs and
practices moved away from the style of traditional Christianity, two of these assistants broke with the church.
The leadership, too, became less like that of traditional
Christian churches.   Access to power was possible only
through Jones.   Although Jones continued to bestow the
title of "assistant pastor" (e.g., on Tim Stoen), such
limited power and confidence as he chose to share was
invested in a largely unofficial elite consisting primarily
of women.

Jones was obviously unable to do all the work of the
Temple himself, but he was reluctant to deputize without
first ensuring the loyalty of those whom he would be com-

pelled to trust. In the highest levels, this was done by making the individual his "property," either by having sex with the women or by taking the "property" of the males by having sex with their wives. Whether these sexual relationships were ongoing or merely a matter of a few incidents, the point had been made and his "property" branded. The women were expected to testify to his prowess, and did, for a fall from favor meant a fall from power.

Within the Planning Commission, the question of loyalty was more explicitly framed. Members signed "confessions," which, they were told, would not be used against them as long as they were loyal. Even within the P.C., however, it was clear that Jones was the one requesting these signs of loyalty, just as it had been Jones who had chosen them to serve on the P.C. in the first place.

Thus the focus of the leaders of the Temple was on proving to Jones that his confidence in them had been justified, and not on serving the rank and file members. This was one important factor in the division between leaders and followers in the Temple, and it was facilitated by the fact that the leaders were not representative of those they led. The two groups both followed Jones, but had very little interaction with each other.

As we have seen the figure of Jim Jones was central to the operation of the Temple. He did not, however, make any realistic allowances for passing his role on to someone else. A five year old child was chosen as successor, but Jones's commitment to the idea of John Victor Stoen as successor was not strong enought to prevent the final White Night. The effect of choosing a child successor, like the effect of the Temple's leadership structures, was to make Jones the only possible source of authority.

We see, then, that Jones was right when he said he was the Temple.[64] The members' relationship to him became so completely intertwined with their relationship to the church that the two became indistinguishable. When Jones saw himself as having no way out, he saw there to be no way out for the Temple--and the members of the Temple agreed. How the members were socialized to the idea that the solution to this was mass suicide is the subject of the next chapter.

FOOTNOTES

[1]H. H. Gerth and C. Wright Mills, translators and editors, From Max Weber (New York: Oxford University Press, 1946), pp. 246-247, emphasis in original.

[2]Gerald Parks, interview, Ukiah, California, 26 June 1981, emphasis in original. Although it was suggested in the previous chapter that the rank and file were more apt to join for religious reasons and the elite for social or political reasons, this distinction is not absolute, as we see here. In addition, the Parks clan followed Gerald's mother Edith into the Temple--and Edith joined because she believed that Jones had healed her of cancer.

[3]Anthony Katsaris, telephone interview, 24 September 1981.

[4]Ibid.

[5]James Reston, Jr., Our Father Who Art in Hell (New York: New York Times Books, 1981), p. 230.

[6]Tim Reiterman with John Jacobs, Raven (New York: E. P. Dutton, 1982), pp. 69-70.

[7]Ibid., pp. 92-93.

[8]Reiterman, p. 93. Cartmell was to become, in later years, Jones's "fucking secretary," the one who made appointments for members to "'learn to relate to the cause' on a more personal level." Jeannie Mills, Six Years with God (New York: A&W, 1979), pp. 244-245.

[9]Reiterman talks about the members of the elite as "staff," and includes only the female members (pp. 157-160). In a sense this distinction is correct, because the staff was the group doing the actual work. The males who are included in the definition of elite being used here, however, are important--they include the Temple attorneys and public relations person. (Reiterman implicitly acknowledges this when he talks about a "p.c. . . . within the p.c., dominated by staff and some men, such as Tim Stoen" [p. 161]. Larry Layton, who was dismissed as "spacey" (Reiterman, p. 172) but entrusted with the instigation of

the ambush at the airstrip, is not really a member of the
elite; his story is included below because of the significance of Jones's appropriation of his two wives.

[10]Buford defected only three weeks before the suicides, and some consider her to still be an adherent. (See
Mark Lane, The Strongest Poison [New York: Hawthorn Books,
1980], pp. 101-105, for a defense of her.)

[11]Min S. Yee and Thomas N. Layton, et al, In My
Father's House (New York: Holt, Rinehart, and Winston.
1981), p. 177.

[12]Reiterman, p. 178. Unfortunately, first person
accounts are not available from Jones's two most important
mistresses, Carolyn Moore Layton and Maria Katsaris, both
of whom died in Jonestown. (Layton bore a son, Kimo,
generally acknowledged to be Jones's, in January, 1975.)

[13]Yee and Layton, pp. 205-206, emphasis in original.

[14]Ibid., pp. 211-212.

[15]Reiterman, pp. 240-247. Ijames, though no longer
a member of the elite, remained a member of the Temple. He
was in San Francisco in November 1978 and thus escaped the
final White Night. According to Jeannie Mills, he was, as
of August 1979, "living in one of the two communes that
still remain with Peoples Temple members in them. They no
longer believe in Jim Jones, but still adhere to the communal beliefs that caused them to join originally." Letter
dated 23 August 1979.

[16]See next chapter, pp.155-158 for discussion of the
role of confession within the Temple.

[17]Reiterman, pp. 171-172.

[18]Yee and Layton, p. 171. Again, Layton should not
be considered a member of the elite (see footnote 9).

[19]This was a privilege marking the Stoens' prestige
within the Temple, and was perceived--and resented--as
such. Reiterman, p. 174.

[20]See above, p. 58.

[21]Ethan Feinsod, <u>Awake in a Nightmare</u> (New York: W. W. Norton, 1981), p. 47.

[22]Reiterman, p. 172.

[23]Susan Brownmiller, <u>Against Our Will</u> (New York: Simon and Schuster, 1975), p. 377, emphasis in original.

[24]Ibid., p. 18.

[25]Yee and Layton, pp. 175-176.

[26]Quoted, ibid., p. 177, emphasis in original.

[27]Brownmiller, p. 271.

[28]Lamaha Gardens was the Temple's headquarters in Georgetown. At the time of the suicides, Maria Katsaris radioed instructions to the members there to join them in suicide. Only Sharon Amos did, of the 75 or so there, killing her son and two daughters before killing herself. Reston, pp. 329-330.

[29]Anthony Katsaris, 9/24/81.

[30]Reiterman, pp. 158-159.

[31]Mills, pp. 294-295. Counsellors served to provide advice and support to members and ensure compliance with Temple rules and norms. As this passage indicates, they were closer to the rank and file than to the elite.

[32]Reiterman, p. 161.

[33]Ibid.

[34]Mills, p. 225.

[35]Ibid. p. 257.

[36]See next chapter.

[37]Mills, p. 295.

[38]These bonds were, in some cases, the reason for the individual's elevation to the P.C., and in others the result of that elevation (i.e., gratitude).

[39]C. Eric Lincoln, The Black Church Since Frazier (New York: Schocken Books, 1974), pp. 122-123.

[40]Ibid., p. 123.

[41]Feinsod does not cite Rhodes or Clayton on this point.

[42]An exception is Jeannie Mills, who says: "I intensely disliked the power structure that Jim had set up among the members. It was disappointing because I still held on to the dream that everyone should be equal. Although I tried to explain to our children that all members were equal, the inequality was evident in this room" where the P.C. was meeting (p. 294).

[43]Reiterman, p. 462.

[44]Mills, p. 285.

[45]From Max Weber, p. 246.

[46]Ibid., pp. 248-249.

[47]Feinsod, pp. 94-95, emphasis in original.

[48]Reprinted from the Georgetown (Guyana) Chronicle of 6 December 1978 by Accuracy in Media Report, 2 February 1979, p. 3. See above, pp.   for a fuller citation of this passage.

[49]Letter dated 17 April 1979. See above, p. 67 for fuller citation of this passage.

[50]Reiterman, p. 160. Bradshaw, a member of the elite, was in San Francisco at the time of the suicides. She remains a loyalist. (Ibid., p. 578.)

[51]See above, p. 76.

[52]Feinsod, p. 94.

[53]Yee and Layton, p. 120.

[54]Anthony Katsaris, 9/24/81.

[55]From Max Weber, p. 250.

[56]See next chapter for further discussion of the role of discipline in the Temple.

[57]John Peer Nugent, _White Night_ (New York: Rawson Wade, 1979), p. 28, emphasis in original.

[58]Yee and Layton, p. 153, punctuated as in original. John Collins is a pseudonym for one of Jones's former sons-in-law who defected and later married Deborah Layton Blakey.

[59]Reiterman, p. 288.

[60]Ibid., p. 315.

[61]For instance, Maria Katsaris' father Steven, who, as an integral part of the Concerned Relatives Group, had extensive contact with Stoen, thinks that John was Stoen's child, not Jones's. (Phone interview, 27 April, 1982.)
[62]Reiterman, p. 558.

[63]Steve Rose, _Jesus and Jim Jones_ (New York: Pilgrim Press, 1979), Appendix 21, "Excerpts of tape of last minutes," pp. 220-221.

[64]Nugent, p. 28.

CHAPTER FOUR

RESOCIALIZATION

Up to this point, the analysis has focused on the structures of the Peoples Temple. In Chapter Two, we examined the ways in which certain structures were designed to draw people into the Temple and to encourage them to commit themselves to it. In Chapter Three, we examined the structures through which Jones led the Temple. It is now time to consider the ways in which the Temple as a whole operated, not in terms of these structures per se, but rather in terms of the everyday living of life through, in, and around these structures. The lens through which we shall do this is that offered by the sociology of knowledge.

Peter Berger and Thomas Luckmann begin The Social Construction of Reality by stating, "The world of everyday life is not only taken for granted as reality by the ordinary members of society in the subjectively meaningful conduct of their lives. It is a world that originates in their thoughts and actions, and is maintained as real by these."[1] We will see in this chapter how this occurred within the Temple.

Berger and Luckmann posit a three step process in the social construction of reality. The first step is externalization, the creation of an object or the articulation of an idea. The next step is objectivation, when this new creation becomes an object--again, whether literally, in the case of a physical object, or figuratively, when an idea is shared with others and becomes a possible subject for discussion. The third step, internalization, involves the reintegration of the created object into the individual's consciousness as reality.

[T]he sum of [these] constitutes the phenomenon of society. Man, because of the peculiar nature of his biological makeup, is compelled to externalize himself. Men, collectively, externalize themselves in common activity and thereby produce a human world. This world, including that part of it we call social structure, attains for them the status of objective reality. The same world, as an objective reality, is internalized

143

in socialization, becoming a constituent part of
the subjective consciousness of the socialized
individual.[2]

In this chapter we will examine each of these three steps
in the creation of the Temple's new reality, focussing
specifically on Jones's role as creator of phrases and
their dissemination among the group (steps one and two),
and then, more specifically, on the question of socialization to the realities of the Temple (step three).

        It is hard to conceive of 913 people all killing
themselves willingly. Obviously not every one of them did.
One member, Christine Miller, tried to protest, but was
shouted down by the rest of the group. Two escaped, and
some, primarily the elderly and infirm, were injected with
the poison, but the rest stepped up and took their paper
cup of cyanide.[3] This was possible because Jonestown was
a society in which death was discussed. The possibility of
committing mass revolutionary suicide had first appeared
among the elite many years before, and drills had been
occurring among the membership as a whole for more than a
year. The idea of suicide was a feature of everyday life.
As Berger and Luckmann tell us:

> [T]he great part, if not all, of everyday con-
> versation maintains reality. Indeed its massi-
> vity is achieved by the accumulation and consis-
> tency of casual conversation—conversation that
> can afford to be casual precisely because it
> refers to the routines of a taken-for-granted
> world. The loss of casualness signals a break
> in the routines and, at least potentially, a
> threat to the taken-for-granted reality . . . .
>   At the same time that the conversational
> apparatus ongoingly maintains reality, it on-
> goingly modifies it. Items are dropped and
> added, weakening some sectors of what is still
> being taken for granted and reinforcing others.
> Thus the subjective reality of something that is
> never talked about comes to be shaky . . . .
> [C]onversation gives firm contours to items pre-
> viously apprehended in a fleeting and unclear
> manner . . . . Generally speaking, the conversa-
> tional apparatus maintains reality by "talking
> through" various elements of experience and
> allocating them a definite place in the real
> world.[4]

It was precisely by means of this sort of process that the idea of suicide became real for the community. Talk about the possibility began in 1973, when the elite, as Bonnie Thielmann tells us:

> assured one another that we would rather die than be taken into fascist concentration camps. We expected to move to a safe haven in another country before America collapsed, but if we didn't, we all agreed that, yes, we'd commit suicide.[5]

Then, in 1976, Jones had the first drills (again, among the ruling elite); this, too, for those who did not defect, became part of their conceptual framework. Naturally, for those who chose to remain with the group, there was an attempt to create a society which was consistent. Thus, there was a tendency to avoid those for whom mass revolutionary suicide was not a matter of conversation.[6] In this way, the creation of the "deviant" form of social expression tended to isolate and define the group. We will return to this point later.

The fact that Jonestown featured a single dominant creator who originated many of the ideas which became "phrases" in their social "language" is not in conflict with the sociology of knowledge approach being used here. Berger and Luckmann argue that with the objectification of the social creation, it leaves the realm of the creator's control and can act back upon him/her as well as on others. It becomes an object in the social universe. For it to become a regular part of the society's "vocabulary," however, it is necessary for it to be used by and meaningful to the rest of the society. If Jones had said, "Let's commit mass revolutionary suicide," and everyone else had said, "No, let's not"--or, more definitively, failed to discuss or consider it--the suicides would not have been possible. It was only through the participation of the group as a whole that the idea's continued existence and power were possible.

At the same time, Jones's position of authority within the group gave special importance to his contributions. For instance, although Ross Case, Jones's assistant pastor in Indianapolis in the late 50s and early 60s, was the one originally concerned about nuclear war, urging retreat to a safer part of the country, it was not until Jones adopted the idea that it became a meaningful part of the group's ideology. By the same token, it is likely that if anyone else had come up with the idea of mass suicide, it would not have been adopted without Jones's approval. His endorsement was a necessary, but not a sufficient, condition for the adoption of a new "phrase."

Stanley Milgram, in his investigation of the nature of obedience, reaches conclusions compatible with this idea. Milgram did a series of experiments in which a subject, thinking he is participating in an experiment on the effects of punishment on learning, was instructed to shock the other "subject" each time he gave a wrong answer, increasing the voltage each time. This other "subject," however, was actually working with the experimenter, and was not in fact hooked up to the electrodes. Most subjects, urged by the experimenter, ignored the pleas, cries, screams and final silence from the other "subject," continuing beyond "extreme intensity shock," "danger: severe shock," and going two full turns beyond the ominous "XXX" to the highest voltage on the board. Milgram concludes from this that:

> There is a propensity for people to accept definitions of action provided by legitimate authority. That is, although the subject performs the action, he allows authority to define its meaning.
> It is this ideological abrogation that constitutes the principal cognitive basis of obedience. If, after all, the world or the situation is as the authority defines it, a certain set of actions follows logically.
> The relationship between authority and subject, therefore, cannot be viewed as one in which a coercive figure forces action from an unwilling subordinate. Because the subject accepts authority's definition of the situation, action follows willingly.[7]

This is precisely what we see happening in the Temple. The members accepted Jones's definition of the situation, because he was the leader.[8] Having granted him this authority, it behooved his followers to perform the actions which were the logical consequence of his definition of the situation.

Milgram is talking about hierarchical situations, which the Temple clearly was. If, as is being argued here, the members continued to be autonomous human beings who participated in the creation and maintenance of their

reality, there would be occasions for both dissent and
disobedience. Milgram wants to distinguish clearly between
the two:

> Dissent may occur without rupturing hierarchical
> bonds and thus belongs to an order of experience
> that is qualitatively discontinuous with
> disobedience. Many dissenting individuals who
> are capable of expressing disagreement with
> authority still respect authority's right to
> overrule their expressed opinion. While
> disagreeing, they are not prepared to act on
> this conviction.[9]

Such dissent occurred within the Temple, even on the final
White Night. One woman, Christine Miller, stood up to
protest the inevitability of their fate. She was shouted
down not only by Jones but by the rest of the group. She
allowed herself to be shouted down because she was still
within a universe where it was possible to die a dignified
death for socialism. She could dissent, but she could not
disobey:

> Disobedience is the ultimate means whereby
> strain is brought to an end. It is not an act
> which comes easily.
>   It implies not merely the refusal to carry
> out a particular command, . . . but a reformu-
> lation of the relationship between the subject
> and authority.[10]

It involves the rejection of the universe within which one
has been living.

   Milgram's work is significant to this argument in two
ways, both of which hinge on the voluntary character of the
group. First, the process of coming into an obedient relationship is precisely that, a process. If a stranger had
walked into Jonestown on November 18th, even granting the
authority of Jones as a minister of the Disciples of
Christ, he would not have been likely to join the others in
suicide. (Mark Lane and Charles Garry, Temple attorneys,
escaped during the suicides by convincing a guard that they
would go back and tell the Temple's story, rather than
joining their clients in mass death.) This is not because
the members were brainwashed, but because they had gradually increased their level of obedience through a series of
increasingly significant acts. Milgram says:

> The obedient act is preservative: after the
> initial instructions, the experimenter does not
> command the subject to initiate a new act but
> simply to continue doing what he is doing. The
> recurrent nature of the action demanded of the
> subject creates binding forces. As the subject
> delivers more and more painful shocks, he must
> seek to justify to himself what he has done; one
> form of justification is to go on to the end.
> For if he breaks off, he must say to himself:
> "Everything I have done to this point is bad,
> and I now acknowledge it by breaking off." But,
> if he goes on, he is reassured by his past
> performance. Earlier actions give rise to
> discomforts which are neutralized by later
> ones. And the subject is implicated into the
> destructive behavior in piecemeal fashion.[11]

This is consistent with the results found in examining the
process of commitment to the group. Investment begins with
a relatively small commitment, which then increases bit by
bit. The process occurs so gradually that there is rarely
a point at which the demand seems _qualitatively_ different
from what you have already done. If you have gone along
with the idea of suicide drills, then suicide makes sense.
This contrasts sharply with the "brainwashing" situation,
in which, as we shall see, complete submission is demanded
immediately.

It is equally important to remember that the followers were the ones who bestowed and maintained Jones's authority. The popular understanding is that Jones's followers
were coerced into following him. Instead, violence played
as much an expressive as an instrumental role in internal
Temple dynamics. As Erving Goffman has observed,

> [T]he most objective form of naked power, i.e.,
> physical coercion, is often neither objective
> nor naked but rather functions as a display for
> persuading the audience; it is often a means of
> communication, not merely a means of action.[12]

This is precisely the role of coercion in the Temple. The
physical and emotional coercion were only too real, as was
the pain they inflicted on both the subject and the other
members watching. This coercion, and this pain, however,
were seen in terms of a much larger context which explained
and justified them. All members participated in the creation and the maintenance of a reality in which the leader

was endowed with the power to use any means necessary to prepare the group for their role as the vanguard of the new socialist society. Al Mills reports that he thought at the time:

> Am I going to let a little whipping stand in the way of the total picture? Jones isn't perfect, but he is the only one who can hold this group together; and this group is going to do great things in this world to make it a better place.[13]

After his defection--his return to the larger reality-- Mills and his wife spoke out strongly against the Temple's violence. Odell Rhodes says of their charges:

> There was discipline all right--no doubt about it. But, to me, it wasn't any big deal. You put a thousand people together and you damn well better have a little discipline. There's discipline in the army that's a hell of a lot worse--and then there's prison, which is a whole different ball game altogether. I don't doubt that things people say happened might be true, but the discipline I saw just seemed like the price you expect to pay for something like the Temple. I guess I figured if the Temple wasn't right for them, they shouldn't be with us. All I knew was that it was right for me.[14]

Reality is maintained primarily through conversation. Obviously, suicide could only become a conversational topic after a long process during which less threatening matters came to be agreed upon. Some of these were matters which it would not be difficult for any group to agree upon, such as the evils of racial prejudice and the undesirability--and possibility--of nuclear annihilation. Other topics developed out of this: the very real social problems of the United States came to be seen as symptomatic of untreatable depravity, and economic equality came to be seen as unrealizable in a capitalist system. From here developed a feeling of commitment to the creation of a new society, one without racial prejudice and economic inequality. For many years there was valid optimism within the group about the attainability of these aims. They were, in simple fact, creating a viable new society which embodied them. Then came a second stage in which this optimism

turned to pessimism--a change clearly attributable to
Jones[15]--and the dream began to seem impossible. Talk
turned to suicide, a gesture designed to demonstrate to the
world the impossibility of attaining these admirable
goals. How did this occur? How could the group's conversation get so far off the track of the more broadly accepted understanding of reality?

Berger and Luckmann discuss the problem of socialization and resocialization at some length. Up to a certain
point, socialization into a "subuniverse" can be achieved
within the larger society. For this to happen, the subuniverse must be accepted as legitimate by the larger
society. Examples of this would be the military, a sports
team, or academia. Each of these areas has its own rules
and norms. Because these rules and norms are not in basic
conflict with those of the larger society, and because the
subuniverse is acknowledged to be in some sense "necessary"
to the operation of society, socialization of individuals
into these subuniverses is generally acceptable. (Obviously, this is not necessarily the case in individual instances: e.g., a Quaker family may object to the socialization of their offspring into the military subuniverse.)
This acceptance is important for the individual entering
the subuniverse, because socialization into a subuniverse
is facilitated by it, in two ways. First, it is easier to
enter such a subuniverse if that entrance is accepted by
the friends and family of the individual entering it.[16]
In addition, the process of secondary socialization is
facilitated when the material being learned is to some
extent consonant with that of the larger society. As
Berger and Luckmann observe, "The more [pedagogic] techniques make subjectively plausible a continuity between the
original and the new elements of knowledge, the more readi-
ly they acquire the accent of reality."[17]

The Temple was founded in Indianapolis in the 1950s
as a church which was to become affiliated with the Disciples of Christ. It started out operating within the
norms--the reality--of the larger society. During this
period, resocialization could take place more or less
through typical techniques of secondary socialization,
i.e., the beliefs of the Temple could be taught. To
facilitate this learning, Jones preached that the Temple
replaced the members' biological families.[18] As Berger
and Luckmann point out, "Socialization in later life
typically begins to take on an affectivity reminiscent of
childhood when it seeks radically to transform the subjective reality of the individual."[19] Ultimately, however,

this simple use of affectivity did not suffice to maintain the new reality, and more extreme measures were necessary.

As some of the tenets of the church shifted from, say, an espousal of an interracial congregation to an espousal of a socialist system, it came to be increasingly dissonant with the reality of the larger society. The members, therefore, were faced with an increasing separation and conflict between the norms with which they had been raised and the norms of their new society. The two realities began to split apart. The larger society came to stigmatize the Temple, pushing them away from the larger reality by labelling them as deviant (for example, because of their healing practices), and the Temple began to pull away from the larger society because of the decadence and unfairness seen there. The latter was more important because of Jones's power to deflect investigations of the Temple which would lead to negative labelling, but the ever-increasing split was a problem. As Berger and Luckmann point out:

> The increasing number and complexity of subuniverses make them increasingly inaccessible to outsiders. They become esoteric enclaves, "hermetically sealed" . . . . to all but those who have been properly initiated into their mysteries. The increasing autonomy of the subuniverse makes for special problems of legitimation vis a vis both outsiders and insiders. The outsiders have to be kept out, sometimes even kept ignorant of the existence of the subuniverse . . . . The insiders, on the other hand, have to be kept in. This requires the development of both practical and theoretical procedures by which the temptation to escape from the subuniverse can be checked.[20]

These procedures, in the Temple's case, involve many of the commitment mechanisms discussed in Chapter Two. The Temple was, throughout most of its maturity, a highly secretive organization which attempted to keep as much as possible of its internal activities secret. This was because the goings-on would not be understood by the larger society. Of course the larger society would not approve of the beating of members for minor infractions of the rules. The idea is repulsive. For members, however, the beatings were seen in the context of their subuniverse, a subuniverse in which they were necessary to prepare a strong and committed group to found the new utopia.

This understanding was not easily achieved. For the adults, the process was extremely difficult, and Jones used a number of physical and psychological techniques. Ultimately, he was forced to move his followers to Guyana in order to continue the process unhampered by the lure of the norms of the larger society.

> The plausibility structure must become the individual's world, displacing all other worlds, especially the world the individual "inhabited" before his alternation. This requires segregation of the individual from the "inhabitants" of other worlds, especially his "cohabitants" in the world he has left behind. Ideally this will be by physical segregation. If this is not possible for whatever reason, the segregation is posited by definition; that is, by a definition of those others that nihilates them.[21]

In other words, Jones led in the creation of a highly polemical reality which not only espoused its own goals, but denied the basic legitimacy of the larger society. The Temple members were socialists: their non-member families and friends were fascist pigs, and need not be heeded. The reality, because of the techniques used to maintain the commitment (viz., violence), was highly precarious. The process of socialization could not be let up for a moment, for fear that the members would begin to think again in the "language" of their previous lives, where violence against the very young and the very old is especially unacceptable. Members constantly persuaded each other of the reality of their reality, of the meaningfulness of the meaning system.

The children of Jonestown were very thoroughly socialized. For them, the Temple was not an alternative reality, a subuniverse, but the ground of their primary socialization. There is no need to persuade children of the reality of reality, because there is, as yet, no alternative:

> Since the child has no choice in the selection of his significant others, his identification with them is quasi-automatic. For the same reason, his internalization of their particular reality is quasi-inevitable. The child does not internalize the world of his significant others as one of many possible worlds. He internalizes it as the world, the only existent and only

conceivable world, the world <u>tout court</u>. It is
for this reason that the world internalized in
primary socialization is so much more firmly
entrenched in consciousness than worlds internalized in secondary socializations.[22]

The primary socialization that the children of the Temple
was receiving, however, was taking place within a milieu
designed more for the secondary socialization of their
parents--a milieu oriented toward those who might be
tempted to deny its reality. The children were constantly
being persuaded of something of which they had no doubt.
For them, their universe made obvious sense.

Jeannie Mills snapped back to the dominant reality
after witnessing the harsh beating of her daughter, who had
hugged a girlfriend she hadn't seen in a long time. The
girl was an ex-member, an "outsider." Jeannie reports this
conversation with her daughter afterwards:

As we drove home, everyone in the car was si-
lent. We were all afraid that our words would
be considered treasonous. The only sounds came
from Linda, sobbing quietly in the back seat.
When we got into our house, Al and I sat down to
talk with Linda. She was in too much pain to
sit. She stood quietly while we talked with
her. "How do you feel about what happened tonight?" Al asked her.
"Father was right to have me whipped," Linda
answered. "I've been so rebellious lately, and
I've done a lot of things that were wrong.
While you were on vacation I was smoking pot and
doing other things I wasn't supposed to do. I'm
sure Father knew about those things, and that's
why he had me hit so many times."
As we kissed our daughter good night, our
heads were spinning. It was hard to think
clearly when everything was so confusing. Linda
had been the victim, and yet we were the only
people angry about it. She should have been
hostile and angry. Instead, she said that Jim
had actually helped her. We knew Jim had done a
cruel thing, and yet everyone acted as if he
were doing a loving thing in whipping our diso-
bedient child. Unlike a cruel person hurting a
child, Jim seemed calm, almost loving, as he
observed the beating and counted off the
whacks. Our minds were not able to comprehend

the atrocity of the situation because none of the feedback we were receiving was accurate.[23]

For the children, there was no atrocity, because it was within the larger society, and not the subuniverse of the Temple, that the beating of a child is atrocious. Is it not therefore possible that it was the children of the Temple who had the fewest doubts about the rightness of the suicides? They had never been in a reality in which such an act did not make sense. As Gerald Parks comments, "They were taught that he was a god to them--the only god they would ever see."[24]

The prevailing understanding of the Jonestown tragedy is that the members of the Peoples Temple were brainwashed by Jones.[25] As will be discussed in the next chapter, this understanding is popular because it makes clear who is the villain, and who are the victims. Our culture greatly values the concept of individual responsibility--unless the individual chooses to do something which is not within the limits of "normalcy." When this happens, the responsibility is detached from the actor and placed upon another. In the case of Jonestown, this "other" is Jones, and he is seen to have brainwashed his followers. The understanding of brainwashing is usually based, whether directly or indirectly, on Robert Lifton's Thought Reform and the Psychology of Totalism.[26] Lifton himself preferred the phrase "thought reform," because of the vague and indiscriminate usage of "brainwashing." Even his theory, however, is not really adequate. He actually stresses the "eight psychological themes which are preominant within the social field of the thought reform milieu."[27] These eight themes constitute the criteria of "ideological totalism" (Lifton's term) and thus are about a state rather than a process.

The eight characteristics of the "thought reform milieu" are as follows:

1. Milieu control: the control of information flow.

2. Mystical manipulation: "Initiated from above, it seeks to provoke specific patterns of behavior and emotion in such a way that these will appear to have arisen spontaneously from within the environment."[28]

3. Demand for purity: "The philosophical assumption underlying this demand is that absolute purity . . . is

attainable and that anything done to anyone in the name of this purity is ultimately moral."[29]

4.   Cult of confession: "Confession is carried beyond its ordinary religious, legal, and therapeutic expressions to the point of becoming a cult in itself. There is the demand that one confess to crimes one has not committed, to sinfulness that is artificially induced, in the name of a cure that is arbitrarily imposed."[30] Lifton outlines three elements of this point: the "purging milieu"; its aspect as "an act of symbolic self-surrender, the expression of the merging of individual and environment";[31] and the maintenance of an ethos of total exposure. With regard to this last point, he says "as totalist pressures turn confession into recurrent command performances, the element of histrionic display takes precedence over genuine inner experience."[32]

5.   Sacred science: "The totalist milieu maintains an aura of sacredness around its basic dogma, holding it out as an ultimate moral vision for the ordering of human existence."[33]

6.   Loading the language: "The language of the totalist environment is characterized by the thought-terminating cliche . . . . Totalist language is repetitiously centered on all-encompassing jargon, prematurely abstract, highly categorical, relentlessly judging, and to anyone but its most devoted advocate, deadly dull . . . ."[34]

7. Doctrine over person: "The underlying assumption is that the doctrine--including its mythological elements-- is ultimately more valid, true, and real than is any aspect of actual human character or human experience."[35]

8. Dispensing of existence: "The totalist environ- ment--even when it does not resort to physical abuse--thus stimulates in everyone a fear of extinction or annihilation . . . . A person can overcome this fear and find . . . 'confirmation,' not in his individual relationships, but only from the fount of all existence, the totalist Organi- zation. Existence comes to depend upon creed (I believe, therefore I am), upon submission (I obey, therefore I am) and beyond these, upon a sense of total merger with the ideological movement."[36]

Lifton concludes his discussion by saying:

> The more clearly an environment expresses these
> psychological themes, the greater its resem-
> blance to ideological totalism; and the more it
> utilizes such totalistic devices to change
> people, the greater its resemblance to thought
> reform (or "brainwashing").[37]

The problem, as has already been suggested, is that Lifton
fails to adequately clarify the distinction between the
state of ideological totalism--a state for which the Temple
would clearly qualify on each of the eight points--and the
process of thought reform. Due to his failure to make this
distinction (apparently even in his own mind), he fails to
really define what is involved in the actual process of
thought reform. In Chapter Four, "Psychological Steps," he
does break these down to the following: Death and rebirth;
the assault upon identity; the establishment of guilt; the
self-betrayal; the breaking point; total conflict and the
basic fear; leniency and opportunity; the compulsion to
confess; the channeling of guilt; re-education; progress
and harmony; the final confession; rebirth; and release.[38]   His analysis of these steps, however, is not
really the focus of his discussion, as it should be to
uncover the psychological process.   By emphasizing the
state rather than the process, he misses the crux of the
distinction between "brainwashing" and other forms of
socialization--the degree of free will involved in the
individual's entrance into the milieu.   In other words,
Lifton cannot conceive of the possibility of entering a
totalistic milieu voluntarily.

This becomes clear in Lifton's analysis of the
Peoples Temple.[39]   In "The Appeal of the Death Trip,"
Lifton boils down the number of psychological principles
behind the totalistic environment to three: the control of
all communication in a given environment; the stimulation
and manipulation of individual guilt feelings; and the
dispensing of existence.[40] Again, these are sociological
generalizations about the totalistic environment rather
than psychological generalizations about the process of
"brainwashing."   The significance of Lifton's failure to
make this distinction is that it blurs the difference
between totalistic environments that are entered freely and
those which are imposed on all without distinction--between
the Peoples Temple and Communist China.

The thought reform in China that Lifton originally
examined was the reorientation of an entire society to a
new ideology.   There was no choice involved as to whether

or not to undergo the process. Although many did enter
"revolutionary colleges" voluntarily, those who did so were
primarily concerned with coming to terms with the new
regime, furthering their careers, and so forth.   The
important point is that there was no alternative to the
process--there was no possibility of not coming under the
system's demands.   For this reason, Albert Somit would
restrict the use of the term "brainwashing" to:

> the technique or process employed in communist-
> controlled states to attain either or both of
> two objectives: (1) to compel an innocent
> person to admit, in all subjective sincerity,
> that he has committed serious crimes against the
> "people" and the state; and (2) coercively to
> reshape an individual's political views so that
> he abandons his previous beliefs and becomes an
> advocate of communism. Both objectives, however
> dissimilar they may initially appear, are
> attempts to make an individual accept as true
> what he previously rejected as false and to view
> as false what he formerly saw as true. Both are
> achieved through the same techniques and proce-
> dures.[41]

Under this more restricted, more precise use of the term,
it is clear that although Jonestown was a totalistic
environment, it cannot be said that its residents were
brainwashed.

First, the use of confession in the Temple--most
obviously, the signing of false confessions by members to
be held against their defection--was not about believing
that these things (child molestation, plotting against the
United States government) had happened, but rather about
showing your commitment to the Temple.   Even the use of
confessions within the Temple (of transgressions of rules
against drinking, for instance) was not so much about
repudiating previous beliefs as it was about commitment to
current beliefs and the necessity of making sacrifices to
attain them. The false confessions were not believed, and
the believed confessions were not false. In other words,
there was a clear distinction being maintained at all times
about what the point of the confession was.   If the
confession was designed to maintain compliance with Temple
rules (e.g., the ban on smoking), the confessions were made
and believed.   The false confessions elicited were also
about commitment, but in a more expressive sense: they
were not designed to change the individual's mind about his

or her sexual preference, for instance, as when Jones required everyone to "confess" to their homosexuality. Instead, these confessions were seen as expressing commitment to Jones and the cause. For instance, Jeannie Mills reports that in one meeting in 1975, Tim Stoen, who had not attended a Planning Commission meeting in some time, was suddenly confronted with this new teaching, but refused to deny his heterosexuality:

> Looks of disbelief and secret admiration were on the faces of the people in the room. Many of us felt the same emotions that Tim was voicing, but we had been too afraid to admit it in the hostile atmosphere of the P.C. Council chambers. Even though we agreed with him, to have voiced our approval would have been considered high treason. Many of us were instructed to confront him.

When Jeannie's turn came, she reports,

> I had been trying to think of another angle to use that would persuade Tim to stop being so stubborn and to say the words that we all knew would satisfy Jim. "Tim, I've often heard you say you were willing to die for this Cause. How could you be willing to die for it if you're not even willing to make a public statement that you're homosexual for this cause? Until you're able to say these words, you'd better never again say you'll die for the Cause."[42]

We see, then, that confessions in the Temple were made by individuals who understood which were true and which were false.

Second, although the new ideology of the Temple stressed communism ("socialism" or "communalism" in Temple usage), it was not a matter of "coercive reshaping" of the individual's political views. As was discussed in Chapter Two, Jones's views were a positive lure. He provided his followers with the language with which they could make sense of their experience:

> Although Rhodes had never spent much mental energy thinking about capitalism or the socialist revolution, the more he listened to Jones, the more he felt as if Jones was expressing his own feelings, feelings he had never been able to put into words.[43]

Michael Prokes made a similar point. Prokes was the Temple
Public Relations person who held a press conference in
March, 1979, saying "the Peoples Temple did not die in
vain" and killing himself in an adjoining bathroom. In the
42 page document distributed before this press conference,
he ruminated on the charges of brainwashing:

> For many blacks who came with no education to
> speak of, often blaming themselves for condi-
> tions they didn't understand, having little
> sense of self-worth and actually feeling infer-
> ior because they had been beat down by white
> standards and white institutions for so long--
> for them, Jones was a hell of an eye-opening
> experience. It wasn't brainwashing that Jones
> was engaged in--it was more like deprogramming.
> Jones was educating and the effect was thera-
> peutic for thousands who heard him and whose
> lives were in a state of confusion from feeling
> imprisoned in a society they were told was
> free. He liberated many minds out of their
> confused states by demonstrating why there are
> huge ghettoes in every city of America and why
> those ghettoes are populated mostly by blacks.
> He laid the blame squarely at the feet of white
> racism and a socio-economic system that clearly
> puts profit motives above human values, resul-
> ting in the lack of opportunity necessary for
> blacks to enter the mainstream of American
> life.[44]

Jones did not force his followers to become socialists. Up
until the time of the final hegira, those who attended a
few Temple services and could not buy into Jones's socialism would have an option--the option not to return. This
is true of all elements of the ideology.

The third difference between the brainwashing and
resocialization explanations is the role of violence, which
was used differently in the Temple than it was in Lifton's
schema. In "thought reform," it is used in the earliest
stages, in the "assault on identity." It is used expres-
sively, as it was in the Temple, but it expresses the
"brainwasher's" control over the individual, creating the
context of that control. In the Temple, it was used as the
assertion of control which had been granted previously, and
thus was a means of expressing obedience as much as obtaining it.[45]

There is a fourth reason why the Temple's totalistic
environment should not be confused with brainwashing—it is
simply not possible to brainwash 1,000 people at once:

> To be successful, [brainwashing] demands a
> uniquely structured and controlled environmental
> setting and an inordinate investment of time and
> manpower. Despite the costs entailed, its
> effectiveness is limited to individual subjects
> or, even under optimum conditions, to a small
> group of persons. Certainly it is not yet a
> weapon that can be turned against large, let
> alone mass, audience.[46]

Brainwashing, when it is achieved, is only possible on a
one-to-one or at best small group basis. The brainwashing
of a large group like the Temple was not possible, although
there are a few cases in which "brainwashing" might seem to
be an appropriate label, such as Larry Layton and Maria
Katsaris.[47] For the rest of the members, however, the
socialization to Temple beliefs was precisely that—resocialization, entered into voluntarily and achieved through
standard, mostly non-coercive means.

The difference between the psychological and the
sociological approaches to this material is really a matter
of degree. In this chapter, we have examined the ways in
which the members of the Peoples Temple participated in a
reality in which they would ultimately choose to commit
suicide. In both the psychological and the sociological
models, the members were converted to a new reality.
According to the psychological model, this was imposed on
the members against their will. The sociological model
developed here acknowledges Jones's significant role, but
also stresses the role of each individual, both in giving
Jones the authority as visionary and spokesperson, and in
helping him maintain the reality which he had shaped. They
did not obey him because he disciplined them; they accepted
his discipline because they had made him their leader.
This is the crux of the difference between the psychological and sociological approaches: the latter, though
focussed on group dynamics, gives individuals far more
credit for their behavior.

FOOTNOTES

[1]Garden City, N.Y.: Doubleday Anchor, 1966, pp. 19-20.

[2]Peter L. Berger, The Sacred Canopy (Garden City, N.Y.: Doubleday Anchor, 1967), p. 81, emphasis in original.

[3]The exact number injected is not known because no autopsies were done. Stanley Clayton, one of the two to escape during the final White Night, reports that he saw about 60 forcibly injected. Tim Reiterman with John Jacobs, Raven (New York: E. P. Dutton, 1982), p. 561.

[4]Berger and Luckmann, pp. 152-153, emphasis in original.

[5]Bonnie Thielmann with Dean Merrill, The Broken God (Elgin, Ill.: David C. Cook, 1979), p. 85.

[6]Leon Festinger, A Theory of Cognitive Dissonance (Stanford, Ca.: Stanford University Press, 1962/1957).

[7]Stanley Milgram, Obedience to Authority (New York: Harper and Row, 1974), p. 145, emphasis in original.

[8]See Chapter Three, pp. 113ff. for discussion of the significance of his role as charismatic leader.

[9]Milgram, pp. 161-162.

[10]Ibid., p. 162.

[11]Ibid., p. 149.

[12]The Presentation of Self in Everyday Life (Garden City, N.Y.: Doubleday Anchor, 1959), p. 241.

[13]Quoted in Mel White, Deceived (Old Tappan, N.J.: Fleming H. Revell, 1979), p. 154.

[14]Quoted in Ethan Feinsod, Awake in a Nightmare (New York: W. W. Norton, 1981), pp. 102-103.

[15]"Rhodes's realization that his leader might be prepared to give up on Jonestown troubled him almost

immediately, not so much because of what Jones said, but
because by the middle of January [1978] he began to notice
that Jones's mood had filtered down and affected the spirit
in which the people of Jonestown approached their work.
'It got so nobody was really working very hard anymore.
You couldn't put your finger on it exactly, but it was like
nobody thought it was very important anymore.' But, although Rhodes did sense that the long discussions about
enemies and attacks, the increased security, and the talk
about moving to Russia were all somehow tied to the passing
of the old pioneer work spirit, he was not all sure how
they were tied together; and he was, in any event, inclined
to attribute the problem in the fields to a more immediate
problem . . . .
    "As resentment about exceptions to the everybody-
works-in-the-fields policy grew, productivity declined.
But by now less interested in productivity than with tan-
gible evidence of his following, Jones allowed the community to divide into classes of workers and managers. His
response to the grumblings in the fields was to institute a
system of Production Reports kept by members of the Security Force who roamed the community taking notes on workers. The result, again predictably, was anything but an
increase in productivity." Feinsod, pp. 130-131, emphasis
in original.

    [16]Cf. Chapter Two, p. 91, on countervailing forces.

    [17]Berger and Luckmann, p. 143.

    [18]See above, p. 79.

    [19]Berger and Luckmann, p. 141.

    [20]Ibid., p. 87, emphasis in original.

    [21]Ibid., pp. 158-159.

    [22]Ibid., pp. 134-135, emphasis in original.

    [23]Jeannie Mills, Six Years with God (New York:
A&W, 1979), pp. 268-269.

    [24]Gerald Parks, personal communication, 25 June
1981.

    [25]See, e.g., James T. Richardson, "A Comparison
between Jonestown and Other Cults," in Violence and Reli-

gious Commitment, edited by Ken Levi, (University Park: Pennsylvania State University Press, 1982), pp. 21-34. Richardson's analysis is helpful despite his failure to recognize the fact that the members of the Peoples Temple were not brainwashed.

[26]Robert Jay Lifton, Thought Reform and the Psychology of Totalism (New York: W. W. Norton, 1961).

[27]Ibid., p. 420.

[28]Ibid., p. 422.

[29]Ibid., p. 423.

[30]Ibid., p. 425.

[31]Ibid.

[32]Ibid., p. 427.

[33]Ibid., p. 429.

[34]Ibid., p. 429.

[35]Ibid., p. 431.

[36]Ibid., pp. 434-435.

[37]Ibid., p. 435.

[38]Ibid., pp. 65-85.

[39]Although Lifton is not completely responsible for the uses to which his theory is put (i.e., in the anticult movement ideology), his willingness to apply it to the Peoples Temple himself shows the relevance of this careful examination of it.

[40]Robert Jay Lifton, "The Appeal of the Death Trip," in The New York Times Magazine, 7 January 1979, p. 27.

[41]Albert Somit, "Brainwashing," in International Encyclopedia of the Social Sciences, Volume Two, edited by David Sills, (New York: Macmillan, 1968), p. 138.

[42]Mills, p. 305.   See ibid., pp.   212-213, for another example.

[43]Feinsod, p. 92.

[44]Quoted, Mark Lane, The Strongest Poison   (New York: Hawthorn Books, 1980), pp. 223-224.

[45]See Goffman's comments above, p. 148 .

[46]Somit, p. 142.

[47]Layton, as described above (p. 119),   had two wives co-opted by Jones; Katsaris was singled out by Jones and was isolated even with regard to the rest of the elite.

CHAPTER FIVE

REACTIONS

The events in Jonestown, Guyana, on 18 November 1978, burst upon a world unprepared to make sense of them. Few had heard of the Peoples Temple, probably almost as few had heard of Guyana. The first reports said there were 400 people dead, with hundreds fleeing through the jungle. Bodies were counted, and parents were found to be stacked in piles on their children, a mass of cheerfully clad corpses strewn around the throne of one Reverend James Jones. Mass suicide.

How on earth could this happen? A world which had thought that it was beyond shock was shocked to the core. We have seen mass death before in our lives, too many times--World War Two, Viet Nam, Cambodian refugees--but these were Americans, and they had _chosen_ to die. How on earth could this happen?

David Weincek found the sequence of reporting about the Peoples Temple to be as follows:

(1) this is what we know about Jim Jones and the People's Temple; (2) this is what happened in Guyana; (3) this is what people tell us about those who belonged to the People's Temple; and (4) this is why and how such a tragedy could occur.[1]

Weincek's formulation is generally true, but to some degree he is splitting hairs: the stages occurred virtually instantaneously. The progression is somewhat clearer in the books which have since come out (19 as of September 1983), but the very answers to the what and who predetermine the why and how. This chapter will be focusing on reactions to Jonestown, primarily on the fourth level of Weincek's typology, the explanations of the suicides. It is important to keep in mind that these explanations are affected by both the progression itself and by the prevailing forms of language available.

The second level should be considered first, for it was the motivation for the other three. The events in

165

Guyana were reported fairly straightforwardly, albeit with occasional inaccuracies. The bodies were found, the reports of the events of the congressman's visit were supplied by those who lived through the airstrip ambush, the bodies were counted and returned to the United States. The reporting of these events was done in counterpoint to the other three levels, and is important primarily in terms of its shock value (viz. the covers of _Time_ and _Newsweek_). It was this reporting that made the Peoples Temple "news."

Much analysis has been done on why news is news. What is it that pulls an event out of the on-going stream of human experience and makes it appear to the media as being worthy of reporting? Two scholars have suggested the following factors: frequency (i.e., news is about events rather than processes); threshhold (i.e., the scale of the event); unambiguity; meaningfulness (i.e., cultural proximity or relevance: "an event may happen in a culturally distant place but still be loaded with meaning in terms of what it may imply for the reader or listener")[2]; cognitive consonance; unexpectedness; continuity ("once something has hit the headlines and been defined as 'news,' then it will _continue_ to be defined as news for some time even if the amplitude is drastically reduced.")[3]; composition (the desire of each medium to present a "balanced" presentation within each reportage-unit); reference to elite nations; reference to elite people; reference to persons (i.e., the event is due to the actions of specific individuals); and reference to something negative.[4]

In terms of these twelve factors, the mass suicide of the members of the Peoples Temple in the wake of a visit by a member of the United States House of Representatives qualifies as "news" in terms of all but unambiguity (e.g., Murder or suicide? How many dead? Who did what when?) and cognitive consonance. The question of composition would refer to the other "news" items reported in conjunction with the reports on the suicides in order to balance the radio or television broadcast, the newspaper edition or magazine issue. This, although an interesting question, will not be dealt with here. In any case, the Peoples Temple's self-extinction qualifies as news: the follow-up and background stories (steps one, three, and four in Weincek's typology) helped it continue to be "news," in terms of resolving the ambiguity and lessening the cognitive dissonance, thus, in a sense, making it a complete news story.[5] Despite numerous examples of exploitative coverage, the news was there, and it had to be made sense of. The rest of this chapter will be examining some of those attempts.

When reporters began to investigate the Temple (step 1), they did so, for the most part, in light of the suicides. Although Marshall Kilduff, co-author of the original _New West_ article, helped Ron Javers, who had been on the final trip to Jonestown, with _The Suicide Cult_,[6] and although George Klineman and Sherman Butler had begun research for _The Cult That Died_[7] in March 1978, the vast majority of the research done on Jones and the Temple was done _after_ the suicides: the questions being asked were asked of people who knew the ultimate fate of the Temple. These people were themselves trying to formulate the answers to the why and the how; the information they provided came out of that context. Thus, for instance, the stories of Jones as a young child took on a sinister significance; our society is one which believes firmly in the adage that "as the twig is bent, so grows the tree." Jones was reported to have had "uncanny" power over animals and over his playmates. A typical example:

> Jim Jones' magnetism which would lead 900 persons to mass suicide in 1978, can be seen in his behavior 40 years earlier. In 1938, he was a boy who led odd processions of animals along the dreary streets of Lynn, Indiana. His way with animals reminded some neighbors of Saint Francis of Assisi.
>
> The boy was born in 1931. His father was a partially disabled worker who met weekly with a fanatical local chapter of the Ku Klux Klan. Like so many hapless humans would, later in life, stray and injured animals fell prey to the boy's charms.
>
> A cousin recalled seeing the boy wandering down a road in the backwater town of 1,300 persons or so. Trailing mutely behind would be a dog, a goat, a cat and perhaps a pig—oblivious to the oddness of their flock, mesmerized by the pudgy, foul-mouthed boy . . . . The feelings of power over other creatures soon yielded fantasies of more power. When one of his animals died, the boy became the minister of their deaths. He would bury them and conduct eerie funeral services. He would bless their graves.
>
> The power he learned to expect from animals he began to seek from humans. Ignored by a father intent upon bigotry, he became known as "the foul-mouthed Jones boy."[8]

These are the opening paragraphs of a chapter entitled "The Foul-Mouthed 'Saint Francis'" in a book which came out immediately after the suicides. In these five brief paragraphs, a number of assumptions are made, all based on a psychologistic understanding of character: if we look closely enough at this madman, we will see the seeds of his madness in his childhood. Jones's madness is not as questionable as the methods used to prove it.

First, these examples are found after the fact, and even those which might seem positive (the boy loved animals and was seen as a sort of St. Francis) are twisted (the appellation is put into quotation marks in the title of the chapter). The practice of giving funerals for beloved pets is surely not an unusual one--whether we performed them ourselves or merely attended them, most of us can remember similar incidents in our own childhoods. This is attributed to his developing lust for power, however, and not to his desire to make sense of death or to imitate what grownups do. The services are described as eerie, and the blessings over their graves, it is implied, were sinister.

Second, Jones's problems are attributed to his relationship with his parents, especially his father. Although Klineman and Butler find no evidence that the elder Jones was, in fact, a member of the Klan (they were told he was not by Barbara Schaeffer, the younger Jones's cousin, perhaps the one quoted above),[9] this is a frequently repeated allegation. It is difficult to determine whether or not Jones should be considered a racist. If he was, however--and this is a favorite explanation for the deaths--it would be convenient to attribute this to his father's influence.

The other significant figure in Jones's childhood was, of course, his mother. Newsweek first publicized a story which has taken on a life of its own:

> Perhaps the story should begin with the dream. Lynetta Jones was once a young anthropologist, working with primitive tribes in Africa and trying to decide between her career and marriage. Torn, she dreamed repeatedly of her dead mother. Finally, from the far side of a river Lynetta's mother called to her that she would bear a son who would right the wrongs of the world. Lynetta accepted a proposal of marriage. Her first child was a boy. And she was

convinced that James Warren Jones was a messiah.[10]

For the most part, this story is repeated as the truth,
without recognition of the unlikeliness of a poorly-
educated woman from rural Indiana working as an anthropologist in Africa. Only one source indicates the basis
for this story:

> [Jones's] mother, Lynetta, was apparently a
> fanciful dreamer. Even when she was a factory
> worker she had time to spin fantasies during the
> monotonous bus rides each day to her job twenty
> miles away. In one of her daydreams, she was a
> young anthropologist working with primitive
> tribes in Africa, trying to decide between
> career and marriage. Then from the far side of
> a river, her dead mother called to her and told
> her that she was to bear a son who would right
> the wrongs of the world. She soon accepted a
> marriage proposal, bore a son, and was convinced
> that James Warren Jones was the Messiah. That
> dream, told often by Jones in solemn tones with
> his mother in the audience, is best understood
> when one understands that Lynetta Jones also
> believed herself to be the reincarnation of Mark
> Twain.[11]

There are two points to be made with regard to this story.
The first is that it is usually repeated as a matter of
fact. For instance, it is the first item in a chronology
in a book of academic articles on the Temple published in
1982.[12] The implication of this factual repetition is
that Lynetta was as crazy as her son, thinking that she had
borne a messiah. The explanatory version takes this one
step further, and implies a folie a deux between the two of
them. In either case, the close relationship between Jones
and his mother is constantly emphasized, in an implicit
reference to the Oedipal complex. One article which is
frequently cited is the "Ragged Tramp" article of 1953[13]
telling of Jones's encounter with a "tattered knight of the
road," friendless, hopeless, whom Jones encountered and
took home to his mother, who got him a job.

Many of the immediate post-suicide articles also
refer to Jones's relationship with Myrtle Kennedy, the
neighbor who sat little Jimmy down on her lap and told him
Bible stories, and with whom Jones attended the Nazarene

church. The source of this is apparently a 1976 newspaper article, "Pastor Stops for Lynn Visit, Brings 600 Friends With Him." Interestingly, none of these accounts quote this article for an assessment of his childhood:

> Mrs. Kennedy spoke up, "Jim was a real active boy and a mischief-maker, a 'captain,' but I loved him just as much then as when he behaved."
> . . .
> Mrs. Nellie Mitchell, who was a neighbor of the Jones family, . . . said he was full of energy and an organizer, even as a boy.[14]

This indicates the extent to which the knowledge of Jones's actions in later life influenced the interpretation of his behavior as a child.

The third main figure in Jones's life was his wife Marceline. Again, his attachment to a woman, a woman who was about four years older than he, is seen as somehow neurotic in the light of later events: Kenneth Lemmons, Jones's college roommate, "said Marceline was a 'mother figure' to Jones. 'He called her at work every day.'"[15]

It is possible to go through the entire corpus of the first level, "this is what we know about Jim Jones and the People's Temple," in this way, but this brief analysis should indicate some ways in which this first level reporting served to influence the fourth level analysis of why and how the suicides could occur. By looking at Jones's early life through a popularized Freudian filter, the most ordinary aspects of his childhood are seen to presage his fate.

The third step, the examination of the stories of people who had belonged to the Temple, followed very quickly on the virtually simultaneous execution of steps one and two. This was done both in the ephemeral media (broadcast, newspaper, and magazines) and in books. Most of these personal stories are examples of the genre that Shupe and Bromley call "atrocity stories."[16] The starting point of their discussion is the recognition that most of the information that the "person on the street" has about the new religions (the Unification Church, the Divine Light Mission, the International Society for Krishna Consciousness [ISKCON], etc.) comes from "apostates": individuals who have left a new religious movement and joined an

organized counter movement.[17]   These individuals have
generally been induced to leave the movement in question by
their parents--in many cases, by being kidnapped and "deprogrammed."   The parents are concerned about their offspring's adherence to a group which challenges the family's
authority structure and the parent's goal of preparing
their offspring for participation in the prevailing economic order. The offspring turn, instead, to a group which
provides "powerful confirmatory experiences";[18] exchanges
between parents and offspring are threatening to the ability of each to make sense of what has happened; and the
parents sense their loss of control.[19]   The parents are
distressed by their offspring's rapid transformation of
behavioral orientation, in an individual who had generally
not been particularly religious previously, and who had
converted to a "bizarre" theology which was not amenable to
discussion.[20]   The parents would therefore conclude that
the movement was pseudo-religious; that the "conversion"
was not, in fact, conversion, but rather brainwashing; that
this brainwashing was physically and mentally deleterious
to the individual; and that this individual must therefore
be deprogrammed.[21]   These are the primary elements of
what Shupe and Bromley call the anticult movement (ACM)
ideology.

If the parents should succeed in having their offspring deprogrammed, the process would be just as difficult
for them as for their wayward offsrping. They had been
humiliated by the offspring's repudiation of their goals
and values; they had expended a great deal of money and
trouble to arrange for the deprogramming; and they were
liable to the possibility of civil or criminal prosecution
for their actions.

These factors dictated that the price of re-
entry into conventional society had now risen,
and only public admission of having been brainwashed as well as testimony about other allegations of heinous cult outrages would suffice to
pay it. _Thus, public contrition for having_
abandoned parental values became the cost of
re-admission into the mainstream community.[22]

This public contrition must usually comes in the form of an
atrocity story:

By atrocity story we refer to the symbolic presentation of actions or events (_real or imagin-_
ary) in such a context that they are made

flagrantly to violate the (presumably) shared
premises upon which a given set of social
relationships should be conducted. The
recounting of such tales is intended as a means
of reaffirming normative boundaries.[23]

Now, despite the fact that no member of the Peoples Temple
was ever kidnapped and deprogrammed,[24] those who did
leave the Temple were in just such a position in which it
was necessary to reaffirm normative boundaries by repudiating the values and understandings of the micro-group. To
return to the language of the previous chapter, it was
necessary for them to make a public statement in the language abandoned and returned to in order to break free of
the language of the subuniverse. They had to tell atrocity
stories in order to be readmitted into the mainstream community. Although a distinction between cults and new religions had been maintained throughout this dissertation,
this is one point on which the distinction is not useful.
As suggested above,[25] both kinds of groups lack legitimacy in the eyes of the larger society; thus, Shupe and
Bromley's argument holds true in the case of the Temple.

Note that Shupe and Bromley point out that the
actions or events so presented may be real or imaginary.
In many cases, the defectors from the Peoples Temple were
reporting real actions and events. The presentation is,
however, symbolic, and emphasizes the dissonance between
the norms of the smaller culture and those of the larger
culture. These atrocity stories are the first person
stories through which we learned about the people who
belonged to the Peoples Temple (Weincek's step three). An
explanation is inherent in the very way these stories are
told.

The main recurrent themes in "atrocity" stories are
zombie imagery and the allegation that the abandoned movement is not a "real religion" because it involves deli-
berate estrangement of the member from his or her family;
because it is economically exploitative; and because it is
overtly political. The first two first-person narratives
to come out, Phil Kerns' People's Temple: People's Tomb and
Bonnie Thielmann's Broken God, stress these themes. Both
Kerns and Thielmann had "born-again" experiences (in each
case at the encouragement of a sibling of the opposite sex)
after their departure from the Temple, and each had their
memoirs published within a few months of the suicides by a
Christian press. Steven Katsaris, who was a major actor in
the Concerned Relatives group, says that Kerns was "enthu-

siastic in his efforts" to have the Temple investigated,
but that his account of his involvement is "highly subjective" and that he has "an extremely vivid imagination." He
describes Thielmann as a woman with a "strong imagination"
whose account greatly over-emphasizes her role in the final
trip to Guyana.[26]

The advertising for these two books is fully indica-
tive of their style. The Broken God:

> Here is the full, uncut, inside story, told by
> the person who lived in Jim Jones' home, idol-
> ized his wife, cared for his children, and
> toiled for his cause . . . until the sexual
> perversion, the blackmail, and the insanity of
> the cult forced her to defect at the age of 28.
> Bonnie Thielmann's devotion to the raven-
> haired preacher-turned-god cost her marriage,
> her faith, her peace of mind--and nearly her
> life. Only at the last moment, in Georgetown,
> Guyana, did Congressman Leo Ryan prevent her
> from following him on to Jonestown, where her
> paranoid "father" had issued orders to gun her
> down.[27]

People's Temple: People's Tomb:

> POSSESSED BY PARANOIA . . .
> It has been said that the love of power is
> the most fundamental of all human motives.
> Driven by an insatiable desire to control his
> followers, Jim Jones tormented, twisted, and
> taunted his "family" until they submitted their
> wills, their bodies, their minds and spirits to
> brutal tyranny.
> No novelist could conceive a more demented
> plot or devise a story so gruesome and strange.
> This is the grim and shocking account of Jones-
> town--and why it happened. Here is Jim Jones
> from a new perspective, with insights into how
> and why this former choirboy and ordained mini-
> ster has found his place in history's gallery of
> madmen. More importantly, it is the story of a
> follower who questioned--and found the truth.
> Under the People's Temple pavilion in Guyana
> there is a fitting epitaph for the victims of
> Jim Jones's brand of religion. It says simply,
> "Those who do not remember the past are con-
> demned to repeat it." This book written with

that thought in mind—so that the world would remember Jonestown and, through greater understanding, never permit a repetition of its atrocities.[28]

Jeannie Mills published her account of her experiences with the Temple as <u>Six Years With God</u>,[29] which came out in the summer of 1979. Katsaris says that she "is a little less self-serving . . . . and more accurate."[30] Her story, although more or less in the atrocity story genre, is far less sensationalistic than either Kerns's or Thielmann's, although it is, in some ways, more sensational, given her position in the Temple as a member of the Planning Commission. It should be stressed again that according to Shupe and Bromley's definition, the truth or falsity of the allegations in an atrocity story is irrelevant: the important point is the repudiation of the norms of the subgroup as a means of "reaffirming normative boundaries." This is precisely what Mills attempts to do in <u>Six Years with God</u>. She states in her Introduction:

> Peoples Temple and Jim Jones appear in these pages as I saw them throughout my years there with Jim. I depict his activities exactly as I saw them. At the time, we all gave Jim credit for performing miracles and healings. Only months after we defected from the Temple did we realize the full extent of the cocoon in which we'd lived. And only then did we understand and deplore the fraud, sadism, and emotional blackmail of the master manipulator. We'd been had by a dangerous maniac. And we set out to warn a world that didn't seem to have the time or the compassion to listen. It took the deaths of 912 persons to spark a series of investigations into the Peoples Temple.[31]

It is her efforts to fight the Temple which place Mills among the apostates.[32]

Mills's book was the last of the books based on firstperson narratives. Two other books have been published which focus on individual stories, but these were written by outsiders. Min S. Yee co-wrote <u>In Our Father's House</u>[33] with Thomas N. Layton, whose mother, sister, and brother were all members, but who never belonged himself. The Layton family was probably the third most important to the history of the Temple, after the Joneses and the Stoens. Deborah Layton Blakey was the defector who tried through her affidavit to bring the possibility of mass suicide to the attention of the world, and her brother Larry was the one who led the ambush at the airstrip in which the Congressman, three reporters, and Patricia Parks were killed. Yee and Layton provide a family history which is heavily flavored with psychologisic assumptions, both implicit and explicit. Although not, for the most part, saying that the individual's childhood has brought on their fates, the lure of the Temple in terms of their personal histories (e.g., family order) is strongly implied. The first third of the book is a family history and examination of its internal dynamics. Again, as with the description of Jones's boyhood, what is presented as statement of fact is actually implicitly an explanation.

Ethan Feinsod interviewed Stanley Clayton and Odell Rhodes at great length for <u>Awake in a Nightmare</u>.[34] Clayton and Rhodes were two of the three members to escape during the suicides (others escaped that day, and one woman simply slept through them). What is fascinating about the book is their refusal to renege on their understanding of what was involved in membership in the Temple. Although they may no longer believe in it, they have not reacted, not gone into an anti-cult organization, not claimed to have been brainwashed during that time. The extent to which <u>Awake in a Nightmare</u> has been quoted throughout is an indication of how unusual this is. Rhodes, especially, has been able to "reaffirm his normative boundaries" without attacking the Temple.[35]

The fourth step, as Weincek analyzes the reportage of the suicides, is the "why and how" of them. This fourth step is not independent of the other three, however. First, the "answers" are influenced by the ways in which the first three steps are reported. This is particularly true of the stories of individuals. Whether they take the form of "atrocity stories" by ex-members or "objective" investigations which imply the seeds of Jones's madness in his childhood, certain underlying assumptions influence the choice of data and the way in which it is presented. This is, of course, a recurring problem in any form of reporting, especially the reporting of deviance, especially the reporting of deviance on a scale of the suicides.

Secondly, the focus on individuals, which was necessary in the case of the Temple, is the result of both a cultural bias and of a fundamental methodological problem.

As for the former, our society is much more comfortable
thinking in terms of the individual, the social atom,
rather than the interrelationship of groups of people.[36]
Even given this bias, however, it was almost a necessity in
the case of the Peoples Temple: individuals, qua individuals, were virtually the only source of information about
the Temple. By extinguishing themselves, they left us
without the opportunity to observe them as a group. (Due
to their maintenance of a public/private split, of course,
participant observation was not really feasible before the
suicides, either.) What are the sources of information
about the Temple? What people report about their
experience with the Temple? Who are these people? They
are, overwhelmingly, ex-members, most of whom had left the
Temple before the suicides, and were apostates in Shupe and
Bromley's sense; they were individuals who feared for the
safety of members of their families who belonged to the
Temple; and they were individuals who had belonged up to
the time of the suicides who felt it necessary to repudiate
their membership in the light of society's overwhelming
disapproval of the group.[36] None of these are likely to
be sources of balanced information about the Temple; even
if accurate as to detail, the information will be presented
in terms of the larger reality, and not the reality of the
Temple. Indeed, this is a serious enough problem that even
when people do not repudiate the Temple, and their words
are reported accurately, a twist is put on it through the
reportage. For instance, "Tim Stoen also remembers
Jonestown with something like fondness."[37] Or, somewhat
more subtly:

> By her own admission, suicide was a very real
> option for Bea Orsot. She was a member of the
> temple [sic] for eight years, the last of them
> in Jonestown. She remembers those years as "the
> happiest in my life, up until the very last
> second."
> She is a thin, high-strung woman, 53 years of
> age, who chain-smokes Merit cigarettes, some-
> times two at a time. She lives rent-free with
> another former temple member, a woman who was
> not in Jonestown, in a neighborhood of San Fran-
> cisco where almost every face on the street is
> black.
> "If I had been there, I would have been the
> first one to stand in that line and take that
> poison and I would have been proud to take it,"
> says Bea Orsot. "The thing that I'm sad about
> is this: that I missed the ending."

How did it happen? "Are you ready for this?
I had to go to the dentist. Some say it's a
blessing. I say it's the worst thing that ever
happened. I wanted to die with my friends. I
wanted to do whatever they wanted to do. Be
alive or dead." . . .

She thinks the C.I.A. had something to do
with what happened in Jonestown. She thinks
that some day the people who lived there will be
viewed as saints. As for Jones, himself: "I
know that the decision he made was a good decision he had to make that would benefit the
greatest number of people for the greatest
good."

In the first days back, she lived with her
son and his family. She watched television.
She had been a well-trained secretary who had at
one point worked for the Internal Revenue Service, but now she would sit and stare at the
wall for hours. She started smoking again after
10 years of abstinence. She began to jot her
thoughts down on little pieces of paper until
she had a shoe box full, and she started writing
a book. The title: "The World Did Not Giveth
and The World Cannot Taketh Away."[38]

Orsot is presented not as a woman who has lost her
community, a woman doing her best to preserve her reality
in the face of overwhelming hostility, but rather as a
chain-smoking neurotic collecting little slips of paper in
a shoe box. In a sense, Gallagher is reporting the facts,
but at the same time she is flavoring the interview to make
Orsot look just a little strange. In this way, even those
individuals who do not repudiate the Temple's beliefs are
made, through the use of this sort of "telling" detail, to
fit neatly into the assumptions of the reporter, whether
blatantly or subtly.

The assumptions on which these attitudes are based
are provided by the anticult movement (ACM). As Shupe and
Bromley point out, the genre of atrocity stories takes
place in the context of an ideology about the "true nature"
of these groups:

atrocity stories were constructed so as (1) to
portray affiliation in a new religious movement
as the product of coercive, manipulative practices rather than of voluntary conversion, and
(2) to portray new religions themselves as vehi-

cles for the personal, political, and economic
aggrandizement of a few leaders at the expense
of the well-being of members, their families,
and the public at large.[39]

These stories both form and are formed by what they call
the ACM ideology, which uses a variety of models of the
nature of the experience for the individual. On one axis,
the model may be secular or religious; on the other, it may
be one of possession or one of deception.[40] By far, the
most popular model is the secular/possession model.   In
this mode, the source of influence is an absolute and inherent evil; the method of control is direct, overwhelming
physical control; the individual's vulnerability is total;
the effect on the individual is the destruction of individuality; the danger to others is extreme; and the solution
is deprogramming. The imagery of this model is that of the
zombie.[41]   The individual, in other words, is seen to be
brainwashed.

Individuals who have left these groups as apostates
tell atrocity stories as a way of "reaffirming normative
boundaries": as a way of making sense of their experience. The media tends to pick up and broadcast these
stories, both because they share the values being reaf-
firmed; because they think that the stories must be true
for the apostates and their parents to make such an effort
to publicize them; and, quite simply, because they make
"good copy."[42] As a result of media repetition, there
has been wide dispersion of these stories and the ACM
ideology has become generally available for making sense of
the new religions.

Thus, these two factors, the bias of the questions
and the bias of the answers in the "factual" description of
steps one through three in Weincek's typology, resulted
from the massive availability of a language to make sense
of the suicides: that of the secular/possession model of
the ACM ideology, brainwashing. Although Shupe and Bromley
demonstrate the ways in which the ACM "used" Jonestown as
the ultimate vindication of their warnings,[43] they do not
deal with the extent to which the ex-members and reporters
"used" the ACM ideology in order to make sense of the
suicides.

I discovered this in my own interviewing.   I did not
talk to Gerald Parks until June, 1981, almost three years
after the suicides, and by then his story was fairly well
set.   It was not really necessary to interview him: the

story came out, a story which he had obviously told many times before. This story was very much influenced by the ACM ideology, in both the language he used and the facts he presented. For instance, he is quoted, soon after the suicides, as saying that "if people were really free to leave, 200 or 300 would go."[44] By the time I spoke with him, he said that at least half (i.e., around 500) wanted to leave.[45] He describes his desire to leave:

> [W]e _were_ going to get out. And I had told my family that one way or another I was going to get them out. So we talked to each other as much as we could, we couldn't stand around and talk very long--we were noticed, anybody was noticed, standing around and talking very long, [if there were] very many [it would be] cause for suspicion. And we had to watch what we was doing . . . .
>
> The food got so bad in a few months that all we were getting to eat was rice, gravy, and greens. And my wife weighed a hundred and thirty-seven pounds up here, and she was down to a hundred and thirteen, and almost everybody--a few people gained weight on the carbohydrates, but . . . most people were underweight. And they would weigh you once a week to see, and if you were underweight, they give you--they would have these butter sandwiches, and sometimes peanut butter but not too often, but that was your basic diet. And it just got to the place where you couldn't understand.
>
> And so the food was bad, he kept us working long hours, and as far as brainwashing techniques: if you work people long hours, if you keep them so tired that they're not able to think for themselves properly, and your diet is insufficient, and things like that, then pretty soon people, you know, they do become practically walking robots, like you said on the phone.[46] But it isn't because of the way they're pushed, it's because of the way they're treated. And people don't get any proper diet over there--had they been given a decent place to live, and recreation and time off and things like that, they would have been able to devise more plans to get out of there, the ones that didn't. So because, if you want to keep people prisoner, if you want to keep them, their minds controlled, then this is the way you would do

it. And there was no reason for Jones to do
that--he had the money to do what he wants.
They were feeding us rice that were fed to hogs,
it wasn't even fit for human consumption. They
had a special crew that would go through the
rice and strain it because it was dirty [inaud-
ible]--and that's what we were eating. And I
first weighed a hundred seventy, seventy five
pounds when I went over there, and I lost
weight, and I gained a little bit since I came
back but I'm still not where I used to be.

Anyhow, this is also a part of control, mind
control: people's diets, working them long
hours, keeping them tired and not really able to
think for themselves. This is basically what,
what was going on.[47]

We see, then, that Weincek's assumption about the four
stages is somewhat naive, in that it implies a separation
of the analysis from the description. The reportage is
highly colored by the "why and hows" in the mind of the
person asking questions and the person answering them.

Not surprisingly, the overwhelming response to the
suicides was that they were the acts of individuals who had
been brainwashed by a psychotic madman. As Newsweek put
it,

Explanations for the disaster could be drawn
only from the murky pathology of madness and
mass indoctrination. Jim Jones, 47, was a
self-appointed messiah with a vision of a
socialist paradise on earth and a lust for
domination over his fellow man (page 54). [Page
numbers refer to this issue.] He attracted
hundreds of followers, whose fierce loyalty and
slavish work on his behalf smacked on the
psychological disintegration that accompanies
brainwashing (page 72). His success, and its
awful consquences, posed disturbing questions
about the flourishing of cults that has given
the U.S. everything from saffron-robed devotees
of Lord Krishna to the weird regimen and ugly
threats of Synanon (page 78). It was as if all
the zany strains of do-it-yourself religion and
personality cult salvation that have built up in
America had suddenly erupted with ghastly

force. And to add a touch of the macabre to the
tragic, the scene was a faraway jungle outpost
where corpses bloated under the tropical sun and
pile of bodies was so thick that the original
count turned out to be too low by half.[48]

The story on page 54 is the one referred to above, in which
Jones's mother is portrayed as a young anthropologist who
bore a Messiah. The story on page 72, "HOW THEY BEND
MINDS," cites such well-known experts of the ACM as Mar-
garet Singer, a psychologist, and Richard Delgado, a legal
scholar. The pictures depict kamikaze pilots, remains of
Jews who took their lives at Masada, "Charles Manson and
his ghoulish groupies," and Hitler leading a Nazi rally at
Nuremburg. "THE WORLD OF CULTS," page 78, focuses on
Synanon, Hare Krishna, the Unification Church, and the
Children of God, but points out that

> Some organizations can come to resemble cults
> even though their members do not live communally
> or share religious beliefs. Werner Erhard, for
> example, has impressive power over thousands of
> Americans who have taken his est courses. He
> promises them spiritual and emotional fulfill-
> ment in 60-hour seminars in which the chief
> techniques are attacking the ego, restricting
> food and drink and inducing mental strain.[49]

Time was much less ready to do a full-brown explanation of the suicides. Compared to _Newsweek_'s 26 full
pages on the Temple, Jones's life, brainwashing, and so
forth, _Time_ had only eight pages (nine, if you include
Lance Morrow's essay, "The Lure of Doomsday,"[50] as _Time_
indicates you should with its death's head logo.)[51] Of
the nine pages, five are text and pictures about the events
in Guyana (level two), with one full-page color picture of
the bodies around the Jonestown pavilion; a page and a half
is devoted to the history of Jones and the Temple (level
one), and a page and a half is devoted to "why and how"
(level four). In "Why People Join," Margaret Singer is
cited again, as are Jim Siegelman and Flo Conway, authors
of the ACM tract _Snapping_. Lance Morrow writes: "Religion
and insanity occupy adjacent territories in the mind;
historically, cults have kept up a traffic between the
two."[53]

Both _Time_ and _Newsweek_, as well as articles in papers
all over the country, relied primarily on the brainwashing
metaphor, emphasizing Jones's control over the group, his

avowed socialism, and his financial and emotional manipulation of his followers. As Shupe and Bromley point out,

> [T]he locus of evil in the brainwashing metaphor
> was found . . . in inherently evil, anti-social,
> anti-democratic ideologies and systems such as
> Nazism and Communism.   This was in no small part
> due to the legacy of post-Korean popular litera-
> ture on brainwashing and mind control which was
> permeated with a hostile anti-totalitarian Cold
> War perspective . . . .
>   In general, some combination of pathological,
> political, and economic motives [were] almost
> always attributed to the [leaders].[53]

The question of whether or not the Temple was socialist was
differentially perceived: it was clearly, however, a political organization as well as (or instead of) a religious
one. Those who explain the suicides in terms of the brainwashing metaphor, however, focus almost exclusively on the
"pathological, political, and economic" motives attributed
to Jones.

     The religious model of the possession metaphor fo-
cuses on the possibility of direct demonic possession.[54]
Paul R. Olson, in a book endorsed by Jim Bakker of the PTL
club, offers this sort of explanation:

> The word charismatic comes from the word charis-
> ma which means that a person possessing it is
> endowed with special powers to sway the masses
> and influence people.
>   What better word to use to describe Jim
> Jones?
>   Jesus warns that in the last days there will
> arise false prophets who will possess this kind
> of charmisma, the uncanny power to sway masses,
> to wield influence and to bring people under a
> satanic influence which will cause them to com-
> mit unnatural acts, as did the people who fol-
> lowed Jim Jones. He also says these people will
> be able to perform miracles.[55]

Olson's analysis is not purely of the "demon possession"
sort; the influence of the brainwashing metaphor is so
strong that he uses it as well, albeit in a rather confused
way:

> Obviously, the people who followed Jim Jones
> were not only brainwashed and manipulated
> through mind control, but most of them honestly
> believed that Jim Jones was a mighty man of
> God. He was their Messiah.[56]

It is not quote clear how these people could <u>honestly</u>
believe in Jones as the Messiah if they were brainwashed,
but Olson obviously believes in psychologists almost as
much as he believes in the Bible:

> Psychologists will have to provide many of the
> answers to the questions as they pertain to the
> psychological make-up of the people involved,
> brainwashing techniques and human motivation.
> However, there are many questions which can be
> answered without any psychological references.
> Not only will these questions be posed in the
> following chapters, but the answers as they are
> found in the Scriptures will be provided.[57]

Most of the religious and theological analyses of the
Peoples Temple, however, are of the "deception" rather than
the "possession" metaphor. The source of influence is not
an absolute, inherent evil, but rather pathological sociocultural conditions; the methods of control are not direct
physical control, but rather indirect control through ex-
ploitation of human weakness; the vulnerability is not
total, but limited; the effects on the victim are not the
destruction of individuality but the distortion of individuality; the danger to others is not extreme, but moderate;
the solution is not exorcism, but witnessing; and the
imagery is not that of the zombie but that of the zeal-
ot.[58]

At the same time, the possibility of demon influence
is still presumed, although not in the activist sense of
the possession metaphor:

> In the deception metaphor used by most religious
> critics of the new religions in twentieth-cen-
> tury America, a satanic power active in human
> affairs was still presumed to exist . . . .
> However, this power's intrusion into the
> everyday world was assumed to be indirect.[59]

Mel White's <u>Deceived</u>[60] is a good example of the religious
deception model, as is implied in his very title. The back
cover reads:

Satan's power is great . . . GOD'S POWER IS
INFINITELY GREATER! DECEIVED is a testimony of
hope.   It turns our eyes upward to God.   He
gives us strength and confidence to deliver us
from the same power that made Jonestown a
reality.   We can resist the manipulation of
Satan.   We must stand firm against his decep-
tions. We will be a vital source for good in
the midst of a troubled world if once we grasp
God's promise of victory.

As Shupe and Bromley argue:

Since individuals were presumed to be misguided
rather than literally possessed by evil themselves, Evangelicals advocated confronting
cultists with the "truth" and therefore they
explicitly rejected deprogramming.[61]

White states in his introduction:

It is too easy to blame the madman Jones, his
henchmen and women, and walk away. It is too
simplistic to give Satan all the credit and just
use Jonestown as one more example of the powers
of darkness at work in this world. And though
it is true that there was very little that was
Christian about the People's Temple Christian
Church, it is not true that Jonestown had
nothing to teach us who see ourselves as "real
Christians."[63]

The text itself focuses primarily on this latter
understanding, a sociologically flavored interpretation
which looks at the success of Jonestown in terms of the
failure of mainline churches. This fits in with what Shupe
and Bromley see as the basic thrust of this model:

The vulnerability of individuals to this indirect satanic influence was conceptualized as
lower than in the direct possession model.   A
given false theology was seen as appealing, but
seduction was mediated both by individual weaknesses which "predisposed" individuals to join
"cults" in search of truth and security and by
manipulation of their weaknesses by "cult"
leaders. Among the traits predisposing individuals to be susceptible . . . were (1) a need for
authority   figures;   (2) alienation/rebellion

toward family, church, and society; (3) recent
emotional trauma and/or emotional desperation;
(4) attraction to an idealistic/absolutist philosophy; (5) spiritual hunger emanating from membership in "dead" churches; (6) recent conversion to Christ not yet accompanied by an
adequate understanding of scriptures; and (7)
mere curiosity and/or boredom.[63]

White mentions most of these, but primarily focuses on the
fifth of them, the "spiritual hunger emanating from
membership in 'dead' churches." For instance, he quotes
ex-member Sherwin Harris:

> You ask about a failure of religion, . . . and
> at some level there was. But on the other hand,
> Jones continuously pandered to the people's
> sense of altruism and higher ideals instilled in
> them by the very religions they rejected. He
> didn't go around religious truth or experience.
> He told them they were creating a brave new
> world. He told them they were the true believ-
> ers doing the true good. And when they had to
> do horrible things, he explained that these
> horrible things they did were necessary for the
> greater good of all. He used the religious
> message to his own ends. He played upon the
> very sensitivities instilled in those people by
> their churches; and by the time people realized
> where they had gone astray, it was too late.[64]

In addition, White closes each chapter designed to
encourage the reader to examine his or her own religious
commitment and with Bible texts to illuminate the unstated
assumptions of the chapter. These Bible texts put Deceived
all the more definitely into the religious-deception model. For instance, he closes the chapter entitled "Jones
Created an Illusion of Respectability" with five citations,
the last of which is 2 Corinthians 11:13-15:

> For such men are false apostles, deceitful
> workmen, disguising themselves as apostles of
> Christ. And no wonder, for even Satan disguised
> himself as an angel of light. So it is not
> strange if his servants also disguise themselves
> as servants of righteousness. Their end will
> correspond to their deeds.[66]

The fourth permutation of the ACM ideology is the
secular deception model, in which the spokespersons

> implicitly or explicitly make reference to the
> sociocultural conditions which were deemed
> pathological in the sense that these conditions
> inhibited normal social adjustment . . . .
> [Members] were believed to be the victims of
> their own misdirected idealism and personal
> inadequacies but not dehumanized.66

This response, compared to the other response on the secular axis, the possession/brainwashing model, is relatively
infrequent.   One good example of this type of response is
Shiva Naipaul's Journey to Nowhere: A New World Tragedy.
His focus is on the conditions in America which made the
Temple appealing, without really being clear about how
these might have led to the suicides:

> The People's Temple was laid out on the latitud-
> inal and longitudinal grid of the fundamentalist
> imagination; an imagination obsessed with sin
> and images of apocalyptic destruction, authori-
> tarian in its innermost impulses, instinctively
> thinking in terms of the saved and the damned,
> seeking not to enlighten but to terrorize into
> obedience. Fundamentalism has no respect for
> the human personality, because to be human is,
> by definition, to be sick.   It was upon such a
> framework that Jim Jones, son of the small-town
> Midwest, grafted his primitive versions of so-
> cialist sharing and racial justice.   The result
> was neither racial justice nor socialism but a
> messianic parody of both.
>   And they came to him. "I was eighteen years
> old when I joined the People's Temple," Deborah
> Blakey wrote in her affidavit.   "I had grown up
> in affluent circumstances in the permissive at-
> mosphere of Berkeley, California. By joining
> the People's Temple, I hoped to help others and
> in the process to bring structure and self-dis-
> cipline to my own life."   They came to him--
> seekers of structure, the I Ching decoders, the
> Tarot interpreters, the higher-consciousness
> addicts, the catharsis freaks, the degenerated
> socialists, those who thirsted for universal
> justice and wanted utopia "real bad."67

As Diane Johnson says of this passage, however,

> This is not who the followers were. And is
> thirsting after universal justice really in the
> same category as the interpretation of the Tarot
> cards?
>   No doubt he's right about many of our native
> forms of foolishness, but wrong to connect them
> to Jonestown.[68]

The problem with this, as with so many interpretations/
explanations of the Peoples Temple, is that it is so
heavily flavored by the assumptions with which the author
begins. These flavor the methodology, which flavors the
results. In Naipaul's case, being Trinidadian, he chose to
wander around California in an effort to get the feel of
the place, to find out what the Temple was really about.
Chapter Eight outlines his journey: he begins in a New
Earth Exposition[69] and ends in "an event that billed
itself [sic] as the 'Men Together Conference,'" at which a
lost and sad looking man may or may not have made a pass at
him.[70] As a non-American, he sees the Temple as being
about fundamentalism being transplanted to that fertile
field of craziness, California.

Naipaul is certainly not alone in seeing California
as being of central importance in contemporary religious
expression. Jacob Needleman, for instance, states in his
introduction to The New Religions:

> I . . . do not claim to understand California,
> but I am certain that it cannot be taken lightly
> from any point of view. Sooner or later we are
> going to have to understand California—and not
> simply from the motive of predicting the future
> for the rest of the country. We are going to
> have to stop thinking about it simply as a phe-
> nomenon of people leaving reality behind. Some-
> thing is struggling to be born here amid all the
> obvious absurdity and grotesquerie.
>   It is, in any case, not reality which Cali-
> fornians have left behind; it is Europe.[71]

Sydney Ahlstrom, however, disagrees:

> [S]ince the 1920's, when the great migration of
> Americans and others to this Western Eden began
> to accelerate . . . , California has come to
> have the largest and most heterogeneous popula-
> tion in the union. More important still, this
> rapid growth prevented the development of power-

ful traditions and restraints. It would thus be senseless to deny the frequently made claim that quantitatively speaking, California leads the nation in the proliferation of diverse religious movements. Perhaps one could say that just as the United States is an extreme form of Western civilization, so California is an extreme form of American civilization.[72]

Naipaul is working out of assumptions similar to Needleman's, whereas Ahlstrom is closer to the truth. California is relevent--highly relevant--to the history of the Temple, but primarily in terms of the absence of traditions and restraints. The social climate in California gave Jones the opportunity to develop his social, political, and religious vision to a degree which would not have been possible in many other places. Thus, when Naipaul goes to California to look for craziness, he finds it, and he mocks it, but he does not understand it. He does not understand the context of it, and he does not understand its basic lack of connection to the Temple.

Throughout this study, a distinction has been drawn between the new religions--on which Needleman is primarily focusing--and the cults. The Peoples Temple was a cult, in that it appealed to the marginal in society. Cults are not the new wave of religion, they are religion in a more Marxist sense: they are opiates and compensators. What Naipaul missed by focusing on the California mystique is the extent to which the Peoples Temple was a middle American phenomenon. It had, as Naipaul correctly points out, quite a bit to do with fundamentalism; but his picture of fundamentalism, too, is warped by distance and distaste.

What is especially distressing about Naipaul's analysis, however, is the extent to which it is taken seriously outside of the United States. The back cover presents various examples of critical praise for Journey to Nowhere:

A brilliant achievement . . . . Brutally, even gloatingly honest, it picks the scabs of a cruelly abraded world and jeers at its panaceas, from Wholism to the Black Panthers, from Marxist-Leninism to est. It is merciless toward all the do-it-yourself doctrines by which the hard questions of life have been given soft or wishful answers, sometimes by blatant frauds but as often by evangelists no less desperate or deluded than their followers.
                    --The Sunday Times (London)[73]

Naipaul's contempt for America, which shines through on every page, is seen as "a brilliant achievement."

It is significant that the most important example of a "secular deception" explanation should be by a non-American. This arises out of two interrelated dynamics: that the rest of the world sees the United States, especially California, as a disturbed society; and that the ACM ideology, expecially in its more extreme, possession-oriented forms, is primarily an American phenomenon. Its extensive promulgation in the United States gave an immediate context into which to place the Temple, i.e., that the members were brainwashed, just like the Moonies, Hare Krishnas, and Scientologists. This is far and away the most popular understanding in the America media. For a foreigner, however, not having that explanation as available, it is easier to look at the general decadence of American culture and attempt to explain the mass suicide of 914 members of an American cult as being the result of their very American-ness; especially their Californian-ness.

There is another kind of response which is parallel to the various manifestations of the ACM ideology examined above. These latter responses are similar in that they come out of a desire--or, perhaps better, need--to fit the Jonestown suicides into an ideological explanation about "what's wrong with America." The difference is that the ACM ideologies see the problem as being cults, pseudo-religions. On the religious axis, "what's wrong with America" is that Satan is luring our children into cults; on the secular axis, "what's wrong with America" is social disintegration and wrong-headed values.

The strong point of ACM thinking is that it correctly focuses on the interrelationship of Jones and his followers as the crux of the process leading to these suicides. The other forms of ideology by which the suicides are explained focus not so much on this interrelationship but on larger forces which perverted the Temple as an undistinguished whole. These explanations are, for the most part, various forms of conspiracy theory. These can be placed on a continuum: What's wrong with America is drugs; drugs and the CIA; the CIA.

For some, what's wrong with America is, quite simply, Drugs. War on Drugs, the magazine of the National Antidrug

Coalition, heads a two page article on "The Jones Cult and Mendocino" with a picture of three Rastafarians captioned "Cultism is an intimate part of the drug world. The Jamaican Rastafarians (above) are no different than Jonestown zombies."[74] Note that the zombies are zombies not because they have been brainwashed, but because they take drugs.

Another example of drug conspiracy theory is an anonymous handbill headed "GUYANA MASSACRE WAS SET UP BY FBI, CIA & MAFIA TO SMUGGLE HEROIN INTO U.S. TO DESTROY THE CHURCHES AND TO ENSLAVE AMERICANS. (A TERRIBLE CONSPIRACY)."[75] It is a long, closely printed description of conversations in which Jones told a friend of the author that

> he [Jones] was working with the government--the CIA people, who were using the People's Temple members as 'guinea pigs' in a mind control experiment . . . .
> [I]n addition to mind control tests, the CIA, with his help, had vast amounts of heroin hidden in the jungle, and when the real suicide order was given 2 1/2 kilos of heroin would be hidden inside each body and smuggled into the U.S. without detection . . . . The plan was to get the heroin into the U.S. where it would be sold cheaply by the mafia. Some of it, Jones said, was to be stored in Fort Knox for later use to enslave the population through drug addiction and mind control.[76]

These examples are offered by way of illustration of the ways in which conspiracy theorists can see the Temple as further evidence of their favorite conspiracy. They were not widely disseminated, however. On the other hand, the various tabloids on sale at supermarket checkout stands are more broadly read, and they, too, found evidence of conspiracy in the Temple.

For instance, on 12 May 1981, The Globe reported that:

> JIM JONES, former cult leader and CIA agent, escaped from the Peoples Temple massacre in Guyana and is now hiding out in Brazil . . . .
> [T]he Ryan family is suing the State Department and the CIA for $3 million for leading the California congressman into an ambush.

The suit claims two cult members, Philip Blakey and Richard Dwyer,[77] were also CIA agents and that Jonestown itself was a "mass mind-control CIA experiment."[78]

Joseph Holsinger, one-time aide to Leo Ryan, explained that

not everyone wanted to commit suicide. Some had to be hunted down, murdered, and their bodies dragged back to Jonestown.

"That would explain why the first count of Jonestown dead was only 385--but rose to more than 900 in six days," he says . . . .

Of course, some cult members were never found--the holders of 300 U.S. passports found in the camp were unaccounted for. They may have fled to another country.

"At the time of the tragedy, the Temple had three boats in the water off the coast," Holsinger says.

The boats disappeared shortly afterwards.

"Remember, Brazil is a country Jones was very familiar with. He is supposed to have had money there. And it's not too far from Guyana.

"My own feeling is that Jones was ambushed by CIA agents who then disappeared in the boats. But the whole story is so mind-boggling that I'm willing to concede he escaped with them . . . ."

Los Angeles private investigator and psychic Jenita Cargile, who helped deprogram former cult members, explains: "The body reported identified as Jones was that of a double . . . .

"Jones is still alive, and I have this uncanny feeling we are going to hear from him again.

"I'm sure he and his inner circle of followers have established themselves somewhere in South America and are waiting to foment trouble in the near future."[79]

Mark Lane, famous conspiracy lawyer, takes a somewhat different tack. As the book cover states,

As with the Kennedy assassination conspiracy, Mark Lane is once again in the right place at the right time, courageously asking the questions that most of us are afraid to ask about the suspect circumstances surrounding the cataclysmic events at Jonestown.[80]

Rather than focusing on the extent to which Jones was con-
spiring with the CIA or other governmental agencies, he
seeks to expose the government's conspiracy against the
Temple. Hired in September 1978, immediately prior to the
suicides, Lane accompanied the other Temple attorney,
Charles Garry, on the final trip to Jonestown. His account, The Strongest Poison, is a mixture of self-justifi-
cation, attacks on Garry, descriptions of the government's
plotting against Jones and the Temple, and descriptions of
the cover-up of that plotting. His main points are the
government's failure to do "adequate" autopsies on all the
bodies, which he says, were not done so that it would not
be discovered that the suicides were, in fact,
murders;[81]   the role of Michael Prokes, who joined as an
agent of a pseudononymous man from an unnamed government
agency;[82] and the role of Tim Stoen, who, says Lane,

> was involved in a close and continuing relation-
> ship with the State Department and the American
> Embassy in Georgetown. The United States gov-
> ernment and its agents, knowing of Stoen's du-
> bious conduct as counsel for the Peoples Temple,
> and the real possibility that he was not the
> father of John Victor Stoen, and doubting that
> his motives were as he stated them, cooperated
> as accomplices with him in a campaign that har-
> assed Jonestown and its leader. This campaign
> surpassed normal conduct by an embassy and was
> blatantly biased in favor of one party against
> another in violation of the rules of the State
> Department. Ultimately the embassy convinced
> the leaders of Jonestown that the American
> government was engaged in a program to harass
> and destroy them.[83]

Steve Katsaris, who was intimately involved with the
Concerned Relatives group, does not believe that any of
these points is valid.[84]

There is also a third group of responses, which are
interesting in that they do not come out of a particular
ideological understanding of "what's wrong with America."
These take the Temple seriously as a religious experiment.
It is possible to talk about some of the ways and means of
its failure, but the experiment itself is taken seriously.

One of these responses is by John V. Moore, who had

two daughters[85] die in Jonestown.   He   had   visited   the
commune and pronounced it good. He says:

> Carolyn and Annie were as free as most of us.
> Of course their freedom was limited.   They ac-
> cepted responsibility for their lives and their
> deaths.
>   It is one thing to be the victim of a mad
> captain.   It is another to choose to sign on and
> in the ultimate trial to choose to go down with
> the ship. I think that this is the way they
> would want me to understand their lives and
> deaths.[86]

A   more   systematic   development   of   this   sort   of
argument   is   James   Reston   Jr.'s,   Our Father Who Art in
Hell.[88]   Having   acquired   the   tapes of the final moments
in Jonestown through the Freedom of Information Act, Reston
discerns a pattern of true religious commitment:

> With Jones's authoritarianism equated with lead-
> ership,   dissent   with anarchy, escape with defec-
> tion,   the   system   was very well worked out. But
> it operated on the plane of belief and commit-
> ment,   and   brainwashing does not describe what
> was at work. If the apostles of Jim Jones held
> on to their beliefs with Jonestown intensity,
> they were right: there was no place for them in
> modern America. Nor does mind control describe
> the control Jones exercised.   As a result,
> Jonestown was very difficult to escape, for
> those who did escape, and in the end destroyed
> Jones, never questioned the overall purpose of
> what Jonestown was trying to say.
>   . . . [T]he success of building Jonestown was
> rooted in a sincere vision, a unique amalgam of
> Christian,   Communist,   and   civil   rights   ide-
> as.[88]

Reston sees the context of the Temple as being the erosion
of the social visions of the 1960s:

> For   the   devoted   and disenchanted alike, Jones
> touched the quick of their belief and their
> helplessness in a passive age of cynicism, mak-
> ing them vulnerable as most of us no longer are
> to political and religious messages.   Once
> touched, they were held by his compound of auth-
> ority,   mystery,   magic,   and   message.   If   the

1970s saw a myriad of strange cults and brief-
lived fads, especially among the young, it was
because America had no central social mission.
It was a time for the country to rest and forget. Forget Vietnam. Forget "civil disturban-
ces." Forget Watergate. With the country's
duty defined so passively and negatively, there
was little center stage on the American scene to
appeal to that basic human yearning to have a
purpose broader than oneself. For those in whom
this yearning was strongest, in whom cashing in
on America's wealth was not enough, only side-
shows were available.[89]

This might seem to be an example of the secular-deception
model discussed above, in which the individuals are still
seen as human, and the phenomenon blamed on "sociocultural
conditions which were deemed pathological in the sense that
these conditions inhibited normal social adjustment."[90]
The distinction, however, should be drawn that Reston is
not seeing the conditions--the desire, as a culture, to
recover from the shocks of the 1960s--as pathological, but
as normal. The phenomenon, itself, is not pathological.[91] The conditions in which it arose, however, were
those of a vacuum in which those with social, political, or
religious ideals could find no place in which to express
such ideals. It is not pathological to have these
ideals. It is not pathological to have no framework within
which to fulfill them given the times--and it is not
abnormal social adjustment to find that framework.

        The effort, in late 1978 and early 1979, was to find
an explanation for the suicides. This was done as quickly
as possible, in order to relieve the cognitive dissonance
created by them. As soon as this explanation was found,
however (and for most people it was the secular-possession,
or brainwashing model), every effort was made to forget
the suicides as quickly as possible. There has been very
little follow-up on the Temple aside from occasional
efforts to provide a new explanation.[92] Again, however,
what news did come out has been presented in a way which is
consonant with the prevailing understanding, i.e., that the
members of the Temple were a bunch of brainwashed crazies.
The alleged existence of a Temple hit squad is a case in
point.

        The origin of the rumors about the hit squad seems to

be the fact that the Temple basketball team was in Georgetown during the final White Night. Since members of the
basketball team were also members of the security force--
and because three of Jones's sons were on the team--it was
generally assumed that there was some ulterior purpose for
their absence from Jonestown, i.e., that they were deliberately exempted from the suicides to "take care of" enemies
of the Temple. This point of view was promulgated by the
FBI when they interviewed the last-minute defectors upon
their return to the United States.[93]

> For once, law enforcement agencies took serious-
> ly the stories of the defectors: public offi-
> cials, reporters, and ex-members all were poten-
> tial targets of those Jones called his "avenging
> angels." But the supposed "hit squad"--the bas-
> ketball team and the public relations team--was
> held under virtual house arrest at Lamaha Gar-
> dens [the Temple's headquarters in Georgetown].
> In the San Francisco Bay Area, as elected
> officials, law agencies and mental health pro-
> fessionals took steps to avert the spread of
> violence and death, ex-members gathered under
> police protection at the Human Freedom Center in
> Berkeley to await word about the identities of
> survivors.
> Unbeknownst to the "traitors" and enemies,
> the same sorts of fears permeated the camp of
> the loyalists. The troops at the San Francisco
> temple expected to be attacked in a backlash
> against the church . . . . [Some] surrendered
> perfectly legal weapons to police through an
> attorney, fearing they might be shot if found
> armed.[94]

This paranoia seemed justified when, on 26 February 1980,
Jeannie and Al Mills and their daughter Daphene were shot
in their Berkeley home. Al and Jeannie died immediately;
Daphene died two days later after doctors disconnected her
life support systems. Although the two articles in the New
York Times[95] stress that investigators had "no evidence
to indicate that any 'hit squad' was involved,"[96] the
public immediately seized upon this explanation. The fact
is that two former members, the Carter brothers, were investigated and cleared, and it seems highly unlikely that
there was a hit squad. This was not reported extensively
in the press, leaving the public thinking that there was.
The extent to which this is true is demonstrated by the
fact that every time I have presented portions of my argu-

ment, whether to a church group, an "Introduction to Religion" class, or a professional group of sociologists, the response is always, "Yes, but what about the hit squad?" The ideology has been formed, and the media itself has done nothing to disturb that understanding of what happened.

Jonestown has become a short-hand way of referring to all the evils of the cults, of religion, of politics, of communalism--of whatever is "wrong with America." It has become a Rorschach onto which the preoccupations of America, of the world, can be projected. This is so precisely because the phenomenon is so completely unexpected, so far out of range of the explicable. Rather than examining the phenomenon in and of itself, as this study has attempted to do, there was a tendency for some simple connection to be found with other problems in the country. It was important to make sense of the suicides as quickly and plausibly as possible. This was done by focussing on Jones's mental health, put into the context of the dangers of the cults. We have examined some of the variations of this explanation, and discovered that such an explanation accounted for virtually all of the interpretations of the Temple. All such explanations, however, are flawed by their presuppositions--that Jones was mad, that cults are evil. By presupposing the answer, only certain aspects are examined, and negative evidence cannot be seen.

The mass suicide of the members of the Peoples Temple was an act almost without precedent in human history. People _had_ to make sense of the suicides, there _had_ to be some explanation for them. Historical precedents were few--the Zealots at Masada, the residents of Saipan, Japan after their surrender to the Allies in World War II--and did not seem to say enough, did not seem to really "fit."

The ideology of the anticult movement provided what seemed to be a natural explanation, or set of explanations, for the deaths. Opponents of the cults--actually the new religions--had long warned of the dangers to the brainwashed followers of these charismatic leaders, and the suicides seemed to prove what they had said.[98] Virtually all of the explanations examined in this chapter have been strongly influenced by the wide availability of the language of the anticult movement.

Aside from its availability, the ACM ideology had a good deal of appeal. As Joost Meerloo has observed,

The awareness of a suicidal tendency in a fellow
being--or the act itself--unwittingly brings
home to the individual his own conscious or
unconscious involvement with the problem of
death. To use the term of William James, suicide gives coercive evidence that death ex-
ists.[98]

How much greater the nomic challenge of mass suicide. The
suicides need to be explained--the people killing themselves needed to be distanced, defined as "other," to avoid
confronting the suicidal potential in oneself. This is the
immediate appeal of the brainwashing imagery. Because the
Temple members were seen as brainwashed, they were somehow
absolved of responsibility for committing mass suicide.
Even for those who do not rely on the ACM ideology, in
either its possession or deception models, the members were
seen to be at effect, through drugs or through mind control
experiments by the CIA. Whatever the specific dynamics,
however, the suicides were seen as something that Jones
"did to" his followers, not something that they did themselves.

FOOTNOTES

[1]Quoted, Anson D. Shupe, Jr., and David G. Bromley, The New Vigilantes (Beverly Hills: Sage Publications, 1980), p. 211.

[2]Johan Galtung and Mari Ruge, "Structuring and Selecting News," in The Manufacture of News: Social Problems, Deviance, and the Mass Media, edited by Stanley Cohen and Jock Young, (London: Constable, 1973), p. 64.

[3]Ibid., p. 65, emphasis in original.

[4]Ibid., pp. 63-68, passim.

[5]George Baker argues that "the desire for information about the events in Guyana had been artificially induced. The desire had not grown out of any long-term commitment to researching the Peoples Temple and certainly not out of any commitment to studying religious communes in rural Guyana. That desire arose from the way in which one was affected by the news media reporting." ("The Ethics and Psychology of Media Consumption" [Program for the Study of New Religious Movements in America: Graduate Theological Union, Berkeley, California, 1979], p. 2). Relying on a self-avowed "Freudian style, medical model" (p. 4), Baker concludes that "The observer was under pressure from the media to consider the subject as a serious matter, but, with each new wave of disclosures, it became apparent that on several levels the event and its simultaneous news coverage had been artificially heated by media tricksters who wanted to 'go down in history'" (p. 12). Baker's reasons for refusing to take the suicides seriously as news are not really clear. Throughout his paper, he cites numerous examples (e.g., Bay of Pigs, the U-2 incident) in addition to the Peoples Temple, and, for all of them, the question is--in what sense is this not news?   Can he seriously be advocating the suppression of the news of 914 American communards killing themselves in Guyana?   (This article has been printed, in slightly different form, in New Religious Movements: A Perspective for Understanding Society, edited by Eileen Barker, [Lewiston, N.Y.: Edwin Mellen, 1982], pp. 312-323.)

[6]Marshall Kilduff and Ron Javers, _The Suicide Cult_ (New York: Bantam Books, 1978).

[7]George Klineman, Sherman Butler, and David Conn, _The Cult That Died_ (New York: G. P. Putnam's Sons, 1980).

[8]John Maguire and Mary Lee Dunn, _Hold Hands and Die_ (New York: Dale Books, 1978), pp. 61-62.

[9]Klineman, et al., pp. 39-40.

[10]Pete Axthelm, et al., "The Emperor Jones," _Newsweek_, 4 December 1978, p. 54.

[11]John Peer Nugent, _White Night_ (New York: Rawson, Wade Publishers, 1979), p. 8.

[12]Ken Levi, Editor, _Violence and Religious Commitment_ (University Park: Pennsylvania State University Press, 1982), p. xi.

[13]See above, p. 15.

[14]_Richmond_ (Indiana) _Palladium-Item_, 29 June 1976.

[15]Kilduff and Javers, p. 14.

[16]Anson D. Shupe, Jr., and David G. Bromley, "Apostates and Atrocity Stories," in _The Social Impact of New Religious Movements_, edited by Bryan Wilson (New York: Rose of Sharon Press, 1981), pp. 179-215. (This is a condensed version of the argument they present in _The New Vigilantes_.)

[17]Ibid., p. 193.

[18]Ibid., p. 184.

[19]Ibid., pp. 184-185.

[20]Ibid., p. 185.

[21]Ibid., p. 186.

[22]Ibid., p. 195, emphasis added.

[23]Ibid., p. 198, emphasis added.

[24]Steven Katsaris and Louis Gurvitch made separate plans to rescue their respective daughters, but neither plan came to anything.

[25]Chapter Two, Footnote 35.

[26]Steven Katsaris, interview, New York, New York, 25 June 1979.

[27]Bonnie Thielmann with Dean Merrill, The Broken God (Elgin, Ill.: David C. Cook, 1979), back cover, elision in original.

[28]Phil Kerns with Doug Wead, People's Temple: People's Tomb (Plainfield, N.J.: Logos, 1979), p. ii.

[29]Jeannie Mills, Six Years With God (New York: A&W, 1979).

[30]Steven Katsaris, 6/25/79.

[31]Mills, p. 9.

[32]This point makes some of the problems with Shupe and Bromley's language clear: it is too heavily loaded against the "apostates." Some groups, such as the Temple, do deserve the investigations which the apostates urge. The problem is, of course, which groups do and which do not.

[33]Min S. Yee and Thomas N. Layton, et al., In My Father's House (New York: Holt, Rinehart, and Winston, 1981).

[34]Ethan Feinsod, Awake in a Nightmare (New York: W. W. Norton, 1981).

[35]Their ability to maintain objectivity may well be the reason that they could escape during the final White Night.

[36]See, e.g., "Interview with Stephan Jones," in Penthouse, April 1979, pp. 85, 86, 88, 167, 168, 170.

[37]Carey Winfrey, "Why 900 Died in Guyana," New York Times Magazine, 18 November 1979, pp. 130, 132, emphasis added.

[38]Nora   Gallagher,   "Jonestown: The Survivors'
Story," New York Times Magazine, 18 November 1979, pp. 130,
132.

[39]"Apostates and Atrocity Stories," p. 198.

[40]The New Vigilantes, Chapter Three.

[41]Ibid., p. 61.

[42]"Apostates and Atrocity Stories," p. 209.

[43]"Jonestown and the Revitalization of the ACM" in
The New Vigilantes, pp. 207-232.   Also reprinted, in
slightly different form, in Violence and Religious Commitment, pp. 105-132.

[44]Maguire and Dunn, p. 39.

[45]Gerald Parks, interview, Ukiah, California,   26
June 1981.

[46]In setting up the interview, I had said that I
was arguing that the members of the Temple were not brainwashed.   It is interesting that he should completely reverse my comment.

[47]Parks, 6/26/81.

[48]Tom Mathews, et al., "The Cult of Death," Newsweek, 4 December 1978, p. 40.

[49]Melinda Belk and Susan Fraker in ibid., p. 81.

[50]Time, 4 December 1978, p. 30.

[51]The American Scene column, about an "Awareness
Extravaganza" featuring Werner Erhard, Wayne Dwyer, Arnold
Schwarzenegger, Masters and Johnson, Jerry Rubin, Buckmin-
ster Fuller, and Dick Gregory, may or may not have been
especially written for the issue. (Frank Trippet, "In New
York: Much Ado About 'It'" in ibid., pp. 6, 8, 10) Cf.
comments about composition of reportage units, above,
p. 166.

[52]Morrow, in ibid., p. 30.

[53]The New Vigilantes, p. 71.

[54]Ibid., pp. 63-65.

[55]Paul R. Olson, <u>The Bible Said It Would Happen</u> (Minneapolis: Ark Books, 1979), pp. 14-15, emphasis in original. It is interesting that this Fundamentalist would be one of the few to be open to the possibility that Jones's miracles were genuine--though, of course, with the proviso that they were Satanic.

[56]Ibid., p. 16.

[57]Ibid.

[58]<u>The New Vigilantes</u>, p. 61.

[59]Ibid., p. 65.

[60]Mel White, <u>Deceived</u> (Old Tappan, N.J.: Spire/ Revell, 1979).

[61]<u>The New Vigilantes</u>, p. 69.

[62]White, pp. 10-11.

[63]<u>The New Vigilantes</u>, p. 66.

[64]White, pp. 25-26.

[65]Ibid., p. 47.

[66]<u>The New Vigilantes</u>, pp. 78, 80, emphasis in original.

[67]Shiva Naipaul, <u>Journey to Nowhere</u> (New York: Simon and Shuster, 1980, 1981), p. 297.

[68]Diane Johnson, "After Jonestown," <u>New York Review of Books</u>, 8 October 1981, pp. 4, 6.

[69]Cf. the juxtaposition in <u>Time</u> mentioned above.

[70]Naipaul, pp. 210-213.

[71]New York: E. P. Dutton, 1970, 1977, p. 3.

[72]"From Sinai to the Golden Gate," in <u>Understanding the New Religions</u>, edited by Jacob Needleman and George Baker (New York: Seabury Press, 1978), pp. 21-22.

[73]Elision in original.

[74]October, 1981, p. 36.

[75]Photocopy of handbill, punctuated as original.

[76]Ibid., punctuated as original.

[77]Philip Blakey was Deborah Layton Blakey's ex-husband; Dwyer was not a member, but rather Deputy Chief of Mission to Guyana.

[78]p. 35.

[79]Ibid.

[80]Mark Lane, The Strongest Poison (New York: Hawthorn Books, 1980), inside back cover, emphasis in original.

[81]Ibid., Chapter 13, "The Massacre."

[82]Ibid., pp. 214, 218.

[83]Ibid., pp. 367-368.

[84]Personal communication, 29 April 1982, telephone.

[85]One of them Carolyn Moore Layton, Jones's mistress.

[86]John V. Moore, "Jonestown: Personal Reflections," Circuit Rider, May 1981, p. 4. Quoted with permission.

[87]James Reston, Jr., Our Father Who Art In Hell (New York: New York Times Books, 1981).

[88]Ibid., p. 230.

[89]Ibid., p. 229.

[90]The New Vigilantes, p. 78.

[91]Cf. Naipaul's characterization above, as the Temple being fundamentalism on which was grafted Jones's "primitive versions of socialist sharing and racial justice."

[92]This is one reason that the main focus of this chapter has been the books which have come out on the Temple: newspapers and magazines have, for the most part, let the story drop.

[93]Parks, 6/26/81.

[94]Tim Reiterman with John Jacobs, Raven (New York: Dutton, 1982), pp. 572–573.

[95]Robert Lindsey, "Two Defectors from People's Temple Slain in California," 28 February 1980, p. A16; "Daughter of Slain Ex-Members of People's Temple Dies," 29 February 1980, p. A1.

[96]Turner, op. cit.

[97]See The New Vigilantes, Chapter Eight, for an analysis of how the ACM was revitalized by the suicides. (Reprinted in slightly different form in Violence and Religious Commitment, Chapter Seven.)

[98]Joost A. M. Meerloo, Suicide and Mass Suicide (New York: Dutton Paperback, 1968/1962), p. 21.

CHAPTER SIX

CONCLUSION

The mass suicide of the members of the Peoples Temple was a phenomenon so far out of the reality of our society that there was an instant of paralysis before any attempt to make sense of it could be undertaken. Once that attempt was started, however, it was only natural that any--and all--explanations should be framed in terms of our reality, a reality in which such an act is impossible. In a very real sense, there is no room for the Peoples Temple's reality within our reality. Jones said, during the final White Night, "I just know there's no point--no point to this. We are born before our time. They won't accept us."[1] He was right, because there is no way we could accept a reality involving mass self-extinction without fundamentally re-experiencing, re-defining, and re-creating our own reality.

The predominant explanations of the suicides were undertaken in the language of pathology and deviance, brainwashing and mental illness. Despite our society's pride in its respect for the individual, that respect is not accorded to individuals who choose to deviate in any significant way from the norms of our reality. In our reality, it is assumed that deviance of any significant magnitude (i.e., beyond mere "eccentricity," which is itself differentially defined and tolerated) is not a freely chosen state, but rather that it must somehow be caused by some external agency.[2] Thus, even when a large group of people participates in a reality which is fundamentally at odds with our reality, there is no way for us to make sense of this without finding this external cause if we are to maintain our own reality intact. We cannot accept the mass suicide of the members of the Peoples Temple without seriously undercutting the reality within which we live.

This is the reason for the popularity of the various permutations of the anticult movement ideology in explaining the suicides. As we saw in the previous chapter, the ACM had provided a language with which we could explain the suicides without disturbing our own reality. By seeing Jones as the brainwashing fiend and his followers as victims, we can avoid confronting the implications of the mass suicide for ourselves.

The sociologist of knowledge, however, forces us to confront some of these issues, as the analysis presented in this study indicates. The starting point is to simply accept the Temple's reality as the Temple's reality. This is, in itself, a radical way of approaching the suicides, and its implications are profound. The members of the Peoples Temple were participating freely in the creation and maintenance of a reality within which a decision to commit mass suicide made sense. Such a premise, of course, raises another series of questions which this study has attempted to answer: Why would individuals choose to join such a group? How would their commitment to such a group become solidified to the extent that this fundamental break with the larger reality would be possible? How was this reality created? How was it maintained? What was Jones's role?

In Chapter Two, the appeals and the process of joining the Temple were examined. It was discovered that the members had a variety of reasons for joining the Temple, most of which clustered around the concept of healing. On the most immediate level, this involved the healing of individuals' physical ailments. The concept of healing in the Temple was in fact much broader than that, however. It included the healing of small units, such as individual families, and, at a higher level, the healing of the larger society through the creation of a healthy sub-society without the inequities of the larger society. Interestingly enough, this hierarchy of appeals parallels the hierarchy of the Temple. The rank and file members, who are typical of the members of a marginal religion ("cult") were more apt to join for the personal and physical healings, while the members of the elite, who are typical of the members of a new religion, were more apt to join for the idealistic reasons of social healing. At the same time, however, these distinctions are far from absolute. Jones had abilities both as healer and as visionary, and the two were intimately intertwined. At the same time that he healed people, he provided them with language with which they could make sense of their experience, so that they could move forward to heal society. Temple services included both Jones's sermons, which frequently included his analyses of current events, and the healings. It was not possible to join the Temple without soon becoming aware that there was a larger social mission for the Temple. In this way, even those individuals who were attracted to the church for reasons at the lowest level of the hierarchy were encouraged to perceive these higher levels. The distinction between the rank and file and the elite remained, however, insofar as for the rank and file the political healing was a secondary benefit, in addition to, and not instead of, the personal.

We saw, then, that the Temple offered a number of very positive appeals for membership: healing, safety, and the opportunity to build a non-racist and economically egalitarian society. Once individuals were interested in joining the Temple, however, they all became involved in essentially the same process of increasing commitment. Through use of James Downton's work on joining alternative groups, we examined the various prerequisites for joining the Temple. Briefly, these involved the reasons for the desire to move into a "deviant" role and the elements of the freedom to do so. In this section, we examined the reasons that members would choose to join any deviant group, as opposed to why they chose to join the Temple specifically. This is important because there were individuals, throughout the history of the Temple, who were healed by Jones or who were persuaded by his social/political vision, but who nevertheless did not join the Temple. Through use of Downton's analysis, we can see the specific dynamics through which an individual who was attracted to the church would make the decision to join.

Next, using Rosabeth Moss Kanter's typology of commitment mechanisms, we examined the various structures of the church to see how individuals, having decided to join, would be encouraged to become committed to the Temple and to break off their ties with the larger society. Specifically, it is necessary for the individuals both to dissociate from the larger society in terms of their roles (instrumentally), in terms of their relationships (affectively), and in terms of their norms (morally)--and to associate with the new society in each of these ways. Kanter sees commitment being as much a matter of breaking off old commitments as forming new ones. She develops a typology of the various specific mechanisms of commitment, both dissociative and associative. It was seen that the Temple used many of these mechanisms--perhaps too many, for the members became almost entirely split off from the larger society and absorbed into the world of the Temple. This is one of the factors which facilitated the creation of a reality within which mass suicide for socialism made snese: the Temple became a world in and of itself, with little interaction with the larger reality to counteract their increasingly deviant theology.

In Chapter Three, we examined another important element in the fate of the Temple: the nature of Jones's leadership. It was argued that his leadership was quintessentially charismatic. His authority was granted by his followers in recognition of his powers of healing and clairvoyance. Recognition of the charismatic basis for his leadership makes certain features of the Temple understandable.

To begin with, this was the reason that his healings and "revelations" (to follow Temple usage) included both the fake and the genuine. In order to ensure the continuance of his authority, it was necessary for Jones to continue to provide proof of the abilities that were the source of that authority. This leads to what is probably the most important question to be raised about Jones's leadership: is authority granted in recognition of certain psychic powers legitimate if those powers are, at least partially, faked? This question, implicitly, is at the basis of the brainwashing analysis of the Temple, and, in the broadest sense, those approaching the Temple from this point of view are correct in saying that such authority is not legitimate. Operating within the reality of the Temple, however, the question is not so clear cut. As we have seen, Jones's authority was predicated on a number of bases. Even acknowledging the outright mendacity of some of his physical healings (e.g., those involving the passing of "cancers"), healing was seen in a much larger context in the Temple, and the higher levels of healing were essentially genuine insofar as they were more about participating in the milieu of the Temple, which was shaped by Jones's vision. Odell Rhodes joined to be healed of his heroin addiction: he was healed by Jones. Jeannie and Al Mills joined to have their fractured family healed: they, too, were healed by Jones. Separating out the faked physical healings as evidence of the invalidity of Jones's leadership ignores the relativey small role physical healing had in the central concept of healing within the Temple once one had joined. Although used as a lure in handbills to attract new members, physical healing was almost immediately contextualized into the total ideology of the Temple.

In any case, since this authority had been bestowed and was being maintained, Jones remained the central source of power in the Temple. This had two implications of fundamental importance.

First, Jones had the right to share his powers with

whom he chose. He chose to share them with a small elite
(primarily young, attractive, white women) which was
neither representative of nor responsive to the membership
of the Temple as a whole. This had important implications
insofar as it meant that the leaders were more concerned
with serving Jones than with serving the Temple. Second,
it was up to Jones to determine not only the present
structures, but the future direction, of the leadership of
the Temple, and he chose not to make any realistic plans
for a Temple apart from his leadership. In these two ways,
the essence of the Temple became very much bound up in the
person of Jim Jones. Because Jones had power, the Temple
had power; because Jones had a vision, the Temple had a
vision. Ultimately, this identification of the Temple with
Jones meant that the Temple's fate was inseparable from
Jones's fate. Because Jones felt backed into a corner
after the Congressman's visit, the Temple as a whole felt
backed into a corner. This, too, was an important element
in the Temple's fate.

In the fourth chapter, the underlying sociology of
knowledge approach being used throughout became most explicit. It was also in this chapter that we saw that despite
the fundamental importance of Jones's role, the role of
each and every individual member must be acknowledged.
Jonestown was a society within which mass suicide for socialism made sense. The creation and maintenance of this
social reality depended upon the participation of all
members of the society. Although Jones was significant as
the primary creator and approver of elements of their
reality, it was only because each member lived in this
reality with him that the suicides became possible. The
members of the Peoples Temple were not drifting through a
dream world, hypnotized by Jones and out of touch with
"reality." They lived in a real world, a world of their
own creation. It was only because they lived in this world
as though it were real that it became real. The usual
understanding of Jonestown can be illustrated by the image
of Potemkin's village. It is assumed that Jones somehow
tricked his followers into living in this sham village with
no awareness of its unreality. By approaching the Temple
through the sociology of knowledge, however, we see that
the village was real, and that it was, in fact, built by
the people living in it. This seems impossible because the
nature of that village--that reality--is so at odds with
our own. It seems impossible that a reality could have as
one of its central tenets the possibility of extinguishing
itself.

This is the root of the popularity of the brainwashing explanation.   Since the Temple's reality is so different from ours, it seems   as   though the only way individuals
could   come   to   live in it is through   either   trickery   or
coercion, both of   which are easily discernable.   As we have
seen, trickery took   place   through   the   faking of healings
and "revelations."   This faking, however, did   not fundamentally   affect the process of commitment, regardless of   its
possible   role in attracting individuals to the Temple.   The
bottom line   is   that   individuals chose to join the Temple.
Similarly, the use of coercion (specifically,   the   use   of
physical   punishment)   within   the   Temple, which is usually
taken   as   evidence that the members were   brainwashed,   was
seen to be not   so   much   a   means of obtaining the members'
obedience as it was a means of   expressing that   obedience,
which   had   already   been   granted.   Just as they were   not
tricked into joining the Temple, members   were not forced to
join   the   Temple, or forced to share Jones's   vision of   a
better world.

These   various   elements,   as uncovered through sociological analysis, are expressed by   Bea Orsot,   a member at
the time of the suicides who has not reneged on her   commitment to the Temple:

> By   her own admission, suicide was a very real
> option for Bea Orsot.   She was a member of the
> Temple for   eight years, the   last   of   them   in
> Jonestown.   She   remembers those   years   as "the
> happiest of   my   life,   up   until   the very last
> second." . . .
> "If   I had been there, I would have   been   the
> first one   to   stand   in   that line and take that
> poison and I would have been   proud   to take it,"
> says Bea Orsot.   "The thing that I'm sad   about
> is this: that I missed the ending."
> How did it   happen?   "Are you ready for this?
> I had to go to the dentist.   Some   say   it's   a
> blessing.   I say it's the worst thing that ever
> happened. I wanted   to   die   with my friends.   I
> wanted   to do whatever they wanted   to do.   Be
> alive or dead." . . .
> She thinks   that   some day the people who died
> [in Jonestown] will be   viewed   as saints. As for
> Jones,   himself: "I know that   the   decision   he
> made was a good decision   he   had   to   make   that
> would   benefit   the greatest number of people for
> the greatest good."[3]

This is the reality which the current study has been trying to uncover. The members of the Temple were living satisfying lives, lives which were bound up completely in the life of the Temple. The Temple was led by Jim Jones, who was almost the incarnation of the spirit of the Temple. He was certainly the decision maker for the Temple. This was not resented by the members, it was not imposed on them: it was accepted and celebrated. The members chose to make Jones their leader, and they chose to follow him to the end.

FOOTNOTES

[1]Quoted, Steve Rose, _Jesus and Jim Jones_ (New York: Pilgrim Press, 1979), p. 221.

[2]See especially Thomas Szasz, _The Myth of Mental Illness_ (New York: Harper and Row/Perennial, 1974).

[3]Nora Gallagher, "Jonestown: The Survivors' Story," _New York Times Magazine_, 18 November 1979, pp. 130, 132.

SOURCES CITED

MATERIAL ABOUT THE PEOPLES TEMPLE

BOOKS

Feinsod, Ethan. Awake in a Nightmare: Jonestown: The Only Eyewitness Account. New York: W. W. Norton, 1981.

Kerns, Phil with Wead, Doug. People's Temple: People's Tomb. Plainfield, N.J.: Logos, 1979.

Kilduff, Marshall and Javers, Ron. The Sucide Cult: The Inside Story of the Peoples Temple Sect and the Massacre In Guyana. New York: Bantam Books, 1978.

Klineman, George; Butler, Sherman; and Conn, David. The Cult That Died: The Tragedy of Jim Jones and the People's Temple. New York: G. P. Putman's Sons, 1980.

Krause, Charles with Stern, Laurence M.; Harwood, Richard; and the Staff of the Washington Post. Guyana Massacre: The Eyewitness Account. New York: Berkely, 1978.

Lane, Mark. The Strongest Poison. New York: Hawthorn, 1980.

Levi, Ken, Editor. Violence and Religious Commitment: Implications of Jim Jones's People's Temple Movement. University Park: Pennsylvania State University Press, 1982.

Maguire, John and Dunn, Mary Lee. Hold Hands and Die: The Incredibly True Story of the People's Temple, Reverend Jim Jones and the Tragedy in Guyana. New York: Dale Books, 1978.

Mills, Jeannie. Six Years with God: Life Inside Rev. Jim Jones's Peoples Temple. New York: A&W, 1979.

Naipaul, Shiva. Journey to Nowhere: A New World Tragedy. New York: Simon and Schuster, 1980, 1981.

213

Nugent, John Peer. White Night: The Untold Story of What Happened Before -- and Beyond -- Jonestown. New York: Rawson and Wade, 1979.

Olsen, Paul R. The Bible Said It Would Happen. Minneapolis: Ark Books, 1979.

Reiterman, Tim with Jacobs, John. Raven: The Untold Story of the Rev. Jim Jones and His People. New York: E. P. Dutton, 1982.

Reston, James, Jr. Our Father Who Art in Hell: The Life and Death of Jim Jones. New York: Times Books, 1981.

Rose, Steve. Jesus and Jim Jones: Behind Jonestown. Pilgrim Press, 1979.

Thielmann, Bonnie with Merrill, Dean. The Broken God. Elgin, Ill.: David C. Cook, 1979.

White, Mel. Deceived. Old Tappan, N.J.: Fleming H. Revell/Spire, 1979.

Wooden, Kenneth. The Children of Jonestown. New York: McGraw Hill, 1981.

Yee, Min S. and Layton, Thomas N. with Layton, Deborah; Layton, Laurence L.; and Valentine, Annalisa Layton. In My Father's House: The Story of the Layton Family and the Rev. Jim Jones. New York: Holt, Rinehart, and Winston, 1981.

Other Published Materials

Axthelm, Pete with Lubenow, Gerald; Reese, Michael; Walters, Linda; and Monroe, Sylvester. "The Emperor Jones." Newsweek, 4 December 1978, pp. 54-56, 59-60.

Baker, George. "The Ethics and Psychology of Media Consumption." Program for the Study of Religious Movements in America, Graduate Theological Union, Berkeley, California, 1979.

Barnes, W. E. "Yet-to-be-Printed Story Builds a Storm." San Francisco Examiner, 11 June 1977.

Belk, Melinda and Fraker, Susan with Shannon, Elaine and Copeland, Jeff. "The World of Cults." _Newsweek_, 4 December 1978, pp. 78, 81.

"The Concealed Confession of Jim Jones." _Accuracy in Media Report_, 6 December 1978, pp. 1-4.

Gallagher, Nora. "Jonestown: The Survivors' Story." _New York Times Magazine_, 18 November 1979, pp. 74-76, 124-126, 128, 130, 132, 134.

Goodlett, Carlton, B. "Inside the Peoples Temple 'Expose.'" _Sun Reporter_ (San Francisco), 12 July 1977, p. 7.

"Guyana Massacre was set up by FBI, CIA, and Mafia to Smuggle Heroin into U.S. to Destroy the Churches and Enslave Americans." Handbill, n.d.

Hall, John R. "The Apocalypse at Jonestown." In _In Gods We Trust_, pp. 171-190. Edited by Thomas Robbins and Dick Anthony. New Brunswick, N.J.: Transaction Books, 1981.

Harrison, William. "New Evidence Reveals Jim Jones Still Alive in Brazil." _Globe_, 12 May 1981, p. 35.

"Interview with Stephan Jones." _Penthouse_, April 1979, pp. 85, 86, 88, 167, 168, 170.

Johnson, Diane. "The Heart of Darkness." _New York Review of Books_, 19 April 1979, pp. 3-7.

_____. "After Jonestown." _New York Review of Books_, 8 October 1981, pp. 3-5.

"The Jones Cult and Mendocino." _War on Drugs_, October 1981, pp. 36-37.

Kilduff, Marshall and Tracy, Phil. "Inside Peoples Temple." _New West_, 1 August 1977, pp. 30, 31, 34, 36, 38.

Kinsolving, Lester. "The Prophet Who Raises the Dead." _San Francisco Examiner_, 17 September 1972.

_____. "'Healing' Prophet Hailed as God at S.F. Revival." _San Francisco Examiner_, 18 September 1972.

Kinsolving, Lester.   "D. A. Aide Officiates for Minor
    Bride." San Francisco Examiner, 20 September 1972.

_____. "Probe Asked of People's Temple." San Francisco
    Examiner, 20 September 1972.

Lifton, Robert Jay. "The Appeal of the Death Trip." New
    York Times Magazine, 7 January 1979, pp. 26-27,
    29-31.

Lindsey, Robert. "Two Defectors From People's Temple Slain
    in California." New York Times, 28 February 1980, p.
    A16.

Mathew, Tom with Harper, Chris; Fuller, Tony; Nater, Timo-
    thy; and Lubenow, Gerald. "The Cult of Death." News-
    week, 4 December 1978, pp. 38-44, 48-53.

"Messiah from the Midwest." Time, 4 December 1978, pp. 22,
    27.

Moore, John V. "Jonestown: Personal Reflections." Circuit
    Rider, May 1981, pp. 3-5.

Morrow, Lance.   "The Lure of Doomsday." Time, 4 December
    1978, p. 30.

"150 Church Disciples Picket the Examiner." San Francisco
    Examiner, 20 September 1972.

"Pastor Stops for Lynn Visit, Brings 600 Friends with Him."
    Richmond (Indiana) Palladium-Item, 29 June 1976.

"Pastor's Own Story." San Francisco Examiner, 24 September
    1972.

Peoples Forum, November 1976.

"Peoples Temple Determined to Remain a Strong Force in San
    Francisco."   Peoples Temple Press Release, 17 August
    1977.

Ramirez, Raul. "Magazine Attacks Peoples Temple." San
    Francisco Examiner and Chronicle, 17 July 1977.

Richardson, James T.   "People's Temple and Jonestown: A
    Corrective Comparison and Critique." Journal for the
    Scientific Study of Religion, 19:3 (September 1980),
    pp. 239-250.

Rogers, Shirley. "Rev. Mr. Jones Raps Rich 'Faith Heal-
    ers.'" Indianapolis Star, 11 December 1961.

Silverman, Art. "Are Investigators Trying to Destroy a
    Progressive Church?" Berkeley (California) Barb,
    23-29 September 1977.

Stumbo, Bella. "Maria Katsaris: Jones Follower All the
    Way to the End." Los Angeles Times, 9 March 1979,
    part 1, pp. 3, 28-29.

Tracy, Phil. "More on Peoples Temple: The Strange Sui-
    cides." New West, 15 August 1977, pp. 18-19.

Treml, William B. "'Mom's Help for Ragged Tramp Leads Son
    to Dedicate His Life to Others." Richmond (Indiana)
    Palladium-Item, 15 March 1953.

Turner, Wallace. "Pastor a Charlatan to Some, A Philoso-
    pher to Wife." New York Times, 1 September 1977.

_____. "Daughter of Slain Ex-Members of People's Temple
    Dies." New York Times, 29 February 1980, p. A1.

"Why People Join." Time, 4 December 1978, p. 27.

Winfrey, Carey. "Why 900 Died in Guyana." New York Times
    Magazine, 25 February 1979, pp. 39, 40, 44-46, 50.

Woodward, Kenneth with Whitaker, Mark and Gayle, Stephen.
    "Temple Trouble." Newsweek, 15 August 1977, p. 79.

Woodward, Kenneth with Hager, Mary; Huck, Janet; Reese,
    Michael; Mark, Rachel; and Marback, William. "How
    They Bend Minds." Newsweek, 4 December 1978, pp. 72,
    74, 77.

Interviews

Case, Ross. Ukiah, California, 24 June 1981.

Goodlett, Carlton. Cascais, Portugal, 5 August 1982.

Katsaris, Anthony. Telephone, 24 September 1981.

Katsaris, Steven. New York, New York, 25 June 1979.

_____. Telephone, 27 April 1982.

Parks, Gerald. Ukiah, California, 26 June 1981.

THEORETICAL AND BACKGROUND MATERIAL

Ahlstrom, Sydney. "From Sinai to the Golden Gate." In Un-
    derstanding the New Religions, pp. 3-22. Edited by
    Jacob Needleman and George Baker. New York: Seabury,
    1978.

Barker, Eileen, Editor. New Religious Movements. Lewis-
    ton, N.Y.: Edwin Mellen, 1982.

Bellah, Robert. "New Religious Consciousness and the Cri-
    sis in Modernity." In The New Religious Conscious-
    ness, pp. 333-352. Edited by Charles Y. Glock and
    Robert N. Bellah. Berkeley: University of California
    Press, 1976.

Berger, Peter L. The Sacred Canopy. Garden City, N.Y.:
    Doubleday Anchor, 1967.

_____ and Luckmann, Thomas. The Social Construction of
    Reality. Garden City, N.Y.: Doubleday Anchor, 1966.

Bird, Caroline. "Nine Places to Hide." Esquire, January
    1962.

Bromley, David and Shupe, Anson. "Moonies" in America.
    Beverly Hills, Ca.: Sage, 1979.

Brownmiller, Susan. Against Our Will. New York: Simon and
    Schuster, 1975.

Downton, James V., Jr. Rebel Leadership. New York: Free
    Press, 1972/1973.

Durkheim, Emile. The Elementary Forms of the Religious
    Life. Translated by Joseph Ward Swain. New York:
    Free Press, 1915.

Enroth, Ronald. Youth, Brainwashing, and the Extremist
    Cults. Grand Rapids, Mich.: Zondervan, 1977.

Festinger, Leon. A Theory of Cognitive Dissonance. Stan-
    ford, Ca.: Stanford University Press, 1962/1957.

Fichter, Joseph. "Youth in Search of the Sacred." In The
     Social Impact of New Religious Movements, pp. 21-41.
     Edited by Bryan Wilson. New York: Rose of Sharon
     Press, 1981.

Fisher, C. William. Why I am a Nazarene. Kansas City,
     Mo.: Nazarene Publishing House, 1958.

Galtung, Johan and Ruge, Mari. "Restructuring and Selec-
     ting News." In The Manufacture of News, pp. 62-72.
     Edited by Stanley Cohen and Jock Young. London:
     Constable, 1973.

Gerth, H. H. and Mills, C. Wright, Translators and Edi-
     tors. From Max Weber. New York: Oxford University
     Press, 1946.

Goffman, Erving. "The Medical Model and Mental Hospitali-
     zation." In Asylums, pp. 321-386. Garden City,
     N.Y.: Doubleday Anchor, 1961.

_____. The Presentation of Self in Everyday Life. Gar-
     den City, New York: Doubleday Anchor, 1959.

Happold, F. C. Mysticism. Baltimore: Penguin, 1963, 1964,
     1970.

Kanter, Rosabeth Moss. Commitment and Community. Cam-
     bridge, Mass.: Harvard University Press, 1972.

_____. "Commitment and Social Organization: A Study of
     Commitment Mechanisms in Utopian Communities." Amer-
     ican Sociological Review, 33:4 (August 1978), pp.
     499-517.

Lifton, Robert Jay. Thought Reform and the Psychology of
     Totalism. New York: W. W. Norton, 1961.

Lincoln, C. Eric. The Black Church Since Frazier. New
     York: Schocken, 1974.

Mannheim, Karl. Ideology and Utopia. Translated by Louis
     Wirth and Edward Shils. New York: Harcourt, Brace,
     and World, 1936.

Meerloo, Joost A. M. Suicide and Mass Suicide. New York:
     Dutton, 1962, 1968.

Melton, J. Gordon and Moore, Robert. The Cult Experience.
    New York: Pilgrim Press, 1982.

Milgram, Stanley. Obedience to Authority. New York: Har-
    per and Row, 1974.

Needleman, Jacob. The New Religions. New York: E. P.
    Dutton, 1970, 1977.

Pirsig, Robert M. Zen and the Art of Motorcycle Mainten-
    ance. New York: Bantam, 1974.

Robbins, Thomas and Anthony, Dick. "'Cults' vs.
    'Shrinks.'" In New Religions and Mental Health, pp.
    48-63. Edited by Herbert Richardson. New York:
    Edwin Mellen, 1980.

Shupe, Anson D., Jr. and Bromley, David. "Apostates and
    Atrocity Stories." In The Social Impact of New Reli-
    gious Movements, pp. 179-215. Edited by Bryan Wil-
    son. New York: Rose of Sharon Press, 1981.

_____. The New Vigilantes. Beverly Hills, Ca.: Sage,
    1980.

Somit, Albert. "Brainwashing." In International Encyclo-
    pedia of the Social Sciences, Volume II, pp. 138-
    143. Edited by David Sills. New York: Macmillan,
    1968.

Stoner, Carroll and Parke, Jo Anne. All God's Children.
    New York: Penguin, 1977.

Trippet, Frank. "In New York." Time, 4 December 1978, pp.
    6, 8, 10.

Troeltsch, Ernst. The Social Teaching of the Christian
    Churches, Two Volumes. Translated by Olive Wyon.
    New York: Macmillan, 1932.

Wallace, Anthony F. C. "Revitalization Movements." Amer-
    ican Anthropologist, April 1956, pp. 264-279.

Weber, Max. Economy and Society, Two Volumes. Edited by
    Guenther Roth and Claus Wittich. Berkeley: Univer-
    sity of California Press, 1978.

INDEX

STUDIES IN RELIGION AND SOCIETY